Russian in Plain English

Russian in Plain English enables complete beginners to acquire the skill of reading words written in Cyrillic independently, with no English transcription or imitated pronunciation, within a short period of time.

This book introduces the Cyrillic alphabet gradually, feeding in the letters and their various pronunciation aspects one by one over its ten units, thus building a complete picture of the Russian sound and writing systems. It also highlights the interrelationship of the two systems and helps learners to see the logic behind the use of the Cyrillic alphabet. In addition, the book teaches learners to produce Russian word stress on a marked syllable, contributing to stress acquisition.

Furthermore, the book explains the basic grammatical features of Russian words and the rules of how to put them into sentences, enabling learners to start saying things in Russian from Unit 1. It employs some findings of research in language processing, helping learners to start building their speaking and reading skills.

This book is an essential guide for all beginners, including students and independent learners.

Natalia V. Parker is a keen educator and language practitioner. Trained in foreign language teaching in Russia, she held a full-time teaching post at Tula University, which she left to set up one of the first non-state, non-profit schools implementing more up-to-date teaching. At the age of 27, she became a head of school. After moving to the UK, Natalia taught Russian for several years, developing a new teaching methodology. She returned to higher education in 2016, doing an MA in Applied Linguistics at the University of Sheffield. Her teaching experiment produced extremely successful results which enabled her to secure an Arts and Humanities Research Council (AHRC) Studentship, awarded by the White Rose College of Arts and Humanities (WRoCAH), for her PhD at the University of Leeds. In 2019 she presented the results of her research at the American Association of Teachers of Slavic and East European Languages (AATSEEL) Conference and at the British Association for Slavonic and East European Studies (BASEES) Conference, among other forums. Currently, Natalia is running another pedagogical experiment on teaching Russian grammar.

Russian in Plain English

A Very Basic Russian Starter for Complete Beginners

Natalia V. Parker

Routledge
Taylor & Francis Group

LONDON AND NEW YORK

First published 2020
by Routledge
2 Park Square, Milton Park, Abingdon, Oxon OX14 4RN

and by Routledge
52 Vanderbilt Avenue, New York, NY 10017

Routledge is an imprint of the Taylor & Francis Group, an informa business

British Library Cataloguing-in-Publication Data
A catalogue record for this book is available from the British Library

Library of Congress Cataloging-in-Publication Data
Names: Parker, Natalia V., author.
Title: Russian in plain English : a very basic Russian starter for complete
    beginners / Natalia V. Parker.
Description: New York : Routledge, 2020. | Includes index.
Identifiers: LCCN 2019054394 (print) | LCCN 2019054395 (ebook) | ISBN
    9780367415365 (hardback) | ISBN 9780367415402 (paperback) | ISBN
    9780367815097 (ebook)
Subjects: LCSH: Russian language—Textbooks for foreign
    speakers—English. | Russian language—Grammar.
Classification: LCC PG2112 .P27 2020 (print) | LCC PG2112 (ebook) |
    DDC 491.78/0071—dc23
LC record available at https://lccn.loc.gov/2019054394
LC ebook record available at https://lccn.loc.gov/2019054395

ISBN: 978-0-367-41536-5 (hbk)
ISBN: 978-0-367-41540-2 (pbk)
ISBN: 978-0-367-81509-7 (ebk)

Typeset in Times New Roman
by Apex CoVantage, LLC

To all those who want to learn and
all those who support learning

Contents

Preface

I'll be your guide to Russian

My name is Natalia, and I will be your guide for learning Russian from the very beginning. I am Russian myself, born and bred, in addition to being a language teacher. I lived in Russia for half of my life (well, a larger half) but have been teaching Russian in the UK for the other half. This book was born out of the questions which my students have asked me, as well as my own questions which came up when I was trying to understand the difficulties that my students had in learning certain aspects of Russian. So, it looks like you have a fairly experienced guide.

Throughout this book, I will do my best to explain the logic behind Russian words and sentences, giving you examples and providing you with lots of practice to apply this logic to your own reading and speaking. As your guide, I will be helping you navigate your way through Russian every step of the way: I will say hello at the start of units and good-bye at the end of them, give you tips and offer prompts, remind you of what is what and advise on how to move forward more effectively. I look forward to helping you learn and hope that you will be excited about turning each new page of this book.

I love my country, its people and its language, and I will also tell you about them the way I see them. I will introduce you to some people and places I know in Tula, the city where I come from, as well as the village where my grandmother lived. Thus, you will have glimpses of Russia outside Moscow and St. Petersburg. I sincerely hope that this book will help you start to know and love my language and my people too.

Before you start

In this book, we are *not* going to start with memorising all 33 Russian letters in one go or reciting them in alphabetical order. Instead, we will learn to handle the new letters in words in order to be able to read them without relying on knowing them or their English transcription.

For this reason, there is no phonetic introduction in this book. I will explain things and we will practice them as we go.

We are not going to start with saying "hello" or "good-bye" in Russian either, as we need to get to grips with a few basics first. I will help you build your knowledge and language skills *gradually*, by adding a bit more information and more practice every time you open this book. This way, by the time you get to the end of the book, you will be able to actually use everything you have studied. For example, you will be able to read out any Russian word unassisted, find your way through short Russian texts and conversations, and make your own simple sentences in Russian (and most certainly say "hello" and "good-bye"). You can also learn to write in Russian, but that will require slightly more time and effort. With regard to listening, there is a world of free listening resources for Russian on the Internet. If you are unsure of the pronunciation of words, you can check in one of the free online translator programmes, which a lot of my students do.

This book aims to help you put into practice everything you learn. They say that you cannot learn to ride a bike by just knowing how to do it – you have to get on and start peddling. Similarly, the best way to learn a language is to use it. Whether you use this book for your own learning or in a class, you will have plenty of opportunities to read and speak Russian, as well as write in it, if you wish. This way you will not only learn *about* Russian but also develop skills for Russian, which you hopefully will be able to use in your further learning.

Finally, we all learn in a different way. That is why this book is organized in such a way that you can do as little or as much as you feel comfortable with or as you need. If you haven't got time or like taking things steady, you can do a page at a time. If you do Russian at a university and devote your day to studying, you might get through this book fairly quickly and be ready for the next stage of your learning, whether it is part of your course or some additional material that you are using. Whichever way, I hope it will help you to make your first confident step into Russian.

Shall we make a start?

Preface for teachers

My dear fellow teachers, tutors and instructors,

I am pleased that this book has made it into your hands and that you are considering using it or recommending it to your students.

As each of us teaches in our own way, I don't think there ever can be a perfect book which would suit every tutor, learner or group. That is why this book has been designed to be as flexible and as adaptable as possible, in order to give you the choice of how much of it to use in your lessons. There is plenty of material for up to 20 classroom hours at the start of semester 1. But I appreciate that our workloads and course requirements vary, so not everyone will be able to allocate 20 hours for its content. In that case, you can easily pick and mix. Whether you will be teaching beginners reading, grammar or speaking, there is an abundance of exercises and activities to start your students up.

What's more, this textbook has been designed with some knowledge of learners' processing of language (e.g., letter-sound correspondences and inflection morphology), synthesising various methods and techniques to effectively help your learners retain what you will be teaching them. When you look inside, you will see some unusual exercises – for example, reading strings that aim specifically to get your students reading Cyrillic as quickly as possible. You might choose to use just those for your students to read Cyrillic unassisted, with no transcription or imitated pronunciation, after eight to ten hours of study. If you are giving a speaking class, you will be able to pick from a range of speaking activities, based on the Interactive Hypothesis, to encourage meaningful communication from the first lesson. If your priority lies with grammar, you will find the most comprehensible explanations of the Russian language grammatical system to help your learners see the logic behind the notorious endings and agreements. At the same time, they will be able to practice certain structures and endings in practical exercises and speaking activities in order to acquire them, not just to learn about them.

Since this book is based on some findings about information processing and language acquisition, the material is presented in small chunks in order to ease its comprehension and retention. Moreover, the illustrations are selected not only with the purpose of illustrating an item or a place but often include writing, inscriptions and signs, which contributes to visual processing of Cyrillic letters, thus speeding up reading fluency. The book also provides a considerable amount of background sociolinguistic knowledge which will help your students acquire language which is alive and flexible, and to feel comfortable in a Russian environment.

Something that is probably important to keep in mind is that this textbook is not structured in a traditional way. You will not find the whole alphabet at the start, declension tables or long lists of vocabulary. This book is learner-friendly and feeds the information gradually, allowing your students to absorb it and retain it. There is no separate workbook – all the exercises are included, so your students will have everything in one place and will be able to use it for reference and for practice. There is no set homework either. You know your students better than anyone, thus you can decide what to do in the class and what to give as homework. Fairly large revision sections provide plenty of exercises and activities to choose from.

If you do decide to use this book or recommend it to your students, I would love to hear from you on either n.v.parker@leeds.ac.uk or at romashka1996@hotmail.com. Your comments and suggestions would be really appreciated, and I will try to consider them in my future work.

Acknowledgements

First of all, I would like to express my deepest gratitude to Dr. James Wilson from the University of Leeds for his inexhaustible support of my research, for his patience in answering my endless queries and for reading numerous versions of my papers. Next I would like to thank Dr. Nigel Harwood and Dr. Oksana Afitska from the University of Sheffield for their belief in my potential and their support of the experimental testing of the materials, as well as their invaluable advice on material writing. Most importantly, this project would not have been possible without the financial support of the British Philological Society, whose Master's Bursary enabled me to test my methodology. Though my research had started long before I was awarded my Arts and Humanities Research Council Studentship (AHRC) by White Rose College of Arts and Humanities (WRoCAH) for my PhD, it has most certainly given my project a huge boost and enabled me to develop this textbook to the point of its acceptance by Routledge Publishers.

In addition to this, I feel I owe an enormous thank you to the Routledge senior publisher Andrea Hartill, who has been with me all the way through the application and submission process, for reading my complex reasoning for this book and for introducing me to the intricacies of the publishing process. For obvious reasons I have to thank with all my heart my participants from Sheffield for volunteering for this project, as well as my adult students from Somerset of the last 20 years, for their interest in Russian and for their dedication in learning with me. They have been absolutely crucial for the shaping of this book, as they helped me see my language through their eyes. I also have to mention Ruth Sindall and other adult education managers for the support they have provided over the years, such as tolerating my everlasting photocopying of my handouts.

One more sincere thank you needs to go to my dearest friend and an amazing Russian philologist from Tula Galina Pavlovna Belyaeva for helping me understand the beauty and the logic of my mother tongue.

Finally, there are no words which can express my gratitude to my husband for his endless moral support, taking me to the railway station at 3.30 am every Monday morning and juggling the logistics of me being away from home, as well as to my 15-year-old daughter for her patience, understanding and interest in what I do and her enormous help in sorting out the illustrations for this book. In conclusion, I have to say that I am eternally grateful to my Dad, who encouraged my learning, because without him, this book would not have happened.

First things first

People often think of the Russian alphabet (often called Cyrillic, as it uses Cyrillic script) as a big challenge, possibly due to not understanding what is behind the Russian spelling system. That is why we will be discovering how it works by gradually moving through the letters, adding *one at a time* to our practice. The points below will help you see how the letters are used in words, thus giving you a general idea how to approach reading in Cyrillic. These will prove useful every time you read Russian. I will keep reminding you about these every now and then too.

DOs and DON'Ts of reading in Russian

▶ In Russian we ***DO NOT*** normally ***omit or skip letters***. One could say that usually ***every letter in a word is pronounced*** (with a few exceptions). Russian letters usually are not silent like *k* in *knot*. So, most of the time you read what you see – every letter. (We have two signs which do not stand for a particular sound, but we will talk about them later.)

▶ Russians ***DO NOT*** normally ***use combinations of two or more letters*** to make one sound. (Compare to English, e.g., *ch* in *child* or *sh* in *shop*). This is one of the reasons why we have more letters (with separate letters for *ch* and *sh*, among others).

▶ The majority of Russian letters, ***if combined, are still read as they are in the alphabet***, e.g., «С» stands for *c* in *cinema* and «К» for *k* in *kangaroo*; together they make «СК» like *sc* in *scout*.

▶ A lot of Russian letters are normally ***read in one way,*** though, as with any language, there are some small peculiarities which we will master one by one. E.g., «С» is normally like *c* in *cinema* or «А» is more or less like *a* in *father*. Compare to the English "a", which can stand for at least four different sounds, or the worst case scenario, the letter "o", where the reader has eight options to choose from, e.g., *o* in *rose, bottle, sport, book, monkey, women* and so on. In Russian, «К» for *k* in *kangaroo*, «Т» for *t* in *tent* and «О» for *o* in *for* produce the same sounds in «КОТ» and «КТО».

▶ Russian does not have as many vowel sounds as English, but it does have many more consonants. So, you will come across some peculiar combinations of those – make sure there are no gaps between them, e.g., «КТО».

The letters in alphabetical order can be found at the end of the book, but we are going to start by splitting them into *four groups*, according to whether the shapes or sounds that they stand for are familiar or not. Note that we are not going to learn the letters group by group but pick and mix them, learning in the most effective way.

Group I (The Easy)	letters which have *similar* (to English) *shapes* and stand for *similar sounds* (not the biggest group but very helpful)
Group II (The Tricky)	letters which have *similar shapes* but stand for *different*, though *familiar, sounds* (a small group which needs a lot of attention)
Group III (Funny Shapes)	letters which have *unfamiliar shapes* but stand for *familiar sounds* (the largest group but not the hardest)
Group IV (The Strangers)	letters which have *unfamiliar shapes* and stand for *unfamiliar sounds* (fortunately, this group has only a very few letters in it)

We are going to start with five letters of Group I and then add others, one at a time.

Getting started

- ▶ to have an idea of how the Russian alphabet works;
- ▶ to recognise five Russian letters from Group I and five others, reading out lots of Russian words made of them;
- ▶ to discover what is what in Russian names and what you need to do to make them sound Russian;
- ▶ to learn the meanings of your first Russian words made of the ten familiar letters;
- ▶ to make your first sentences in Russian with the words you have learned;
- ▶ to introduce yourself and others;
- ▶ to find out some surprising facts about Moscow.

GROUP I (The Easy)

These letters have the *same* (or almost the same) *shape* as some English letters and (even better!) stand for *similar sounds*. There are not that many of them, but they will be our starting point. We are going to name all the letters phonetically as we would read them in a word. This means that we will call the letters by the sounds that they stand for, rather than by their names (which can be found in the table at the end of the book).

М м stands for *m* in *empty*   **А а** stands for *a* in *father* but not as long and not as back

Т т stands for *t* in *tent*   **О о** stands for *o* in *for* but not as long or as back either

К к stands for *k* in *kangaroo*

Keep in mind that a lot of Russian letters are usually pronounced in only one way. Be particularly careful with the *vowels*: «A» is close to *a* in *father* and «O» (for now) stands for *o* in *for* (NOT for *o* in *rose*). To help you remember to read the Russian letters the Russian way at all times, I will put them in Russian inverted commas « » in text.

> **To make it clear:** If you have a closer look at the letters above, you will see that Russian **lower case letters** generally have the same shape as capitals, e.g., «M м», «T т», «K к». (There are three exceptions to this rule, with «A a» being one of them.) So, if you intend to write in Russian, you need to make sure that little «м» is pointed and not rounded like an English "m", and little «т» and little «к» are not tall like the English "t" and "k". Also, you can write «a» like handwritten «*a*».

Check that whenever you see «A» or «O» you name them
*the Russian way: like **a** in **father** or **o** in **for**.*

> **WORTH REMEMBERING:** *In Russian there is **NO distinction between long and short vowel sounds** in different words (compare English "peel" and "pill", or "pool" and "pull") – most Russian vowels are somewhere in between.*

Thus, for Russians it is not important whether you pronounce «KOT» as *court* (with *o* in *for*) or *cot* (with *o* in *spot*) – they will hear it as the same word (meaning "*a cat*").

With these basics on board, we can now start using what we have learnt, like pedalling the bicycle.

Ex.1 a) Decoding Cyrillic. Just read ALOUD! In an exercise like this you do not need to remember the words or look them up in a dictionary (though if you are curious there is nothing to stop you). The meanings of these words are not of much use to us at the moment, as our main purpose is to sound them OUT LOUD, pronounce them and get used to combining Russian letters into words! To start with, we can concentrate on reading words without thinking about what they mean. (The words to remember will come later.) So, read aloud! These are best read in columns.

Tip! Every letter here is read only one way! Look at the two Russian vowels again, «A» *(like **a** in **father**) and* «O» *(like **o** in **for**), and read them aloud.*

TAM - TOM	TOK - TAK	TA - TO - KTO	ком - кома
MAT - MOT	MOK - MAK	OT - TOT - KOT	мама - Кама

To make it clear: The only words which start with a capital letter in the middle of a sentence in Russian are names. For example, «Кама» is a Russian river; later we will have «Тома», which is a short version of the Russian name "Tamara".

NEW WORDS (these are to remember!)

KOT - *cat (male)*   КТО? - *Who?*

MAMA - *Mum*   КАК? - *How?*

TAM - *there*

The best way to learn words is to put them into sentences. Now we can do just that. In any language there are rules of putting words together into phrases and sentences; that's what grammar is, in a simplistic kind of way. In different languages there are some rules which are similar and some which are different. We will start with things which you will not need to worry about in Russian.

WORTH REMEMBERING: Sentences in Russian DO NOT have little words like "A"
or "THE" (called "articles" in linguistics), which you often need in front of nouns in English. Russians have other ways of identifying nouns. So, when you want to say something in Russian you do not need anything for those.

The word for "is" actually exists (both in dictionaries and very formal documents), but Russians tend not to use it in the present tense in everyday speech. So, you DO NOT need anything for "IS" either! Thus, our first sentence «Кот там.» means "The cat is there." and is a full correct sentence.

b) Reading for meaning. Read each sentence and, before reading the next, translate it into English (using in English all the words which are not used in Russian). E.g., Кот там. – *The cat is there*.

Мама там.   Как мама?   Тома там. («Тома» *is a girl's name*)

Кот там.   Кто там? *(e.g., at the door)*   Как Тома?

c) Say it in Russian. Try to do this without looking at the sentences above. You can check the words in boxes if you need to, but construct your own sentences, rather than reading those above or trying to remember them. Speaking is a different language skill from reading or memorising. Make sure that you say everything aloud.

The cat is there.   Who is there? *(e.g., at the door)*   Natalia is there.

Mum is there.   How's Mum?   How is Natalia?

3

GROUP II (The Tricky)

These letters have a *familiar shape* but stand for a *different sound* to their English "look-alikes."

Cc «C c» stands for c in *cinema* and never ever for anything else! In English this shape can give us different sounds (Compare: *cinema* or *cat* or *ocean*), while in Russian – only ONE!

Ex.2 a) Decoding Cyrillic. (Remember: you do not learn or translate these. They are here to help you get used to finding correct sounds for Russian letters.)

КОТ - COT	CAM	COK - KOC
КОМ - COM	COK	COM - MOCT
KOK - COK	COC	COT - TOCT

Check that you remembered to pronounce «C» as in "cinema" every time.

NEW WORDS: COK - *juice*

MOCT - *bridge*

b) Reading for meaning (sentence by sentence).

Сок там.   Мост там.   Кто там?   Как сок?

c) Say it in Russian. Try not to look at the words or sentences above.

Mum is there.	The juice is there.	How is the juice?
How is Mum?	Who is there?	The bridge is there.

Check that you remember that you don't need anything for "is" or "the".

If you are learning to write, try writing the phrases above in Russian without looking at the words in the box and then check them. If you are not sure which letter should be there, say the Russian word aloud and listen to the sounds, then assign one Russian letter to each sound you say, and you are there. It is also good to read all the sentences that you have written aloud.

d) Try not to trip up! You will find that the combination «СК» (like *sc* in *scout*) is very popular in Russian words. Remember: always read ALOUD.

Скот, скок, скос, скат, маска, каска, соска, Омск, Томск

> *Check that you realise that the last two words are names*
> *(they are two large Siberian cities).*

Next, we will try reading longer words, but I've got something to tell you about these first.

How does it sound? The crucial part of pronouncing longer words in Russian is STRESS – it makes them sound right, so people understand you better. **Russians struggle to understand words with a wrong stress,** so it is important to learn to produce correct stress. Also, the meaning of words can depend on where the stress is. On the down side, in Russian, like in English, there are no easy rules of where to put the stress. On the plus side, in all dictionaries and textbooks Russian words have a special sign (′) indicating where the stress should be placed (e.g.: ма́ма). So, your job when you are learning a new word is to pay a little attention to where the stress mark is and give yourself a second to make sure that you put the effort in the right place. This way you will learn the stress while learning the word.

Also, it is extremely important to remember that there is normally **ONLY ONE STRESS** in a Russian word. So, do not split your words, putting two or three stresses like in English (e.g., " ‚compre'hension"). Russian athletes performing at international competitions always say that one of the hardest challenges, believe it or not, is to recognise their names announced by foreign speakers, because two or more stresses sometimes make them sound unrecognisable. Let us get it right! Try, for example, pronouncing "Sha'rapova" with one stress on the "ra", or "Gorbachyov" with one stress on the "ov".

You might remember that earlier on I mentioned that in Russian, there is no distinction between long and short vowels sounds in different words (like *pill* and *peel*). Well, there is a **distinction between the length of stressed and unstressed vowels within Russian words** – stressed vowels are so much longer (up to 1.5 times) and much louder. So, to produce Russian stress correctly, put all the power of your breath and your voice only on the stressed vowel, making it **longer and louder**. If the stress mark is at the front of the word, put all the power of your voice onto the first vowel (e.g., «А» or «О») – that would be the longest vowel in the word – and let the rest of the word fade away (e.g., ма́ма). If the stress is at the end, do some kind of run-up towards the end and put all your effort into the last vowel (e.g., *Gorbachyóv* or като́к). If the stress is in the middle, you would need a bit of both techniques to emphasise the marked vowel (e.g., *Sharápova* or ата́ка). It is easier to do than to describe how to do it. And it gets even easier with practice.

When you write you do not have to mark the stress; textbooks only do it to help you. Although stresses are not normally marked in Russian texts, by the time you are able to read them, you will have an idea of where the stress goes in certain types of words.

Ex.3 a) Watch your stress! No translating – just reading ALOUD. Remember that «C» is like *c* in *cinema*.

Tip! There will be NO stress mark in very short words (e.g.: кот *and* мост) *where there is only one vowel. They are called monosyllabics. The stress is obvious in these words and you wouldn't be able to put it anywhere else in them.*

ТАК - ТА́КСА	ТОК - КАТО́К
САМ - СА́МКА	ТАК - МАСТА́К
СОТ - СО́ТКА	МА - САМА́

If you would like to hear exactly how a particular word sounds in Russian, you can use any of the free online translators. To type in Russian, you might need to activate Russian on your device. (To type Russian on your laptop, you would need to download a virtual Cyrillic/Russian keyboard or buy a USB one. Some of my students use Russian-English stickers for computer keys.)

Do you think it is time for a new letter? We can then have more words to practice our single stress.

GROUP II (The Tricky - *familiar shape, different sound*)

Нн «Н н» stands for *n* in *nut*. I agree it can be misleading. So let's try to get used to it.

Ex. 4 a) Decoding Cyrillic.

Tip! As in Russian we do not normally omit or skip letters. Make sure you read «Н» everywhere you see it.

НА	НОС - СОН	КАНТ - КАНА́Т	НОТ - НО́ТКА
НО	НОТ - ТОН	СТАН - СТАНО́К	СНОС - СНО́СКА
ОН	НАС - САН	НА́ТА - НАТА́Н	КО́МА - КО́МНАТА

Check that you read «Н» at the end of the words;
that «СН» in СНОС came out as "sn" in "snow".

> NEW WORD: КО́МНАТА - *a room*
>
> *(Did you put only ONE stress?)*

Tip! *The stress pattern in «кóмната» is very common in Russian but is often challenging for English speakers, who tend to put a second stress on the first «A». To avoid that, make sure that your «O» is much longer and louder than the «A»-s. Have a few goes. Try saying in Russian "The room is there." or "How is the room?"*

Before you start a new page, see whether you remember the words from the previous boxes. It is good to make sentences with words, rather than memorising a list – this way you learn to use them.

> **How does it sound?** As stressed vowels in Russian words are longer and louder than others, it makes them very pronounced and in a way superior to those away from the stress. Thus, *unstressed vowels are often much weaker* and sound very unclear or faint (are "reduced" in linguistic terms). I guess that, as Russians put so much effort into that ONE vowel under the stress, there is not much breath left for the others, so they fade away. For example, the unstressed «O» sounds somewhat between «O» and «A», *not as rounded* as «O» but not as open as «A», sort of weakened. But DO NOT try to pronounce a different sound in place of an unstressed «O» – concentrating on it too much might lead to stressing it accidently, thus putting two stresses in a word (double-stressing), which is an absolute taboo in most Russian words. It is better to concentrate on the stressed vowel, directing all your attention and all the effort to it, to make it longer and louder. This will naturally weaken the others. Just check that there is no rounding of unstressed «O»-s.

Check that you read «A» and «O» the Russian way.

It might be reassuring to know that if you forget about the weak «O» and read the words exactly as they are spelt, any Russian would still understand you (unlike with the wrong stress or with double-stressing). It is helpful to be aware of weak unrounded «O»-s, though, when listening to Russians. In addition, not putting any effort into unstressed vowels helps to strengthen ONE stressed vowel.

c) Watch your stress! Read these aloud. Make sure that you put only ONE STRESS in each word and direct all your effort onto it. Try not to round the unstressed «O»-s.

МОТ - МОТÓК	ТОМ - ТÓМОМ	том - котóм - котóмка
НОС - НОСÓК	МАТ - МÁТОМ	мат - космáт - космáта
НО - ОКНÓ	СОК - СÓСКА	сок - сосóк - осóка

> **NEW WORDS:** **ОКНÓ** - *a window*
>
> **СТАКÁН** - *a glass, a tumbler*

Check that your «O»-s in «окнó» sound different.

Let's have a look at a letter from Group III now.

GROUP III (Funny Shapes - *unfamiliar shapes, familiar sounds*)

 «Э э» stands for *e* in *end* and is a vowel. Can you name the other two vowels that you know in Russian?

Ex. 5 a) Decoding Cyrillic. Watch out for weak and unrounded «O»-s.

ЭТА - ЭТНА- ЭТА́Н   ЭТО - ЭТОТ - ЭТОМ

NEW WORD: Э́ТО - *this*

(Have you made «Э» longer than «O»?)

«Э́то ма́ма.»   «Э́то кот.»

> **WORTH REMEMBERING:** *The word* Э́ТО *gives us plenty of chances to make more phrases in Russian. In the same way that in English you say "This is . . ." when you introduce someone or something, Russians start their introductory sentences with* «Э́то». *With no word used for "is," it makes it fairly straightforward. E.g.,* **Это Э́мма. – *This is Emma.*** Э́то ко́мната. *– This is a/the room. (Did you have only one stress in «ко́мната»?)*

b) Reading for meaning:

Кто это? *(when pointing)* – Это ма́ма.   Это Стас. Анто́н там.   Это ко́мната. Окно́ там.
Кто там? *(at the door)* – Это Э́мма.   Это сок. Стака́н там.   Это Ка́ма. Мост там.

c) Let's try it in Russian. Using the Russian words that you know, make similar sentences. Make sure you use both «там» and «это», keeping track of what you are saying. If you work with someone else, you can make sentences (or blocks of two sentences similar to those in the second column) for each other to translate. In a class, you can go round asking «Кто это?» about different people, giving names as answers. There is one condition – you need to do it with the book shut (peep if you need to, but speak without looking into it, as speaking and reading are different skills).

GROUP III (Funny Shapes) «И и» stands for *ee* in *see*

Ии «И» is a vowel. Can you name the other three vowels?

> **How does it sound?** As I mentioned earlier, there is no distinction between long and short vowels in Russian, and most vowels are somewhere in between the two. It matters only for *one* vowel – «И». It will make your learning easier later on if you remember to say **«И» a bit longer** (like *ee* in *see*).

Ex.6 a) Decoding Cyrillic. Watch your stresses – ONE per word, and keep an eye on weak unrounded «О»-s. Note that the stress patterns are different in different columns (watch your «ко́мната» pattern in the first column).

кит - ни́тка - ни́тками	Ка́ма - ками́н - ками́ном	ко́сит - оси́на - мокаси́н
иск - ми́ска - йскоса	си́то - сати́н - сати́ном	э́ти - ико́на - эскимо́
сан - са́ни - Са́нина	тис - тиски́ - тиска́ми	э́тика - Ники́та - никоти́н

Check that you remembered to pronounce «И» long and that you read «СК» like "sc" in "scout".

NEW WORD: И - *and*

b) Reading for meaning. Remember to read aloud.

Tip! As well as not using anything for *"is"*, we **do not need anything for the word *"are"*** either, *e.g.,* Анто́н и Ни́на там.

Э́то Омск и Томск.	Как Макси́м и Ни́на?	Сок и стака́н там.
Анто́н и Антони́на там.	Э́то ко́мната. Окно́ там.	Кто э́то? – Э́мма и Ники́та.

c) Now it's your turn. Imagine that you are having a Russian visitor. Introduce the members of your group or your family using their names. It works exactly as in English, e.g., Э́то А́нна. Try two people together, e.g., Э́то Ники и Ти́на. You can use pictures on your phone and say who is who, using names.

How does it sound? In addition to Russian consonants combining in peculiar ways, in some Russian words you may have a **double consonant** (like in «Áнна»). These two letters are not read separately but make a slightly longer sound than a single one – Russians sort of stretch consonants. This does not normally affect the meaning but does help you sound more Russian. Let's give it a go – the longer the better. Russian names: Áнна, Ѝнна, Нóнна and Russian words: мácca, тóнна, кácca.

NEW WORDS:

КИНÓ - *cinema (watch the stress!)*

ТАКСИ́ - *taxi (watch the stress!)*

КÁССА - *cash-desk or till, "Pay Here", box-office*

d) Let's try it in Russian. With my suggestions below, say blocks of two sentences, using «Это» with the first word and «там» with the second. Translate what you said, or if you are in a class, get somebody else to do the translation.

cinema, box-office	room, window	Kama (*river*), bridge
Omsk, Tomsk	Anna and Inna, Emma	juice, glass

🅱 *GROUP II (The Tricky)* «В в» which stands for *v* in *van*

Can you name the other two Tricky letters that we know?

Now we can read the name of the Russian capital in Russian. Make sure you note the stress and put all your effort onto the long «А», leaving the «О» weak and unrounded. Ready. Steady. Go! **МОСКВÁ**

RUSSIASCOPE: **МОСКВÁ**

Moscow is the most northern city on the planet to have a population above 10 million people. It is also the most populous city in Europe and the sixth largest city in the world. With the Soviet days long gone, Moscow now is rated as the third most expensive city in the world. According to some statistics it also has more billionaires (79, apparently) than any other city, including New York.

Ex.7 a) Decoding Cyrillic. Watch your stress - make sure there is ONE per word and in the right place!

ВОСК - ВА́КСА - ВИСО́К   Ива́н - и́ва   сно́ва - осно́ва
ВИНТ - НИ́ВА - ОВИ́Н   вино́ - ви́на   свист - свисти́т
ВИСТ - СВИ́ТА - ОТВИ́С   вати́н - ва́тка   сви́нка - свини́на

Check that you remembered to pronounce «И» long
and not to round the unstressed «О»-s.

> **NEW WORDS:** ВИНО́ - *wine (watch the stress!)*
>
> ВА́ННА - *a bath (often used by Russians to mean a bathroom too)*

Check that you tried to stretch «нн» in «ва́нна».

b) Watch your stress! From the list below, pick five monosyllabics (words with one vowel only); you can underline them. In all other words, try to remember where the stress goes; you can mark it over the stressed vowel. Do you remember what these words mean? Now, read aloud all words with the stress at the front (these do not include monosyllabics), and then all those with the stress at the end.

кино, ванна, как, стакан, такси, это, мост, комната, Москва, кто, окно, сок, касса, вино, там

c) Let's try it in Russian. Try to see how many different sentences you can make with the words from Ex.7b. You can make a rule of using each word once or, if you are learning with someone else, compete to see who can make more sentences (you can do it in writing or by taking turns). Have fun.

RUSSIASCOPE: RUSSIAN NAMES

People in Russia, as in England, have first names and surnames (family names). The first name is chosen by the parents. The formal versions of first names can tell you whether they are male or female. **Most female names have «А» at the end.** *Try to spot them:* Áнна, Антóн, Антони́на, И́нна, Макси́м, Ива́н, Ни́на, Ким. *One of the very rare exceptions is a male name* Ники́та.

A child gets his/her parents' surname at birth. Boys keep it throughout their lives. Girls may take their husband's surname when they marry (if they wish, nowadays). Many Russian surnames end in «-ОВ» (for men) or «-ОВА» (for women). There are others, e.g.: Сóнкин, Сóнкина. *We also have the second name which is a "patronymic" – we will discuss this later.*

How does it sound? In the same way that Russians do not put too much effort into unstressed «О»-s, they do not make some consonants at the very end of words sound clear either. For example, **«В» (like *v* in *van*) at the end of Russian male surnames sounds more like "ff"** (e.g. "Smirnov" (Смирнóв) is pronounced like "Smirnoff"). This is called devoicing. Keep in mind that if you say the words exactly as they are written, you are not going to confuse anything or anybody (as long as you get your stress right!), but knowing about devoicing will help when you listen to Russians. Also, if you have long-term plans for Russian, it might be a good idea to start making good habits. If you wish to have a go at saying these as Russians would, read this list of some Russian male surnames with the final «В» pronounced as "ff" (check your stresses!): Кóтов, Нóсов, Мáков, Иванóв, Максímов.

d) What's in a name? Read ALOUD and keep in mind which surnames are male and which are female. Note that «В» in female names sounds as *v* in *van* – it is only devoiced to "ff" if it is the last letter.

Tip! Make sure that there is ONLY ONE STRESS in each name – it's important for the names to sound right. Keep it on the same syllable in male and female versions of the same surname (no double-stressing!).

Кóтов - Кóтова	Титóв - Титóва	Максímов - Максímова	Иванóв - Иванóва
Сóмов - Сóмова	Носкóв - Носкóва	Анíсимов - Анíсимова	Сíтников - Сíтникова

Check that you did not add a second stress in female surnames.

To make it clear: There is no sound for "w" in Russian. It sometimes appears as «В». For example, "Doctor Watson" has become «Дóктор Вáтсон». Similarly, Russian does not have the sound for "th." It is replaced with «Т», for example, "Smith" turns into «Смит».

Now that we can introduce other people, we need to learn how to introduce ourselves. To learn the Russian word for "I", we will have a quick glance at one more letter, the last one for this unit.

(яя) *GROUP III (Funny Shapes) «Я я» stands for ya in yak.*

This is an unusual "*two-in-one*" letter in Russian. It is often read as TWO sounds – /y/ and /a/. Actually, when Russian children are learning to read, they do not realise that there are two sounds in this letter; they learn «Я» as *ya*, just as any other letter. «Я» is classed as a vowel and can carry stress. Try these syllables first:

AM - ЯM   AC - ЯC   AT - ЯT   AH - ЯH

NEW WORD: Я (я) - *I*

«Э́то я.»

«Э́то Я́на и Анто́н.»

Check *that you realise that* «Э́то я.» *is translated as "It's me".*

Ex. 8 a) Reading for meaning.

*Tip! As Russians do not use words for "is" or "are", you would be right to think that they **do not use a word for "am"** either.*

Я Макси́м. Э́то Антони́на.   Э́то Ива́н Со́мов. Я Ни́на Макса́кова.   Э́то Анто́н и Я́на.

«Я» when meaning "I" is NOT normally written in its capital form, unless it is at the start of a sentence, e.g., «Я и Анто́н» or «Анто́н и я». There is no preference in Russian of who goes first, «Я» or names of others.

b) Now it's your turn! Practice how you would introduce yourself and your group mates or your family and friends. See examples above. If you are learning in a group, have a round introducing yourself and the person on your right and then, if you wish, go in the opposite direction. You can use pictures from your mobile to talk about names in your family. This is how you learn to speak – by speaking!

c) If you are learning to write, try to write some English names below in Russian. Don't panic! Your name will sound the same in all languages (perhaps with a slight accent). There are Russian versions of foreign names, but that's a different story. To write a name in Cyrillic, try not to think about its English spelling. Instead, say it aloud, listen to the sounds in it and find one Russian letter for each sound, e.g., Samantha – Сама́нта

Also, we are not learning Russian handwriting at this stage as it feels that we have plenty on our plate as it is. If you feel you can cope with more, you can find a table of Russian cursive letters on the Internet.

Tip! Double letters will appear double in Russian too.

Emma, Tony, Kitty, Nick, Monica, Max, Anthony, Viv, Tina, Evan, Vicky, Thomas, Anita, Yvonne, Mina, Steve, Timothy, Nancy

> ***Check*** *that you remember that small* м, т *and* к *look the same shape as the capitals; that you have written* «КС» *for "x" in "Max".*

d) What's in a name? Read these names aloud. There is a lot to think about: stresses, tricky letters, unrounded «O», devoiced «B». Remember: after decoding the Cyrillic letters, Russian stress is paramount; the rest is a bonus.

Стас Носко́в	Ви́ка Токмако́ва	Ники́та Са́ввин	Анто́н Ми́тин
А́нна Ко́сова	То́ма Со́ткина	Инна Осо́кина	Но́нна Макса́кова
Ива́н Восто́ков	Макси́м Вито́в	Ким Со́тников	Антони́на Москвина́

WELL DONE! YOU HAVE COMPLETED UNIT 1!

It is good to think of what you can say in Russian in between your sessions with the book. We don't always have time to go back to the book, but we can THINK RUSSIAN. When you have a minute in your day (waiting in a queue or washing up), make your little sentences with Russian words you know, as this is the best way to learn to use words, that is, to start speaking. This is not to say that you have to memorise phrases (though that is OK too) – try to do some sort of mix and match, combining different words you know into small sentences. For example, think how you would introduce your friend in Russian, show your Russian visitor their room, point somebody towards a glass and so on. If you can say things aloud it would be even better. Keep peddling!

To say good-bye in Russian, we need one more letter – «Д» for *d* in ***dentist***. Practicing it might be best left for our next unit, but for today we can try ДО СВИДА́НИЯ (no separate stress on «до» is required – these two words sound as one).

Something old, something new (*revision of unit 1*)

Hi. I am glad you are back. I hope it means that you are happy to keep going. Before learning something new, we need to make sure that you remember and can handle the important things from Unit 1. Here are a few questions and exercises which will jog your memory and give you a chance to have another go at your Russian. Please do not treat these as a test – this is just to make sure that you've got what you need to move on.

1. Why does the Russian alphabet have more letters than the English one?

2. Can you name five letters that look and sound similar in Russian and in English?

3. Do you remember which of them are vowels?

GROUP I (*The Easy*): «Мм», «Тт», «Кк», «Аа», «Оо»

> ***Check*** *that you named* «А» *as **a** in father and* «О» *as **o** in for!*

Ex.1 a) Jog your memory. Can you remember our first Russian words? Can you make five sentences with them?

мáма, кот, там, кто? как?

4. What is so tricky about *The Tricky* letters? Can you name the three we have learnt?

5. Are they vowels or consonants?

GROUP II (*The Tricky*): «Сс», «Нн», «Вв»

b) Try not to trip up! (As before, these are not for translating or remembering. You just need to read them out loud – this is your reading practice.) Make sure that your tricky «С» is always like *c* in *cinema*.

СОК - КОС - СКОК
СОТ - ТОСТ - СТО
ТОМ - СОМ - МОСТ

МАК - САМ - СМАК
МÁСКА - КÁСКА - КÁСТА
СКОТ - СКОС - СÓСКА

(?) 6. How many stresses are there normally in a Russian word?

7. Why is it so important to get the stress right in Russian?

8. How do we know where to put stress in a Russian word?

9. Why aren't there any stress marks in words with only one vowel (monosyllabics)?

10. What happens to «О» if it is NOT under the stress, for example in Москва́?

11. Why do we need to remember about weak and unrounded «О»-s, since Russians would understand you if you say all «О»-s as *o* in *for*?

Ex.2 a) Watch your stress! Try to put only ONE stress in each word. Remember that all the power of your voice falls onto the long stressed vowel, so the other vowels are much weaker. Try not to round unstressed «О»-s. Note that the stress patterns are different in different columns.

воск - восто́к	кос - ко́смос	квант - окта́ва	окно́ - о́кна
мост - Москва́	ма́ма - ма́монт	ос - оста́ток	тонка́ - то́нок
сон - сосна́	ко́ма - ко́мната	ка́ска - каса́тка	носо́к - но́сом

b) Try not to trip up! Read Russian anagrams. Watch your stress.

кот - кто	То́ма - а́том	смо́ква - Москва́
скок - кокс	ко́смос - ско́сом	со́ков - сово́к

c) Jog your memory. Can you remember the words below? Now read them aloud, putting ONE stress in each. Then, try covering the stresses (for example, with a pen), and read the words again, trying to remember where the stress mark is, putting most effort into the marked syllable.

сок, мост, ка́сса, ко́мната, окно́, стака́н, ва́нна, Москва́

Check that you tried to stretch double consonants.

(?) 12. Do you know a Russian word for "is"?

13. What other words are not used in Russian sentences?

d) Reading for meaning. Remember to read aloud and translate one by one. Note that there are no stress marks – try to remember the stresses without them. I will be gradually removing stress marks in familiar words, so you would get used to reading them correctly without stresses being marked.

Анна там.	Кто там?	Сок там. Стакан там.
Москва там.	Как мама?	Комната там. Окно там.

(?) 14. What letters have we put into Group III?

15. Can you remember the three we had? Are these three vowels or consonants?

GROUP III (Funny Shapes): «Ии», «Ээ», «Яя»

Check that you pronounced «И» as a long sound (like ee in see).

Ex. 3 a) Try not to trip up! Don't forget to read everything aloud. And watch your stress – ONE per word! Remember that «И», «Э» and «Я» are vowels, so they can carry the stress.

маска - миска - Максим   таксист - токсин - такса

свист - свиток - свисток   сосок - сосиска - соска

эти - этика - этаном   окис - оскомина - оникс

Check that your unstressed «О»-s are weak and not rounded.

b) Jog your memory. Can you remember the following words? Don't forget to read them aloud.

это, вино, такси, и, кино, я

Check that you put the stresses in the right places and that you read the «И» long.

NEW WORD: **А** - *and (ONLY at the start of a sentence or a clause)*

When Russians speak, they often start their sentences with "And". Note that «И» is normally used to link words inside a sentence.

Check that you read «А» as "a" in "father"

c) Reading for meaning. Check that you apply the correct stresses where they are not marked.

Tip! When two sentences are joined into one, they become clauses (they are always separated by the comma in Russian). «А» can be used at the start of a clause as well as at the start of a sentence, e.g., Сок там, а стакан там

Это кино, а это касса.   Это вино, а сок там.   Это Иван и Эмма.

Это Токио, а это Москва.   Это комната, а ванна там.   Это Никита, а это Антонина.

Это мама, а это я *(looking at pictures)*.   Это Нина, а Инна там.   Это Омск и Томск.

d) Let's try it in Russian. Introduce the following pairs of people or things using the word «а» at the start of the second clause, e.g., Это Стас, а это Ким. Make sure you are *not* reading anything from the exercise above.

Иван - Анастасия;   мама - я *(looking at the pictures)*;   киоск - касса;

комната - ванна;   Минск - Иваново *(looking at a map)*;   вино - сок

> **RUSSIASCOPE:** *The names of some* **RUSSIAN CITIES** *can often look a bit long. Sometimes it is because they are made of two or more words. For example,* Новомоско́вск *has part of the word "new"* (ново) *and part of the word "Moscow", so it could possibly be translated as "New Moscow" (almost as New York). Similarly,* Новока́мск *is made of "new" and the name of the river* Ка́ма. *In famous Vladivostok (*Владивосто́к*) in the Far East,* «влади-» *is part of the verb "to own" and* «восто́к» *stands for "east".*

? 16. Why have we called «Я» a two-in-one letter?

Ex. 4 a) Decoding Cyrillic. Watch your stress!

Tip! If you have two vowels (e.g., «А», «О», «И», «Я») next to each other in Russian, you need to read them both, one after the other. One or neither of the two vowels can be stressed, but you cannot have stress on both, e.g., Ма́я, мая́к, маяка́ми.

я́мка	Ма́я	мая́к	но́во - но́вая	мая́к - маяка́ми
я́сно	со́я	стоя́к	ста́я - ста́ями	кая́к - каяка́ми
я́вно	стоя́	воя́ка	я́сно - я́сная	стоя́к - стояка́ми

> **Check** *that you noticed that there is NO letter* «а» *after* «Я» *as* «Я» *has the /a/ sound in it already.*

b) Just read and recognise! You do not need a dictionary for these Russian words, because they will remind you of English words when you pronounce them ALOUD! They might look odd, but they will sound similar to their English equivalents, so you need to pronounce them to recognise them. Watch your stress.

тост, ки́ви, кая́к, конта́кт, ви́ски, эскимо́с, як, коми́ссия, со́я, кака́о, анато́мия, инсти́нкт, такт, моски́т, тома́т, эконо́мика, ко́микс, кано́э, сава́нна, твист *(as in dance)*, кио́ск, ма́ска, стати́стика

? 17. What kind of words start with a capital letter in the middle of a sentence in Russian?

18. Which letter do most Russian female names have at the end? Do you know a male name that ends with «А»?

19. How do Russians pronounce «В» at the end of Russian male surnames?

20. What is more important: to say this «В» at the end correctly or to get the stress right?

c) What's in a name? Read Russian names (aloud). Watch your stress! (Remember: stress is very important for the names to sound right.) Note which names are male and which are female.

Tip! Keep in mind that names with «Я» at the end are female names, e.g., Анастасия. (Check that your stress in Анастасия is on the «И» and that «С» is read as "c" in "cinema.")

Я́на Ста́сова	Макси́м Ки́син	Ма́я Анто́нова
Анто́н Носко́в	А́нна Косо́нская	Анастаси́я Со́нкина
И́нна Яки́мова	Ники́та Ивано́в	Стас Са́ввинов

Check that you have ONE stress in each name.

? 21. Which of these two questions can be asked when looking at pictures: «Кто это?» or «Кто там?»

22. Where do Russians write «Я» (for *I*) as a capital?

Ex. 5 a) Reading for meaning:

Tip! «Я» can also stand for "me" when saying "It's me" – «Это я», for example, when showing your photograph or maybe responding to "Who's there?" at the door. E.g., Кто там? – Это я. (Who's there? – It's me.)

Я Анастаси́я. А это Ви́ка.

Это Макси́м Я́ков. А я Ма́я Ивано́ва.

Это Анто́н и Я́на, а я И́нна.

Кто там? *(at the door)* – Это я, Таи́са.

Кто это? – Это Стас. – А кто это? – А это Вика.

Кто это? – Это я. – А кто это? – А это ма́ма.

b) Now it's your turn. Have a round introducing yourself and people next to you, similar to what we did in Unit 1, but this time have a go at using «А» at the start of your second sentence, as in the examples above. Remember that you can use pictures from your mobile to practice your Russian.

To make it clear: Do not worry if you do not use «А» at the start of your sentences when you speak – it does not add any meaning, but works as a sort of connective. It is important, though, to spot the use of «А» when you read or listen to Russians.

Reading Challenge: Наискосо́к

This section will have only one word which will be made of letters that we have already learnt, sometimes in challenging combinations. It might be on the long side too. To read a long word in Russian, you need to do exactly the same as with shorter words – pronounce every letter, one after the other, and try putting one stress only, which is crucial. Do not try to read fast – do it as slow as it is comfortable, making sure the stressed vowel is the longest. It might pay to have a few goes. Today your reading challenge is **наискосо́к**. You don't need to learn this word or know what it means – just read it out letter by letter, with most effort on the stressed vowel.

c) Let's try it in Russian. Let's try putting it all together in your speaking. Using pairs of words below, introduce the first person or item (using «Это») and then say that the second person or item is there (using «там»). Make sure you don't look at the Russian words above! E.g., Это Во́ткинск. А Ива́ново там.

Nina – Inna;	Moscow – Omsk;	wine and juice – glass;
cinema – box-office;	room – bathroom;	Anton and Maya – Maksim and Anna

Check that you had two different Russian words for "and"
in the last column.

2

Questions and answers

► to read five new Russian letters;
► to read names of different countries written in Cyrillic;
► to learn more Russian words made up of the letters you know;
► to find out how many dialects Russians have;
► to ask and answer simple questions in Russian;
► to try starting a telephone conversation in Russian;
► to find out whether you put tea in your *samovar* and how fast a Russian *troika* can be.

GROUP III (Funny Shapes - *unfamiliar shape, familiar sound*)

Лл

«Л л» stands for l in fall. Can you name (and write) the other three letters of this group?

How does it sound? In English, "L" can be read in two different ways: like *ll* in *fall* and like *l* in *lit*. Russian «Л» also has two versions, but at the moment we are only interested in the first one, plain or hard, like *ll* in *fall*. To make sure you're pronouncing it correctly, move the body of your tongue back and down a bit, while keeping the tip behind your front teeth.

Ex.1 a) Decoding Cyrillic. (No translating - just reading aloud.) Note the stress in each word before reading, to see which of the vowels should be strong, long and loud, and which need to be weak and faded.

ЛОТ - ЛОТÓК - МОЛОТÓК   МÓЛНИЯ - МОЛÓКИ - МОЛОКÓ
КЍСЛО - КИСЛÁ - КИСЛОТÁ   СÁЛО - СОЛÓМА - САМОВÓЛКА
ÉЛЛА - ЭЛЍНА - ЭТАЛÓН   ЛÁВА - ЛАВЍНА - КОТЛОВЍНА

Tip! *When learning new words always check that you know where the stress goes.*

NEW WORDS:

КЛАСС - *a classroom, a class*   **САЛÁТ** - *salad*

СТОЛ - *a desk, a table*   **МОЛОКÓ** - *milk* (Watch the stress!)

Check that the last «О» in молокó *is the loudest and the longest of the three;*
that all your «Л»-s here sound like **ll** *in* **fall***.*

b) Reading for meaning:

Это класс, а стол там.   Это Áлла, а Éлла там.   Как салáт? А как сок?

Это салáт, а сок там.   Это молокó, а стакан там.   Как Слáва?

Это Клáва и Мѝла.   Кто там? – Это я, Лóла.   Кто это? – Это Таѝсия.

Check that you read all FOUR vowels in «Таѝсия», with one very
long and loud stress on the «И».

To make it clear: In addition to not having "a" or "the" in Russian, we do not use "some" and "any" in front of nouns as often as people do in English (although the words do exist in Russian). E.g., "some milk" will often translate to just «молокó».

c) Say it in Russian.

some milk and a glass;   This is the classroom, and the desk is there.
some juice and some salad;   This is a/the room, and the bathroom is there.
some juice and some wine;   This is some juice, and the salad is there.

Check that you translated "and" as «И» in the left column
and as «А» in the right column.

Tip! If you decide to write the above in Russian, make sure that you say each sentence (or phrase) aloud first and then write it down. Watch that the unstressed «О»-s appear as «О» in your writing.

d) Watch your stress! (as well as weak unrounded «О»-s). You don't need to worry about reading fast – make sure that you read all the letters correctly and get your stress right – you will get faster with practice. Remember: lots of effort on one stressed vowel in each word, to make it louder and longer; this makes unstressed vowels weak and indistinct.

склон - скло́ка - оско́лок   ло́кон - наколо́л - ко́локол   во́лки - во́локом - волноло́м
та́ял - та́лая - тала́нтом   свал - самосва́л - сва́лками   сла́ва - Сла́вик - Станисла́в
сло́во - ствол - столо́вая   о́клик - около́ток - о́коло   ло́мка - ла́комка - локомоти́в

Check that you realise that Russians would read «В» at the end as "ff"

> **NEW WORD: АЛЛО́** – *Hello (on the phone only!)*

Check that your «Л» here sounds like ll in fall.

Ex.2 a) How does it work in Russian? The following are the opening exchanges in three telephone conversations. Read them aloud, trying to work out what is going on in each of them as you are reading. If you practice with someone else, you can read in parts. Try to formulate two rules about how Russians use words to ask questions on the phone, then check whether they are similar to those in the boxed sections following the conversations.

1) – Алло́. Это Ма́я.   2) – Алло́. Это Та́я. А это кто?   3) – Алло́. Это Ми́ла.
    – Алло́.   – А это Станисла́в.   – Кто?
    – Кто это?   – Это я, Ми́ла Вла́сова!
    – Это А́лла.   – А-а-а, Ми́ла! Алло́.

Check that you realise that «А-а-а» is similar to "Ah" in English.

> **To make it clear:** «Это» *can be used when we are referring to something close to us or something further away. That's why we use* «Кто это?» *when speaking on the telephone, whereas in English one would ask "Who is that?"*

> **WORTH REMEMBERING:** *There are NO strict rules about* **WORD ORDER** *in Russian, which means that when Russians speak, words can appear anywhere in the sentence. Compare: «Кто это?» and «Это кто?» (Both questions mean exactly the same). For you it might be best to follow the English word order. This way you will be able to keep track of what you are saying. Just do not expect Russians to do it!*

b) Step-by-step guide on how to start a conversation on the telephone in Russian. Imagine that you are calling a Russian friend. You can try it with different names and vary it slightly. Here are some guidelines.

1. To start with, you need to say "*hello*!" (**Алло́.**).

2. Then you *introduce* yourself (on the phone) by saying "This is . . . ." in Russian (**Это . . . .**). In this exercise you can use your name or any Russian name from the previous exercises.

3. Now it is your *partner's turn* to say "hello" and introduce themselves (on the telephone). If they don't say who they are, ask them "Who is that?" (**Кто это?**) and wait for them to reply.

4. Now put it all together and do it without using any English, and possibly without looking at this guide!

If you don't have a partner to practice Russian with, you might end up with even more practice, as you can play both parts. Try not to lose track of whom you are speaking for, though. You can try it a few times using different names or different word order when asking, until you feel comfortable and don't need to look the words up.

> **WORTH REMEMBERING:** *Coming back to the WORD ORDER issue, in English sentences the word order is fixed and is absolutely crucial to linking words in a sentence. As a classic example, the English sentence "Kids eat free." only makes sense in this order, and you can't change it without changing the meaning (you can try it for fun, though). As Russian has very flexible word order, it uses a different method to link words into sentences – it adds little* **"identifiers" to the end of words to show which is linked to which** *(similar to how female names have «А» at the end). Thus, the word order stops being important. These "identifiers" tell you whether the word is a noun, a verb or an adverb. This means that in Russian you normally CAN swap the words round within a phrase, and as long as they have their identifiers, the phrase still has the same meaning. This is something to keep in mind for the future – for now you need to know that words in a Russian sentence might not necessarily follow the English word order, and sometimes you might need to rearrange them to make sense in English.*

> **How does it sound?** All «Л»-s above should have sounded more or less like *ll* in *fall*, with the body of your tongue slightly down and towards the back. Note that «ЛИ» in Russian sounds like *l* in *lit*, with your tongue closer to the palate.

Ex. 3 a) Just read aloud and recognise. Before reading, underline all cases of «ЛИ». When you read, try to pronounce all «Л»-s as *ll* in *fall*, except in «ЛИ» (where it should be like *l* in *lit*). Watch your stresses!

ла́ва, со́ло, кли́мат, лото́, лими́т, ли́лия, коло́ния, ло́тос, ова́л, кли́ника, сало́н, си́мвол, тала́нт, лимо́н, сала́т, ла́ма, оли́ва, сла́лом, кла́ссика, эли́та, кока-ко́ла, а́тлас, миллио́н, талисма́н, ало́э

b) What's in a name? Try to differentiate between «ЛА» and «ЛИ». Are the names all male or all female?

Ли́ка, Али́на, Ли́я, Ло́ла, Али́са, Э́лла, Ната́лия, А́лла, Ми́ла, Ли́лия, Васили́са.

Check that you read both letters in «ИЯ»: long «И» + «Я» like ya in yak.

Note that the Russian letter «Л» can have a slightly different shape, for example «Λ», which stands for absolutely the same sound. In books, newspapers and other printed materials you normally have «Л», while the other shape «Λ» sometimes appears in street and shop signs. E.g., «АΛИСА» and «АΛИНА» are popular names for cafés; you can come across «ЭΛИТА» as a name for a boutique or a furniture shop.

> *WORTH REMEMBERING:* As I mentioned before, the word order in English is crucial. To ask a **QUESTION** in English we normally need to put a verb first. For example, if we swap "is" and "this" in "This is Emma." we would be asking "Is this Emma?" In Russian, as the word order is not important, «Это Эмма» can be used as a question or as a statement. The tone of your voice indicates which one is which. So, when you ask "Is this Emma?" in Russian, the tone of the voice would go up on the last word, as if you are surprised «Это Э́мма?».
>
> So, to ask a question in Russian, you **DO NOT NEED TO CHANGE THE WORD ORDER.** You do **NOT** need to add any special words (like "do" or "does") either. The only thing you have to do is to put a question mark at the end when you write, and **RAISE THE TONE OF YOUR VOICE** on the last stressed syllable when you speak. E.g., **Это Э́мма?** – Is this Emma?

Ex.4 a) Reading for meaning. Check the stress before you read, as that is where you need to raise the tone of your voice for each question for it to sound like a question!

Это Алѝна?	Алло́. Это Москва́?	Это сок?	Макси́м там?
Это Ива́н?	Алло́. Это А́лла Мосоло́ва?	Это молоко́?	Касса там?

To start answering questions we need one more Cyrillic letter. We will start with positive answers.

GROUP III (Funny Shapes) «Д д» stands for *d* in *dog*

Do you remember the other *Funny Shapes*? Which three of them are vowels?

Now you can recognise the name of the British capital written in Russian: **ЛО́НДОН** (*Do the two «О»-s sound different when you are saying it?*)

> **NEW WORD: ДА -***Yes*

b) How does it work in Russian? Read the question-answer exchanges aloud and remember to raise the tone of your voice at the end of the questions. Summarise three common ways of giving a positive answer in Russian.

– Это Ли́да?	– Алло́. Это Москва́?	– Это молоко́?
– Да. Это Ли́да.	– Да, Москва́.	– Да.

In English there are all sorts of attachments to *Yes*, like "*(Yes), he is*" or "*(Yes), they were.*" In Russian, as the word order is quite loose, the grammar structure does not require any of those attachments. «Да» is a full, sufficient and polite answer. Sometimes Russians use full answers (e.g., Да. Это Ли́да.) or repeat the most important (often the last) part of the question (e.g., Да, Москва́.) to confirm things. More often than not, though, they just say «Да», which is not rude or abrupt. When you are learning, it is probably better to give full answers to make sure people understand what you agree with – and for some extra practice.

c) Question time. Using the Russian words that you know, make up questions in Russian similar to those above – you can use pictures, things or even people in the room. If you are working with someone else, try giving different kinds of answers – just «Да», a full sentence or confirming the most important word. Make sure that the tone of your voice is different in questions and answers.

The answers in the classroom might be pretty easy, but things are not always obvious when you are in a different country. For example, in Russia juice and wine are often sold in similar cartons, so you want to be sure you're buying the right thing. So, keep practicing questions. For Russians to know that you are asking, raise the tone of your voice.

Ex.5 a) Try not to trip up! This exercise will help you differentiate between the shapes of «Л» and «Д».

ДИ́МА - ЛИ́МА   ЛИВА́Н - ДИВА́Н
ВА́ДИК - ВА́ЛИК   КОЛО́ЛА - КОЛО́ДА
ДО́СКИ - ЛОСК   НАЛОВИ́Л - НАДАВИ́Л

> ***Check*** *that you differentiated between the two ways of reading «Л».*

In our conversations we do not always refer to other people by name – we often use words like "he" or "she". Let's have a look at their Russian equivalents. Before you read the new words in the box below, decide in which of the two words the «О» is stressed and strong (that is, long and loud), and in which it is unstressed, thus weak and not rounded. So, make sure that your effort goes on the correct vowel. The right stress will help you make «она́» sound different from «А́нна». (Stretching the double «нн» in «А́нна» will complete the job.)

> **NEW WORDS: ОН** (он) - *he*
>
> **ОНА́** (она́) - *she (Watch the stress and the unrounded «о»)*

Tip! To remember which is which, you might want to think that in both Russian and English, the word referring to a female has one letter more than that for a male: he - он; she - она́. Watch the stress! OR Think of она́ *as* он *with an added «А», which most Russian female names have at the end.*

b) Let's get this right. Read questions aloud, remembering to raise the tone of your voice. Use either «ОН» or «ОНА́» instead of the names in your answers, e.g.: Ли́я там? – Да, она́ там. However easy it might seem, these two words are commonly confused in foreign languages.

Tip! Try to make «Л» in «ла» and «ли» sound slightly different: the first more to the back and the second closer to the palate.

Дани́л там? – Да, ... там.
Ли́дия там? – Да, ... там.
Ники́та там? – Да, ... там.

Это Али́на Довла́това? – Да, это. . . . .
Это Кла́вдия Воло́дина? – Да, это . . . .
Это Станисла́в Лива́нов? – Да, это . . . .

Check that you worked out that «Это он» means "It's him"; and that you remembered that «Ники́та» is a male name in Russian.

> **RUSSIASCOPE:** *You know that similar gestures can have different meanings in different cultures. As Russians are Europeans, most of their gestures are identical to those in Britain and have identical meanings, for example, nodding for "yes" and shaking the head for "no". The only little twist is that Russians use «Да» to agree with any statement, whether it is positive or negative, e.g., Doesn't he like it? – Да. Since a direct translation "Yes, he doesn't" doesn't make sense in English, we would translate this as "No, he doesn't". That's why for you as a learner, it is always safer to give full answers and to ask straightforward questions.*

c) Say it in Russian. Keep an eye on your stress in «она́». Remember to raise the tone of your voice in questions. If you are learning to write, you can write these down.

I am Natalia, and she is Leah.
Is Ivan there? – Yes, he is.
Is she Ella? – Ella is there. She is Emma.

Who is that? – It's him.
Who is he? – This is Stanislav.
Who is she? – She is Maya.

How is he?
It's her.
She is there.

d) If you are learning to write, write the following English names in Cyrillic. Remember to say them aloud first and listen to the sounds they are made of. To make your job easier, you can write «Л» as «Λ» and «Д» as «Δ».

Sid, Donna, Elsie, Linda, Neil, Cindy, Dominic, Leigh, Amanda, Quintin, Adam, Cathleen, Maximilian, Nadine

Check that you wrote "Neil" as «Нил» and "Leigh" as «Ли».

How does it sound? Similarly to how «В» at the end of male surnames sounds like ff (so «Смирнóв» sounds like "Smirnoff"), some other Russian consonants (hard voiced sounds like «Д», for example) "lose their voice", that is, get devoiced. For example, **«Д» at the end of words sounds like /т/**, e.g., the name «Влад» sounds like /в л а т/. Again, as with devoiced «В»-s, it is not essential for you to follow this precisely to be understood, but you do need to be aware of this to understand Russians when they speak. Our new word «САД» (for *garden*), for instance, is most likely to sound like /с а т/. Try reading the following words like Russians would, to get the idea: сад, над, клад, склад, свод, вид

To make it clear: Words in slanting brackets, e.g., /с а т/, show us how words sound. This is called transcription. Technically, inside the brackets, there are NO letters (!) but letter-like transcription signs, each representing one sound. Compare: we write «сад» and pronounce /с а т/.

Ex.6 a) Let's get this right. Before you read, find those devoiced «Д»-s at the end, which Russians would pronounce as /т/. (There are ten altogether). Remember that the single stress is more important than anything else!

Влáда - Влад	сад - садовóд	отвóд - отводи́л
нáдо - над	яд - ядови́т	лимóн - лимонáд
кóдом - код	клад - кладовáя	скотá - скотовóд

«Это дом.»

NEW WORDS: ДО СВИДÁНИЯ - *Good-bye!*

ДОМ - *a house, a home*   ВОДÁ - *water*
ДÓМА - *at home*   СТАДИÓН - *a stadium,*
САД - *a garden*   *a sports ground,*
   often a sports centre

Check that водá *has the stress at the end and a weak unrounded* «о»; *that you notice the difference between* «дом» *and* «дóма».

> **RUSSIASCOPE**: The Russian word «ДОМ» is much roomier than the English word "house". «Дом» stands for any kind of building where people live or used to live: "a cottage", "a house", "a bungalow", "a block of flats", etc. In Russia all of these are «дом». Russian do have another word which means "building", but it is not as conversational.

b) Reading for meaning. Remember to raise the tone of your voice in your questions.

Это дом, а это сад.	Это вода? - Да, вода. Сок там.	Алло́. Это до́ктор Дани́лов? - Да.
Это стадио́н «Дина́мо»?	Это мост, а стадио́н там.	Алло́. Я до́ма.
А́лла и Влад дома.	А Ли́дия до́ма? - Да. Она́ до́ма.	Кто до́ма? - Вади́м и мама.

c) What would you say in Russian? Think of what you or others would say or ask in Russian in the following situations. Try to make at least three sentences which you might hear or use. Then check my suggestions below. Make sure your intonation is different in questions and in statements.

1) A Russian estate agent is showing you around a house where you might rent a room.

2) You are phoning a Russian friend. You know his Mum is supposed to have come out of hospital.

3) You have brought a Russian friend to a drinks-only party.

1) This is the house. This is the room. Is this a bathroom? Is the garden there? Yes, it's there. How is the house?

2) Hello (*on the phone*). This is . . . . Is (your) Mum at home? How is she?

3) This is wine, vodka and lemonade. A glass is there. Is this juice? This is some wine. Some water is there.

⟨чч⟩ GROUP III (Funny Shapes) «Ч ч» stands for *ch* in *child*.

Do you remember that Russian does not use combinations of letters to make different sounds? Now you can recognise a word which came into Russian from English – СА́НДВИЧ.

Ex. 7 a) Decoding Cyrillic. Watch your stresses and unrounded «О»-s.

ЧИН - ЧИНИ́Л - ЧИ́ННО	о́чи - то́чки - очка́ми	на́чал - начи́н - начина́л
ЧАД - ЧАДИ́Л - ЧА́ДО	ма́чта - мо́лча - моча́ло	кли́чка - кача́л - каланча́
ЧИСТ - ЧИСЛО́ - ЧИ́СЛА	ми́чман - ли́чно - отли́чно	до́чка - дичо́к - одино́чка

RUSSIASCOPE: ДА́ЧА.

If you are interested in the Russian way of life or have been to Russia in summer, this word might be familiar. ДА́ЧА is a place in the country or just outside the city where families often go in summer and might spend their holidays. Many Russians have a ДА́ЧА. In Russian cities, people mostly live in blocks of flats, not bungalows or cottages, so a ДА́ЧА is their chance to enjoy the summer. It might sound a bit grand, but most people use their ДА́ЧАs to grow vegetables and fruit, so a ДА́ЧА often brings a lot of work with it. The size of a ДА́ЧА depends on how much you earn; sometimes it is just a hut which provides shelter if it rains. Government officials' ДА́ЧАs of course have nothing to do with vegetables or sheds — they are more like country residences.

How does it sound? It is worth noting that our new word «ЧТО?» *(meaning "What?")* is pronounced as /sh t o/ and is more of an exception than a rule. So, if you say it as /ch t o/, nobody is going to get confused. However, «ЧТО?» is a very popular word, and to recognise it when Russians say it, you might want to get used to saying it like /sh t o/ yourself. Keep in mind: Russians often use «ЧТО?» for *Pardon* (as there is no special word for it in Russian), sometimes doubling it into «Что-что?». Make sure that you read «Ч» as "*ch*" everywhere else.

NEW WORDS:

ДО́ЧКА - *a daughter*   ЧТО? - *What?*
ОТЛИ́ЧНО - *excellent, great*

b) Reading for meaning. The questions with question words, e.g., «Кто?», «Что?», «Как?», do not require the rising tone – it is obvious that it's a question. Note the word order in questions and try to read «ЧТО?» as /sh t o/.

Что это? – Это лимона́д.	Что там? – Стадио́н.	Это кто? – А это до́чка, Ли́дочка.
А это что? – А это вода́.	А там что? – А там кино́.	Как она́? – Отли́чно.

c) Question time. Using «Кто?» or «Что?», ask blocks of TWO questions, following English word order in the first and swapping words round in the second. E.g., Что это? – Это стол. – А это что? – А это окно́. You can use my list below for answers or get your own things and pictures. Great to do with a partner.

класс, сала́т, мама, Вади́м, мост, сад, вода́, дочка, стол, Ли́дочка, комната, Владисла́в, дом

Russians add bits to ordinary words not only to link words in sentences but also to create new forms with slightly different meanings or to add some emphasis. For example, «ма́ма» often turns into «ма́мочка» for Mummy (with the same stress). Similar bits are often added to Russian names to make them sound nicer or lovelier, e.g., «Ли́да» can become «Ли́дочка» (still with one stress at the front, but now a similar pattern to «ко́мната»). Eventually we will learn to understand the meanings of different "bits", but for now you need to learn to read the words with added "bits" keeping only one stress in each word!

d) Watch your stress! Make sure that you read «Ч» as *ch* in *child* everywhere.

ва́нна - ва́нночка	коса́ - коси́чка	стака́н - стака́нчик
ви́лка - ви́лочка	лиса́ - лиси́чка	дива́н - дива́нчик
са́ло - са́лочки	вода́ - води́чка	вола́н - вола́нчик

Pp *GROUP II (The Tricky - familiar shape - different sound)* «P p» stands for *r* in *error*

but it rolls.

How does it sound? The Russian sound for «P» sounds more like /r/ in Scots English. This might seem easier said than done. Try starting with the English /d/ or /t/ and push the air between the tip of the tongue and the alveolar ridge, at the same time making an effort with the tip of your tongue not to let the air go through. This should result in a repetitive tap. Have a few goes. It might be comforting to know that Russian children do not learn to say «P» properly until the age of 4 or 5, and that does not stop them talking! **What you CANNOT do is skip «P».** If you are not good at rolling it yet, read «P» as an English /r/ but do not omit it – you might be making different words!

Now we can read the Russian name for Russia! Note the stress and make sure that the «O» is not rounded.

«Это Россия.»

Do you remember the Russian name for the capital of Russia?

Tip! *The main trap with the letter «P» (like* **r** *in* **error***) which a lot of learners fall into is that in English you are not used to pronouncing /r/ after vowels (for example, in "car" or "doctor"). In Russian, normally* **all letters in a word are read,** *so «P» will be read wherever you see it, even after «A» or «O». Compare: "doctor" and* ДО́КТО**Р***, with a strong «P» after «O».*

Ex.8 a) Decoding Cyrillic. Make sure you read all your «P»-s. Look out for unrounded «O»-s too.

РОТ - ВОРО́ТА   СОР - СОРО́КА
РОВ - КОРО́ВА   ВОР - ВОРО́НА
РОК - МОРО́КА   КАР - КАРТИ́НА

*Check that you realise that Russians would pronounce «В»
in «ров» differently from «В» in «корóва».*

RUSSIASCOPE: **САМОВА́Р** *(Did you pronounce «P» at the end?)*

A САМОВА́Р *is a very peculiar kind of a kettle which was invented by Russians and surely came in handy during our cold winters. My home city of Tula (120 miles to the south of Moscow) is commonly considered the homeland of samovars. There is even a samovar museum there.*

Originally, the water was heated by glowing embers, which were put into a pipe going through the middle of the metal container, with water filling the space around the pipe. The boiling water was then poured into a teapot which was placed on top of the samovar to keep it hot. Thus, no tea inside a samovar!

Nowadays all samovars are electric. You can find various sizes, from tiny souvenirs to enormous 50-litre giants in large office buildings. Traditionally they were polished, but these days they are often painted with various Russian patterns. Many Russian families still keep a samovar for special occasions or honoured guests, or just as a decoration.

b) Try not to trip up! In each word make your «Р» is heard and make sure there is *one* stress only.

рост - росто́к   дар - дари́л - мандари́н   страна́ - стра́нная - страни́чка

риск - раски́с   тир - касси́р - канони́р   равно́ - ра́вная - равни́на

три́ста - трико́   вор - вара́н - навари́л   трава́ - тра́вная - тракто́вка

ро́дина - родни́к   торс - торо́с - трактори́ст   кварта́л - ква́ртами - кварти́ра

Check that you read «АЯ» as two separate vowels and did not put additional stress; that you noted five unrounded «О»-s.

c) Just read and recognise. Sort out the words into three groups: 1) where «Р» is read after «О», 2) where it is read after other vowels (e.g., «А», «И»), and 3) where «Р» is read after a consonant. One word will be in two groups.

корт, кардамо́н, до́ктор, дра́ма, эква́тор, команди́р, кроссво́рд, кора́лл, контра́кт, монито́р, корридо́р, сарди́на, кориа́ндр, радиа́тор, эскала́тор, кардина́л, санскри́т, марина́д, кало́рия

NEW WORDS: КВАРТИ́РА - *a flat, an apartment (NOT a block of flats, which is* дом*)*

КА́РТА - *a map*   **МА́РКА** - *a postage stamp*

ТОРТ - *a gateau (as a whole)*   **КАРТИ́НА** - *a painting*

                                   *(**карти́нка** - a picture, an illustration, NOT a photograph)*

RUSSIASCOPE: Most Russians in cities live in flats, which is **КВАРТИ́РА**. *Note that a block of flats is «дом». If you look at a Russian address you might spot a letter «д.» for «дом» (like English "No.") and two letters «кв.» for «кварти́ра» (which is the actual apartment). The order in Russian addresses could vary, so this might turn out to be handy to know.*

Ex. 9 a) Reading for meaning. Remember your intonation in questions.

Это ка́рта. – А это Росси́я?

Это дом. – А кварти́ра там?

Что э́то? – Это ма́рка.

Как карти́на? – Отли́чно!

А это что? – Это торт.

Это кварти́ра, а ко́мната там.

Лари́са там? – Да. А это Мари́на.

Это кто? – Это до́чка, Ри́та.

Алло́! Это Росси́я?

Йра до́ма? – Да, до́ма.

Ви́ктор там? – Да, он там.

Она́ до́ктор? – Да.

Check that you tried to pronounce «что» as /sh t o/.

b) Let's get this right. Fill in the gaps using the words below.

Это кварти́ра, а это.............. .

Что там? – Там.............. .

Это самова́р? –.............. .

Кто она́? – Она́.............. .

Это сок, а .... там.

Карти́на там? – Да,.............. .

Это дом и.............. .

Как до́чка? –.............. !

А это что? –.............. торт.

сад, отли́чно, там, стадио́н, это, ко́мната, да, стака́н, до́ктор

c) Big sort out. Using Google maps (you can try them in Russian), rearrange the list of cities below going from Moscow to the Far East. You can write them out in the correct order or number them. Read the correct list aloud, watching your stress (one per word). If you have not got time, you can just read the names aloud as they are.

Сара́тов, Орск, Владивосто́к, Чита́, Сама́ра, Омск, Москва́, Красноя́рск

d) If you are learning to write, remember to write «Р» after a vowel in Russian even if you do not hear it in English, e.g., Mark - Марк.

Nora, Lorna, Rory, Sandra, Dorothy, Orville, Richard, Eric, Roxana, Miriam, Oscar, Christina.

Check that you wrote «КС» for "x" in Roxana.

(йй) *GROUP III (Funny Shapes)*

We have come across six of these so far: three vowels in Unit 1 and three consonants in this unit. Can you name them?

How does it sound? The sound for «**Й**» can probably be described as *y* in *employ* with no /o/ (quite different from *ee* in *employee*) or as *y* in *yes* with no /e/. A similar sound is found at the very start of some English words like *yet, yacht, yak* and *yule*, just before the vowels. The Russian «**Й**», though, is much more tense and a bit more abrupt than the English sound. To say it correctly, you need to start with English /i/, to tense your tongue up and push the air through the slot between the tongue and the palate in a short burst with a lot of effort, without making it long. It should come out as a ***tense and rapid*** sound. «**Й**» is classed as a consonant and is a very important sound in Russian!

To make it clear: Note that the v-shape at the top of the letter «Й» is part of the letter and not a stress mark. «Й» (like *y* in *employ*) and «И» (like *ee* in *employee*) are two different letters which **stand for two different sounds**: «Й» is a tense and rapid consonant, while «И» is a long and effortless vowel. Keep an eye on them.

Ex.10 a) Decoding Cyrillic. Remember to tense your tongue up and put some short burst of effort in pronouncing your /й/.

МОЙ	МАЙ - МА́ЙКА	мой - доло́й	тайни́к - та́йна
ВОЙ	ЛАЙ - ЛА́ЙКА	Ной - родно́й	двойни́к - дво́йка
ДАЙ	ЧАЙ - ЧА́ЙКА	рой - настро́й	тройни́к - тро́йка
КРАЙ	СЛОЙ - СЛО́ЙКА	дай - отда́й	стройни́т - стро́йно

Check that you spotted weak unrounded «О»-s in the last two columns.

NEW WORD: ЧАЙ - *tea*

b) Reading for meaning:

Это чай и лимо́н.

Это чай, а молоко́ там.

Что э́то? – Это самова́р. Чай там.

Это чай, а это торт.

Это чай? – Да, чай.

А это что? – А это молоко́.

c) Try not to trip up! Watch the stress!

Tip! «Й» *cannot carry a stress as it is a consonant; thus,* «мой» *or* «рай» *do not have the stress marked as they are monosyllabics. Keep an eye on the stress marks elsewhere. If the stress is over the* «И» *(in the first column here), all the effort needs to go into it, making the unstressed* «О» *weak and unrounded. Note the stress is on the «А» in the second column, which makes «И» less important, but not too short.*

мой - мой   сва́и - свай

рой - рой   ста́и - стай

стой - сто́ит   Ра́и - рай

RUSSIASCOPE: **ТРО́ЙКА** *stands for three horses harnessed in a particular way pulling a sleigh, carriage or cart. The word «тройка» comes from the Russian word «три», which means "three". In the past a* тройка *was used in Russia to get around fast — it can reach 50 km per hour, or over 30 mph. Since one of our writers, Gogol, compared Russia to a* тройка *flying through the time and space into the unknown,* тройка *has become a symbol of Russia. In modern Russia,* тройка-s *are as rare as horse carriages in Britain. You can have a* тройка *ride during some festivals such as the New Year season or Pancake week (the last week before Lent); sometimes you can see newlyweds in a* тройка. *On a bright frosty day, with the sparkling snow around and little bells jingling on the horses' harnesses, it is absolutely thrilling!*

To make it clear: «**Й**» in Russian normally **follows** one of the **vowels** («А», «О», «Э» etc.), for example, чай, тро́йка, Никола́й.

---

d) If you are learning to write, write the following English names in Russian. First say the name in English (aloud), listen to how it sounds and decide which of the following letter combinations you will use: «**ЭЙ**», «**АЙ**» or «**ОЙ**». E.g.: Michael – Ма́йкл.

Simon, Ray, Roy, Amy, Kylie, May, Troy, Sadie, Miles, Eileen, Clyde, David, Irene, Ivy, Lloyd, Myra, Adrian, Raymond, Silas

We have finished for today and you have got the Unit 2 under your belt! **ДО СВИДА́НИЯ**.

«До свида́ния» is made of two words written separately: «до» which means "until" or "up to", and «свида́ния» (with one stress) which stands for "seeing somebody". Together they make «До свида́ния», which is "till seeing you" or "See you", except it does not have to be informal.

ДО СВИДА́НИЯ. Don't forget to THINK RUSSIAN (perhaps questions and different positive answers this time?) and keep peddling!

Something old, something new (*revision of unit 2*)

Hi. I can't say «Алло́» as this is only for when we speak on the phone, but by the end of Unit 3 we will learn our proper Russian "hello". Before we get to the new things though, we need to check that you are comfortable with what we have learnt so far. Let's have a go. Try answering questions before reading on. If in doubt, you can find some prompts later on, or you can always go back to the previous units – all the answers are there.

1. Which of our letter groups needs most of our attention? Can you name the four letters that we have put in it so far?

2. Are they vowels or consonants?

3. Why do we need to be extra careful with Russian «Р» (like *r* in *error*)?

GROUP II (*The Tricky*): «Сс», «Нн», «Вв», «Рр»

Ex.1 a) Decoding Cyrillic (ALOUD!). Watch the stresses – only ONE per word, even if the word is long! Keep an eye on unrounded «О»-s too. Finally, make sure that you read «Р» after vowels, like in «до́ктор».

я́р - я́рка - я́рмарка

сва́ра - сва́рка - ва́рварам

трос - тра́сса - тро́сиком

вар - кова́рна - сокова́рка

вор - воро́там - воротни́к

кран - экра́н - киноэкра́н

Check that you realised that the last word in each string of the first column has the same pattern as «ко́мната».

b) Let's try it in Russian. Match the words on the left with those on the right to make meaningful sentences. Translate each phrase. Note that there is one combination which does not quite make a straightforward meaningful sentence. If you work with someone else, you can take turns in making sentences for each other to translate.

КТО	ОН
ЭТО	ОНА́
КАК	ТАМ

? 4. Can you name five Russian vowels that we have come across? (two from Group I and three from Group III)

Check that you name the vowels the Russian way, e.g.: «О» like o in
for (not like in "rose").

5. How many sounds does «Я» represent?

RUSSIAN VOWELS: «Аа», «Оо», «Ээ», «Ии», «Яя»

c) **Just read and recognise** and big sort out. Sort out the following words into three groups: 1) monosyllabics, 2) those consisting of two syllables, and 3) those made of three or more syllables. Note that the number of syllables equals the number of vowels in Russian. You can either put an appropriate number over a word or rewrite them into three columns. Read all words aloud with all the effort on one stressed syllable. Make sure you pronounce all your «Р»-s.

риск, тра́ктор, а́рмия, старт, актри́са, контра́ст, самова́р, экстра́кт, арома́т, ритм, мото́р, астроно́м, экскава́тор, карате́, мини́стр, трон, са́ри, каранти́н, исто́рия, кани́стра, монито́р, авиа́тор

Ex.2 a) Jog your memory. Can you remember the following words? Read them aloud watching your stress.

торт, стака́н, сок, он, она́, ко́мната, ка́рта, окно́, ма́рка, ва́нна, карти́на, ка́сса, кварти́ра, мост

b) **Spot the difference.** Mark the stresses in the words below, without looking them up in the line above. Compare the two lines and name (in Russian!) the words which changed places. What do they mean?

торт, стакан, сок она, он, комната, марка, окно, карта, ванна, квартира, касса, картина, мост

If you feel you might need more work with the words above, choose two or three which are most challenging for you, highlight or just underline them, have a good look at them (note the stress) and then look away or shut your eyes and try to remember them (not all – just those that you have marked). Try it a few times till you feel you remember them. Make a few sentences with them. Next time you open the book, have another go at the same words. Then you can pick the next two or three.

? 6. What are the two possible translations of «Кто это?»?

7. What are the *three* types of words that Russians don't use in their sentences?

8. What is the difference between the two Russian words for *and*: «А» and «И»?

c) Reading for meaning:

Это Россия, а это Москва.	Это я, а это он.	Это картина? – Картина там.
Это карта. – А это Ростов?	Кто это? – Это Роман и Кирилл.	А она кто? – Она Кира.
Как Виктор? – Отлично.	Это квартира. А это комната и ванна.	Это Арина, а Ирина там.

? 9. What can you say about word order in Russian?

10. Does it have to change when you ask a question?

11. How would Russians know that you are asking a question?

12. When Russians answer "yes", what do they do about "it is", "I was", "they do" etc.?

d) Question time. Using the words from Ex. 2b, make statements (e.g., Это квартира.) and then turn them into questions by raising the tone of your voice (e.g., Это квартира?). Great to do in pairs: one of you says a sentence, and the other acts quite surprised, asking a question with the tone of the voice up. Don't forget to take turns.

GROUP III (Funny Shapes): «Ээ», «Яя», «Лл», «Дд», «Чч», «Ии» (like ee in see or employee), «Йй» (like y in employ (with no "o"), but more tense and rapid).

This group is getting bigger. It is the largest of the groups, but not the most challenging, except perhaps «Й». Can you pick out the three vowels in this group?

Ex. 3 a) Try not to trip up! Read the Russian anagrams below. Take your time.

НАДО - ДАНО	ВИДАЛ - ДАВИЛ	СОЛДАТ - ДОСТАЛ
ДОМНА - МОДНА	НАВОД - ДАВНО	ДЛИНА - ЛИНДА

? 13. A lot of Russian «Л»-s are read as *ll* in *fall*. What do you do with your tongue to achieve this?

14. When do we know «Л» is read slightly differently? Where do you need to move your tongue?

b) Big sort out. Sort out the words below into three groups: those with «Л», those with «Д» and those with both. You can write them out in different groups or just number them. It is also good to read them aloud as you go.

дом, класс, миллио́н, лава́нда, сала́т, стадио́н, мандари́н, Ло́ндон, молоко́, лимона́д, алло́, да, сканда́л, соли́ст, стол, лими́т, кома́нда, лимо́н, мандоли́на, кандида́т, авока́до

Check that your «л» in «ли» sounded different from the other «л»-s, and that the last sound in авока́до *is unrounded /o/.*

? 15. Are names with «Я» at the end male or female?

16. How do we need to read TWO vowels next to each other (e.g., «АЯ» or «ИЯ»)?

c) Decoding Cyrillic. Make sure you read two vowels as two vowels, with unstressed «Я» being weak. Watch the difference between «ЛА» and «ЛИ» too.

Ма́я - Та́я - Ра́я   Ли́лия - Ли́дия - Кла́вдия   ма́лая - ста́рая - ми́рная
Ли́я - Мари́я - Анастаси́я   Ита́лия - Австра́лия - Молда́вия   а́рмия - та́лия - ми́дия

Check that you realise that the first three strings are female names; that the fourth string is country names.

d) What's in a name? Imagine that you are sorting out a group of Russian visitors (see the list below) into shared rooms. Say who is male and who is female, e.g., Ири́на – э́то она́. If you work with somebody else, choose a *random* name from the list, determine whether it is male or female and ask your partner a question for them to give you a positive answer. E.g., Ири́на – э́то она́? (Watch your stress in «она́» and remember to raise the tone of your voice for the question.) After your partner finds the name in the list and answers («Да.», «Да, она́.» or «Да, э́то она́.»), it is their turn to ask a question. Try varying your answers.

Рома́н, Вла́да, Ли́я, Ки́ра, Станисла́в, Лари́са, Марк, Варва́ра, Ники́та, Ли́дия, Тама́ра, Вади́м, Ви́ктор, Ната́лия, Ари́на, Мака́р, Владисла́в, Я́на, Кла́вдия, Родио́н, Кири́лл, Васили́са

Check that you can find two names where «В» would sound like ff; *that your «Л» in «ЛА» and «ЛИ» sound slightly different.*

? 17. How many stresses do we put in a Russian word?

18. How would Russians pronounce the «О» in «Москва́» and «Росси́я»? Why?

19. Why is it important to know about unrounded «О»?

> ### *RUSSIASCOPE: RUSSIAN DIALECTS*
>
> *In Russia there are over a hundred ethnic groups who are not of Russian origin and speak their own language. For them Russian is a second language. They are most likely to speak Russian with an accent (like Welsh speaking English). Like England, Russia has regional dialects, meaning that people from different areas speak differently but have no problem understanding each other. In Russia though, there are only three main dialects: northern, central and southern, which is not many, considering the size of the country.*
>
> *The main difference between the dialects is in how people pronounce those unstressed «O»-s. In the north they say them exactly as o in for, and all «O»-s are rounded, which makes it heaven for beginning learners. In the central dialect, which is spoken in Moscow and St.-Petersburg and is considered standard Russian, all unstressed «O»-s are weak and unrounded (e.g.: in Москва́ or она́). In some southern or Far Eastern areas the unstressed «O»-s become even more open and sound more like a in father, which, I agree, can be confusing. There are other differences, but they never seem to be as sharp as between some dialects in English.*

Ex.4 a) Watch your stress and unstressed unrounded «O»-s. Make sure you have ONE stress even in longer words. All «Ч»-s here are read as *ch* in *child*.

ка́чка - качо́к	сачо́к - сачки́	ка́рта - ка́рточка	моло́чник - стано́чник - ло́дочник
мо́чка - молчо́к	волчо́к - волчки́	ма́рка - ма́рочка	москви́чка - води́чка - во́дочка
то́чка - толчо́к	роднично́к - роднички́	са́нки - са́ночки	яи́чко - яи́чник - я́мочка

 20. How do Russians pronounce «Д» at the end of words (e.g., in «сад»)? And what about «В»?

21. Why do we need to know about this, since Russians would understand us even if the words are pronounced exactly as they are written?

22. When we talk about transcription, what do we see in slanting brackets: letters, sounds or signs representing sounds?

b) Try not to trip up! Before you start, find and highlight five words which have «Д» at the end (which Russians would devoice into /т/). Watch your stress patterns in each column.

сад - доса́да - досади́л	ра́да - маскара́д - ра́дости	кача́й - кача́лка - раскача́л
час - часо́к - часосло́в	ча́рка - очаро́ван - ча́рочка	эско́рт - эстра́да - эскадро́н
род - наро́д - кислоро́д	э́ра - Эвриди́ка - э́врика	кара́т - квадра́та - кавардак
яро - ярка́ - ярова́я	ско́ро - сковоро́дка - ско́рая	роди́т - сморо́дина - саморо́док

c) Big sort out. Sort out the words below into four groups: monosyllabics, those with the stress on the first syllable, those with the stress on the last syllable (on the very last vowel) and those which are stressed somewhere in the middle. Make sure you read them ALOUD! If you want more practice, write all the words without marking the stress and then read them (aloud) across the columns or even in a random order. If you are not learning to write or are short for time, you can highlight different groups in different colours or put numbers above the words. Make sure that you know what the words mean.

алло́, дом, тро́йка, ка́рта, он, окно́, мост, до́чка, касса, карти́на, кто, такси́, самова́р, да, ванна, до́ма, Ло́ндон, кино́, она, Влади́мир, стол, как, сала́т, молоко́, сад, стадио́н, да́ча, чай, Росси́я, стакан, отли́чно, ма́рка, кварти́ра, торт, комната, что, Москва, до свида́ния

> *Check that you remember that Russians would read «что» as /sh t o/, and that your «Л»-s in «молоко́» and in «отли́чно» are read slightly differently.*

Ex. 5 a) Reading for meaning. Make sure that you raise the tone of your voice in your questions.

Это Влади́мир? – Да. Это он.   Алло́. Это Москва́? – Да. – А это Ло́ндон.   Лари́са до́ма? – Да, до́ма.
Это до́чка? – Да.   Это ванна? – Ванна там. Это ко́мната.   Стол там? – Да, там.
Что это? – Это ма́рка.   Это молоко? – Да, молоко. А это чай.   А это что? – Это самова́р.

> *Check that you remember that Russians would pronounce «что» as /sh t o/.*

b) Question time. Before we start, try to find as many things and pictures which you know Russian words for (make sure that you include a few people); you can search for images on your mobile. It is fun trying to type it in Russian – you might get different images. You will be asking and answering two different types of questions in Russian: 1) questions with question words (e.g.: «Кто?», «Что?», «Как?»), which do *not* require «Да» in the answers (or "No", which we will learn in Unit 3), e.g., Что это? – Это торт. ; 2) questions with raising intonation, which *do* need «Да» (or "No"), e.g.: Это торт? – Да. (or «Да, торт.» or «Да, это торт.»). This is great to do with someone else – you can even score points and compete for more correct answers (with or without «Да»). In our own language, we choose a correct form for an answer automatically – in a foreign language, we need to pay attention and to practice.

Wow! We know nearly half of the Russian alphabet! Let's have a look at where the letters that we have learnt are in the alphabet. Here we go:
А ... В ... Д .... И Й К Л М Н О ... Р С Т .... Ч .... Э ... Я
There are two good reasons to have an idea of where to find letters within the alphabet: dictionaries and lists. It might come handy if you need to look up a Russian word in a dictionary or to find something in a Russian directory or any other sort of list. Though you might not want to spend time learning the whole of the Russian alphabet, it might help to divide it roughly into

three parts: the *start* section, the *middle*, which sounds a bit like the English alphabet (К Л М Н О. . . .), and the *end* section. Then try to remember which part a particular letter belongs to. For example, it is good to know that «В» (for *v* in *van*) is at the start in Russian, and not at the end like in English, or that «Э» is at the end, and that «Я» is the very last letter.

c) **Big sort out.** Below there are the names of some Russian cities. Put them in alphabetical order, as they would appear in a train timetable in Russia. Read them aloud with ONE stress in each name. If you have a few words starting with the same letter, list them according to their second letter.

Орск, Ростóв, Самáра, Москвá, Ивáново, Кисловóдск, Сочи, Костромá, Лиски, Элистá, Армавир, Ялта, Красноярск, Читá, Владивостóк, Томск, Донскóй, Новодвинск

Reading Challenge: Смородиновая

(try putting ONE stress only, making the stressed «О» the longest and the loudest)

? 23. What kind of a building can be called «дом» in Russian?

24. What is the difference between «дом» and «дóма»?

Ex. 6 a) Reading for meaning. Read the following opening exchanges of three telephone conversations (slightly longer than in Unit 2). Make sure that you follow what is going on – you might want to read a bit slower to understand the meaning, as well as pronouncing the words.

1)	2)	3)
– Аллó. Ярослáв.	– Аллó.	– Аллó.
– Аллó. Это я, Лия. Мама дóма?	– Аллó. Кто это?	– Аллó. Это дом Кóтова?
– Да, дóма.	– Это Влад Дмитрóв.	– Да. А это кто?
– Как онá?	А дóктор Чáлин там?	– А это Лида. Николáй дóма?
– Отлично.	– Да.	– Да-да, Лидочка. Дома он.

b) **Let's try it in Russian.** Let's try to do something similar–that's good to do with someone else. We can start as we did in Unit 2, but this time we'll ask for somebody at the other end. Pick a Russian name from somewhere above, or if you already have a real friend in Russia, use their name. Imagine that you are calling them but get someone else instead. What would you say? Do it without using any English! If you do not have a partner, try playing both parts.

? 25. What do you need to do with your tongue to pronounce «Й» correctly?

26. If we compare «Й» (like *y* in *employ*) and «И» (like *ee* in *employee*), which one is tense and rapid?

27. Which is a consonant and which is a vowel?

28. Which of them requires more effort?

Ex. 7 a) Decoding Cyrillic. Remember to tense your tongue up to make «Й» tense and rapid.

мой - домо́й - домово́й

дай - дава́й - отдава́й

рай - сара́й - карава́й

вой - во́йлок - война́

чай - ча́йник - чайнво́рд

строй - стро́йка - настро́йка

RUSSIASCOPE: **ТОЛСТО́Й**

This name is from the field of Russian literature, as they would say in a quiz. You might have heard of his mammoth book "War and Peace" («Война́ и мир»). Some people find it fascinating, while others say it is a bit challenging. Nevertheless, it is definitely considered remarkable and ranks among the world's classics.

Tip! As male names in Russian normally end with a consonant, Russian names with «Й» at the end are male names, e.g.: Никола́й, Толсто́й.

29. After which letters do you normally find «Й»: vowels or consonants?

30. Can «Й» have a stress on it? Why or why not?

b) Try not to trip up! Keep an eye on long «И» – whether it is stressed («И́») or unstressed («И»), it is different from tense and rapid «Й».

Tip! Watch your stress too! In the first two columns, make «И́» («И» under the stress) stronger than «О» or «А». And make it long! Note that the stress pattern in the last two columns is different from the first two.

МОЙ - МОЙ	КРОЙ - КРОЙТ	СТО́ИТ - СТОЙ	ДО́ИТ - ДО́ЙКА
СЛОЙ - СЛОЙ	ЧАЙ - ЧА́ЙНКА	СТО́ИК - СТО́ЙКА	ВО́ИН - ВО́ЙСКО

c) Just read and recognise and a big sort out. Underline all the words that have «Й» in them and then read the list carefully, making sure that your «Й» and «И» sound different.

диск, ла́йкра, И́ндия, домино́, данти́ст, Тайла́нд, санда́лия, Чи́ли, райо́н, Ирла́ндия, майо́р, Владивосто́к, Никола́й, майо́лика, Си́рия, Яма́йка, ра́дио

45

To make it clear: You might have noticed that «Й» normally follows a vowel, producing combinations like «АЙ», «ОЙ», «ЭЙ» and similar. Traditionally, Russian words do not start with the letter «Й». However, you can come across possibly half a dozen words with «Й» at the start. They have come into Russian from other languages – for example, the name of the English city of York is spelt as «Йорк».

d) Say it in Russian:

Who is he? – He is Doctor Smith.

What is this? – This is a sports ground.

Who is there? (*at the door*) – It's me.

How is the flat? – Great!

Is this Lidia? – Yes. It's her.

Is this the house? – Yes, it is.

Is the tea there? – Yes, it is.

Is Victor at home? – Yes, he is.

Good-bye.

Check that you raise the tone of your voice at the end of the questions with no question words; that all your answers in the right column are different.

3

Mine or yours?

WHAT'S THE PLAN?

- ► to recognise and use four new Russian letters;
- ► to learn more Russian words using our 20 letters;
- ► to say "hello" and "thank you" in Russian *(we are getting there!)*;
- ► to use Russian words for *my* and *your* in your sentences;
- ► to say "no" in Russian and give negative answers;
- ► to have a go at saying what you and others eat or don't eat;
- ► to find out what a balalaika is and how old it is.

Chain of chemists in Russia

NEW WORDS: МОЙ - *my, mine*

ТВОЙ - *your, yours*

*Check that there is no vowel between the sounds /т/ and /в/ (like v in **van**) in «твой».*

Ex. 1 a) How does it work in Russian? Read the small exchanges below and see how Russians use the new words.

- Это твой дом?   - Это мой класс.   - Твой чай там?   - Что это?
- Да, мой.   - А мой там!   - Да.   - Это твой самовáр.

> *Check that you raised the tone of your voice at the end of the first two questions.*

b) Let's try it in Russian. Using my suggestions below, ask different questions and give different forms of positive answers, similar to the above. It is good to do this in pairs.

house, glass, tea, samovar, juice, lemon, garden, desk, gateau, classroom, lemonade, salad.

Well done! There is something else that you need to know about using the words «мой» and «твой», but first we need to have a good look at how our /й/ sound is represented in different words.

Ex. 2 a) How does it work in Russian? Read aloud and compare the syllables. Listen carefully to the *sounds* and see how the Russian /й/ sound appears in spelling.

АМ - ЯМ   АК - ЯК   АН - ЯН   АР - ЯР   АС - ЯС   АЛ - ЯЛ

> *Check that you have noticed that in each pair, the second syllable sounds like*
> *the first syllable with a /й/ sound in front;*
> *that you realise that we do NOT write the letter «Й» in front of «А» as we have*
> *a two-in-one «Я» for that. E.g., yak - як*

b) Decoding Cyrillic. Read the word pairs aloud. Note that the second word in each pair sounds like the first word with an /a/ sound added to the end. E.g.: чай /ч а й/ - чáя /ч á й а/. Watch your stress, particularly in the last two columns.

> *Check that you remember that transcription in slanting brackets*
> *shows how a word sounds.*

мáй - Мáя   стой - стóя   мой - моя́   трóйка - троя́к
рáй - Рáя   строй - стрóя   стóйка - стоя́к   мáйка - мая́к

> *Check that you noticed that in the last two columns, in the second word of each pair*
> *«О» is weak and unrounded, while «Я» is long and loud, e.g., МОЯ́ sounds more like*
> */м а й á/; (compare it to the name «Мáя» (from the first column) where the stress is*
> *on the «a»).*

c) If you are learning to write, write the following English names in Russian, using «Я» (as part of «ИЯ») at the end. E.g.: Lydia - Ли́дия. Make sure there is NO «Й» before «Я» and no «А» after it!

Antonia, Emilia, Maria, Olivia, Silvia, Victoria, Delia

> **WORTH REMEMBERING**: *In the same way that full Russian names can be easily identified as male or female by their endings, other Russian words also have gender and can be* **masculine** *or* **feminine**, *depending on whether they have «А»/«Я» or a consonant at the end. For example, «Мари́я» and «ко́мната» are both feminine, while «Ви́ктор» and «стол» are masculine. Russian also has neuter, but we will concentrate on the first two at the moment.*

Ex. 3 a) Big sort out. Sort out the words below into two columns – masculine and feminine. If you are not practicing writing, read out all the masculines first and then all the feminines. If you are not sure which letters are consonants, skip back to the start of the revision of Unit 2.

дом, кварти́ра, стол, стака́н, сок, до́чка, ма́рка, сала́т, ко́мната, чай, ка́рта, сад, да́ча, карти́на, стадио́н, мост, ванна.

b) Let's get this right. Name some Russian words that you know and say whether they are masculine (with a consonant at the end) or feminine (with «А» or «Я» at the end). Note that, among the words you know, it is only nouns that can have gender, while, for example, «как» would not. Also, some of your nouns might be neuter (e.g., окно́), but we will concentrate on identifying masculines and feminines for now. This can be fun to do as a group or in pairs: one person says a word and asks for its gender – masculine or feminine, or neither. You might agree that whoever gets it wrong is out, and the last person remaining is the winner.

> **WORTH REMEMBERING**: *You might remember that in Russian there is no strict word order, and words are linked into sentences by different "identifiers" attached to the end of them. Thus, words connected to feminines often have «А» or «Я» at the end. For example, to say "my Mum" we need to put «А» at the end of «мой». This will give us something like /м о й + а́/, which is spelled as* **«МОЯ»** *(as we do not normally write «Й» before «А»). This word sounds more like /м а й а́/ because the stress falls on the «Я», and «О» becomes weak and unrounded. As a result, we will have* **«МОЯ́ МА́МА»** *(with the effort at the end of «моя́»).*
>
> *So, when you want to use "my" in Russian, you need to keep an eye on the end of the words it relates to, in order to know whether to use «мой» or «моя́». «Мой» is only used with masculines, e.g., мой до́ктор, мой дом, while for feminines we would need «моя́», e.g., моя́ мама, моя́ ко́мната.*

---

c) Reading for meaning. After you read a sentence, find the words for *my* and decide whether it has a masculine (мой) or a feminine (моя) form. Underline the word which it is linked to, which is the same gender. Remember to put your stress at the end in «моя» with *no* effort on the unstressed unrounded «О». Keep track of the meaning too.

Это мой стол, а это моя картина.

Это моя комната. Моя ванна там.

Это Владимир Чалин. Он мой доктор.

Кто это? – Это Ирина, моя дочка.

Что это? – Мой сад. – А это? – А это стадион.

Мой стакан там? – Да, там.

Моя мама дома.

А это что? – Это мой атлас и моя карта.

d) Let's get this right. Say in Russian that the following are yours.

Tip! Before speaking, have a glance at the end of the word and decide which gender it is. Then choose the right form of "my": мой *or* моя. *Only then say it aloud. E.g.,* класс *(consonant at the end > masculine >* мой*) –* Это мой класс.

дом, квартира, стол, стакан, дочка, чай, марка, салат, комната, карта, сад, дача, картина, самовар

> **WORTH REMEMBERING:** *Similarly to how* «мой» *has a masculine and a feminine form,* «**ТВОЙ**» *(your/s) also changes its ending depending on whether it refers to masculines or feminines. E.g.,* твой дом, **твоя комната**.

Check that there is no gap between /т/ and /в/ and that the stress in «твоя» is on the «Я».

Ex. 4 a) Let's get this right. Choose correct forms of «мой» and «твой» to match the genders of the words they refer to. Mark the stress on the feminine forms (моя/твоя) to make sure you pronounce them correctly. Remember to raise the tone of your voice at the end of the questions when reading.

Это мо. . . квартира, а это мо. . . комната.

Это тво. . . стол? – Да, мо. . . .

Это Лидочка. – Она тво. . . дочка? – Да.

Алло. Тво. . . мама дома? – Да.

Мо. . . класс там? – Да, там.

Это мо. . . карта? – Да, тво. . . .

Это мо. . . стакан.

Это тво. . . чай?

Тво. . . дача там?

b) Now it's your turn. Think of how you would ask somebody whether the following things are theirs. First, decide on the form of the word for *your/s* («твой» or «твоя»), and only then ask your question, e.g., Это твой дом? Это твоя картина *(not photo)*? If you work with somebody else, find some pictures on your mobiles, for example, of some people or the place where you live. Have a go at asking and answering questions using мой/моя and твой/твоя. Remember to give full as well as shorter answers. If you have no pictures at hand, use my suggestions below:

desk, juice, room, tea, classroom, map, gateau, flat, daughter, garden, samovar, stamp, glass, doctor, bathroom, salad, house, dacha, picture *(not a photograph)*

Here is one more opportunity to THINK RUSSIAN! Every time you have a chance in your day, try to use the Russian words you know with «мой»/«моя» and «твой»/«твоя» - say which things are yours or think of how you would ask somebody if they are theirs. Now, though, it might be time for a new letter.

🄳 *GROUP III (Funny Shapes)* «Б б» stands for *b* in *bar*

Tip! To differentiate this new letter «Б» from the familiar but tricky «В» (for v in van), think that it has some sort of a bar at the top ("bar" starts with "b"). Every time you seee one of them, look for a "bar".

Ex. 5 a) Watch your stress! Note that the stress patterns are different in different columns.

блин - блондин - блондинка	набок - набор - набрана	бай - байка - балалайка
бой - отбой - набойка	бочка - бочок - бабочка	оба - облако - облаками
бар - барак - баранина	битва - ботва - области	баян - боярин - обаяния

RUSSIASCOPE: БАЛАЛАЙКА

Балалайка is a traditional Russian musical instrument which looks like a triangular guitar but sounds a bit like a mandolin. It usually has only three strings and can be of all sorts of sizes from prima (the most common) to contrabass. Despite its popularity, the балалайка is not as old as people often think – it appeared only at the end of the 19th century but gained almost instant popularity. During the Soviet time, when folk art was promoted as part of national identity, there were a lot of balalaika groups and even orchestras created. Some of them have become world famous.

---

b) Spot the difference! In every word there is one letter changed or added to make the following word. Make sure that you put one stress and do not stress or round the first «О» (which is not stressed here). You can name each new letter (in Russian!).

обои - обил - облил - обвил - обвал - облава - обивал - обвалил - обвалила

How does it sound? Similarly to «В» and «Д» which get devoiced, or "lose their voice" at the end of words (like in «Смирнóв» and «сад»), **«Б» sounds like English "p"** if it is the last letter in a word. For example, Russians would pronounce the English name "Rob" as /r o p/. This can also happen before some consonants, often before «К». So, in your new word «корóбка», do not waste your effort trying to make «Б» voiced and clear next to voiceless «К» – it will sound exactly like the English "p".

NEW WORDS: БРАТ - *a brother*

РАБÓТА - *work (a place of or a piece of), a job*   **ЯБЛОКО** - *an apple*
КОРÓБКА - *a box (made of paper, card or cardboard)* **СОБÁКА** - *a dog*

*Check your stresses and unstressed «О»-s, and that /л/ in «я́блоко» sounds like **ll in fall**.*

«Это мой брат»

«Это моя́ собáка»

To make it clear: «Собáка» is a general word for a dog. Russians have specific words to indicate whether an animal is male or female. Note that «собáка» (although it refers to all dogs) is a feminine word, so when you use it in a sentence you need to link it to «моя́» or «твоя́».

c) Let's get this right. Pick all the feminines from the box above and use them with the word «твоя́», e.g.: Это твоя́ корóбка?

d) Try not to trip up! Keep an eye on «Б» (for b in *bar*) and «В» (for v in *van*). Make sure that you put one stress even when you have more syllables.

волáн - баллóн - болвáном   Я́ва - я́вно - я́блоко
барáн - варáн - барáнчик   Вáнда - бáнда - вóдная
соврáл - собрáл - собáка   бóдро - вóбла - вóбрана

Ex. 6 a) Reading for meaning. Keep an eye on your «Б» and «В».

Он твой брат? – Да.

Я́блоко, бана́н и абрико́с там.

Это моя́ соба́ка Ди́на.

Как твоя́ рабо́та? – Отли́чно!

Моя́ коро́бка там? – Да, там.

Это кто? – Это Бори́с, мой брат.

Что это? – Это твоя́ коро́бка.

Алло́. Брат до́ма? – Да, дома.

Это брат и я, а это мама.

Check that your «Бори́с» is stressed at the end.

WORTH REMEMBERING: *You might have noticed that in the last two examples, there were no «мой» or «твой». This is very common, as Russians do NOT use words «мой/ моя́» or «твой/твоя́» as much as "my" and "your" are used in English. The reason is that in English, words like this (called "possessive pronouns" in linguistics) are often used to replace "the", e.g., "I'll put my coat on". You are most likely to put your own coat on — here "my" has a grammatical function, to indicate a noun. In Russian, there is no need for that, as "the" is not required in the first place. «Мой/моя́» are used mainly when it is important to specify that something belongs to you, rather than to somebody else. The same applies to «твой/твоя́» and other similar words. So, Russians can easily say «Это брат» instead of «Это мой брат», unless the distinction from somebody else's brother is necessary. Nevertheless, having a habit of using «мой/моя́» and «твой/твоя́» correctly is very important, as gender "identifiers" are a big part of Russian grammar. Also, note that if «мой/моя́» or «твой/твоя́» are used, they are normally placed in front of a noun.*

---

b) Let's try it in Russian. This activity will help you to start developing a skill of noting the gender of Russian words and linking words correctly when gender is involved. Let's start with small phrases made of two words connected by «и», e.g., дом и рабо́та. Next, identify genders of each of the words and use «мой/моя́» with them, e.g., мой дом и моя́ рабо́та. This is great to do with someone else. Then you can move to sentences, and finally try different questions, e.g., Это твоя́ ка́рта и твой а́тлас? or Как твоя́ мама и твой брат? Keep peddling.

③₃ *GROUP III (Funny Shapes)* «З з» stands for *z* in *zebra*

How does it sound: Russian sound for «З» is normally very **distinctive, voiced and reasonably loud** (unlike «С», which is always quiet and voiceless). You need to make «С» and «З» noticeably different from each other, as they make different words.

Ex. 7 a) Try not to trip up! Make sure that you differentiate between «С» and «З». (Spot one pair where Russians would read «Д» as /т/.)

ЗАМ - САМ	ЗИЛ - СИЛ	КОСА́ - КОЗА́	ЗАСО́Р - ЗАЗО́Р
ЗАД - САД	ЗАБО́Р - СОБО́Р	ЛИСА́ - ЛИЗА́Л	ЗАНО́С - ЗАНО́ЗА

To make it clear: Sometimes the shape of our new «З» is confused with that of our old «Э». They do not normally cause any problems when you read (as «З» is a consonant, while «Э» is a vowel), but watch them when you write. The new letter «З» is made of two small semicircles and looks like the digit "3", while the old «Э» is all rounded, making one big semicircle. To make sure you remember the difference, you can copy the following pairs of words. Read each word aloud before writing it, making sure that «З» and «Э» are different shapes. Watch your stresses: зато́ - э́то, задо́к - э́дак, заро́с - э́рос, зако́ном - эконо́м.

---

b) Decoding Cyrillic. Make sure you do not slip into /c/ when reading these. When two consonants are next to each other, try not to make a gap or insert a vowel between them. Watch your stress too.

знак	засло́н - засло́нка - заслони́л	Зи́на - корзи́н - Карамзи́н - Зи́ночка
злак	разбо́р - разбо́рка - разбира́л	зной - козо́й - козодо́й - ко́зочкой
звон	затво́р - затво́рник - затвори́т	я́зва - язви́л - заяви́л - я́звочка
изба́	зада́ча - разда́ча - раздава́л	ко́зам - каза́к - казано́к - ска́зочно

NEW WORDS:

ЗАВО́Д - *a factory, a plant*   **ЗА́ВТРА** - *tomorrow*
ВОКЗА́Л - *a big station (a terminal)*   **ВИ́ЗА** - *visa*

Check that you remember that Russians would pronounce the final «Д» in «заво́д» as /т/.

c) Reading for meaning:

Что э́то? – Э́то радиозаво́д.

А э́то что? – А э́то автовокза́л.

Э́то вокза́л? – Да. – А ка́сса там? – Да, там.

Э́то ви́за? – Да. Э́то твоя́ ви́за. – Отли́чно.

Твой брат до́ма? – Он за́втра до́ма.

– Алло́. Э́то заво́д?

– Да, заво́д «А́том».

– А Зо́я Раки́тина там?

– Да. А э́то кто?

– Э́то Зинаи́да Козло́ва.

До свида́ния.

До за́втра.

d) Let's try it in Russian. See how many different sentences you can make with the new words; questions count too. If you work with someone else, you can compete, taking turns until you run out of options – whoever made the last sentence wins.

e) Just read and recognise. Read out only those words which have the stress at the front, then those which have the stress at the very end, and finally those which are left, with the stress in the middle.

ви́за, кри́зис, зодиа́к, диви́зия, ро́за, моза́ика, визи́т, Кирги́зия, диза́йн, транзи́т, эро́зия, ва́за, диноза́вр, оа́зис, экзо́тика, озо́н, тонзилли́т, до́за, транзи́стор, казино́, ли́нза, бизо́н, виско́за, зо́на, борзо́й, транквилиза́тор

(Ee) *GROUP II (The Tricky)* «Ee» stands for *ye* in *yes*.

This letter might be the trickiest of them all. Thus, as it is one of the most frequently used letters in Russian, it needs a lot of our attention.

> **How does it sound?** «Е» (like *ye* in *yes*) is one of the four two-in-one letters in Russian. Similar to the first one that we have learnt, «Я», which has /й/ and /а/ in it, «Е» contains **two sounds - /й/ and /э/**, both combined in one letter. «Я» (like *ya* in *yak*) is quite open, while «Е» (like *ye* in *yes*) is narrower.

Ex. 8 a) Decoding Cyrillic. Read the syllables below aloud. All of them should start with a /й/ sound.

ЯМ - ЕМ   ЯЛ - ЕЛ   ЯР - ЕР   ЯН - ЕН   ЯТ - ЕТ

Tip! Try not to call the Russian letter «Е» as you would in English, even if you talk in English about it. Always name «Е» like ye in yes! To get used to it, you might even stop before reading it and say to yourself: "Yes, I know it!"

> **To make it clear:** «Е» (for *ye* in *yes*) is a different letter from «Э» (for *e* in *end*)! To begin with, unlike «Э», we need to start «Е» with a /й/ sound and to make sure that there are TWO sounds for this letter - /й/ and /э/. Also, «Е» is incomparably more popular in Russian than «Э», which is rare. From my experience, getting this difference right saves learners a lot of hassle!

b) Let's get this right. Read the syllables below aloud. The first syllable in each pair has our old «Э» (like *e* in *end*), while the second syllable should have a /й/ sound at the front to make our new «Е» (like *ye* in *yes*).

ЭМ - ЕМ   ЭН - ЕН   ЭЛ - ЕЛ   ЭР - ЕР   ЭТ - ЕТ

> **How does it sound:** Whenever you see two Russian vowels next to each other (the same or different) you need to read them separately, one after the other. Together they produce exactly the same sounds as when they are on their own. Make sure you read **«Е»** *as* ye in *yes* after any vowel. Have a go: АЯ, ОЕ, ИИ, ИЕ, АЭ, ОО, ОЯ, ЯЯ, ЕЕ.

c) Decoding Cyrillic:

ЕМ	ÉЛИ - ÉСЛИ	ест - наéст	доéл - надоéл
ЕЛ	ÉВА - ÉВРО	éла - заéла	короéд - дармоéд

Check that you realise that Russians would pronounce «Д» as /т/ in the last pair.

> **NEW PHRASES: Я ЕМ** (я ем) - *I eat (I am eating)*
> **ОН/ОНÁ ЕСТ** (он/онá ест) - *He/she eats (He/she is eating)*

> **To make it clear:** Most Russian verbs have only one form in the present tense. This means that they use the same form to say "I eat" and "I am eating" (or "I read" and "I am reading"). Thus, «Я ем салáт.» might mean "I am eating some salad." or "I eat salad.". If Russians would want to specify that they do it with some kind of regularity, they would use words like "often", "sometimes" or "always" (we will learn them when we need them).

d) Reading for meaning. Keep an eye on your «Е» (or «е») (like *ye* in *yes*).

Я ем салáт, а Зóя ест сáндвич.

Лúда ест банáн. А я яблоко ем.

Борúс ест «Кит-кэт», а Úра – «Твикс».

Кто торт ест? – Николáй и Зúна.

А что ест Кирúлл? – Он банáн ест.

Онá ест тост? – Да, ест.

The Russian verb "to eat" is a rather unusual verb: it does not follow any regular rules or patterns. We are going to learn it first, before we get to all others.

> **How does it sound?** Two-in-one letters (we know «Я», like *ya* in *yak*, and «Е», like *ye* in *yes*, out of the four of them) are very special in Russian as they include that all-important /й/ sound. To understand what's so special about it, let's compare two English words, *canyon* and *cannon*. If you listen carefully, you might notice that the first *n* in *canyon* sounds slightly different, sort of softer, than the first *n* in *cannon*. Something similar happens in Russian, for

example, in the word **«НЕТ»** (for "no"). However, in the Russian «нет», /й/ (from «Е») is not distinct or separate, like in *canyon* – /й/ sort of merges with /н/ and produces a slightly different version of /н/ which is **pronounced closer to the palate, thus called *"palatalised"***. So, «нет» has three sounds and is pronounced as /н'э т/, with *no* separate /й/.

NEW WORDS:

НЕТ - *no*   **НЕ** - *not*

Tip! To remember which one is which you can think of these as being opposite to their English equivalents: «нет» has «Т» at the end while "no" does not, and vice-versa for «не». E.g., **Нет**, это **не** мой сок. – *No, this is not my juice.* You might also compare the number of letters in these – Russian «нет» has three, while English "no" has two, and the other way round for «не».

Ex. 9 a) Reading for meaning. Remember to raise the tone of your voice in your questions.

Это твой чай? – Нет, не мой.

А это моя коробка? – Да. – Отлично.

Это твой дом? – Нет, это моя дача.

Это твоя квартира? – Нет. Моя квартира там.

Это завод? – Нет, это не завод. Это вокзал.

А это не Саратов. Это Саранск. – Да? – Да-да.

А Ева дома? – Нет. Она дома завтра.

Это Неводов. – Он доктор? – Нет, не доктор.

Check that you put only one stress in the surname «Неводов»,
and that it is at the front (a similar pattern to «комната»)

b) Say it in Russian. Make sure you get «нет» and «не» the right way round. Try to give different versions of negative answers: full, shorter or short.

She is not Lidiya. She is Liliya.

Is he a doctor? – No, he isn't.

Is this your job? – No, it isn't.

Is your brother at home? – No, he isn't. He is at home tomorrow.

Is this your dog? – No, it's not mine.

This is not a station. The station is there.

c) Let's try it in Russian. Find things or pictures which you know the Russian words for. If you work on your own, have a mix of those which are yours and those which are not. Make positive and negative sentences, e.g., Это мой сад. OR Это не моя собака. It is great to do this with someone else. Before starting, *swap some* of the things and pictures. Ask each other questions (you can use «твой»/«твоя») and answer them using a lot of «да» or «нет». Try to vary your answers. Remember that we also have questions with question words. Take turns.
E.g., Это твоя квартира? – «Да.» OR «Да, моя.» OR «Да, это моя квартира.»
– А это стадион? – «Нет.» (OR «Нет. Это не стадион.») Что это? – Это твой сад!
Enjoy speaking Russian.

How does it sound? Similar to how Russian «Н» can be read as an ordinary /н/ (like in «он») and as palatalised /н'/ (like in «нет»), **most Russian consonants have two versions: plain and palatalised.** You might remember that we had two ways of reading «Л» – the /л'/ in «ли» (with the tongue closer to the palate) is the palatalised version of the ordinary plain /л/ (with the body of the tongue back and down). The difference is subtle and, for English speakers, does not matter much, while in Russian these two versions can make different words, making it much more important for you as a learner. So, most consonants *BEFORE* **«Я» and «Е»** are *palatalised*, that is, need to be pronounced with the tongue closer to the palate and slightly tensed up; very much as we did for /й/, except here /й/ is not pronounced as a separate sound. Have a go at these syllables:

НЭ - НЕ	МЭ - МЕ	ДЭ - ДЕ	ВЭ - ВЕ	РЭ - РЕ
НА - НЯ	МА - МЯ	ДА - ДЯ	ВА - ВЯ	РА - РЯ

Ex. 10 a) Attention: palatalisation! Read the pairs of words below, making sure that in each pair the second consonant sounds slightly different from the first. Remember that «Я» is more open than «Е».

МАК - МЯК	МЭР - МЕР	НАМ - НЯМ	РАД - РЯД
МАЛ - МЯЛ	СЭР - СЕР	ВАЛ - ВЯЛ	РА́СА - РЯ́СА

Though palatalisation might sound a bit tricky, it is quite manageable. The contexts of the words above are never the same, so you are not going to confuse anything by not getting them exactly right. All you need to do is to try making them sound slightly different. The difference is subtle, and a small move of the tongue towards your palate is normally enough. As palatalised consonants are very common in Russian, it is good to practice them so that Russians will be able to understand you easily.

b) Attention: palatalisation! Watch your consonants *BEFORE* «Я» (which is open) and «Е» (which is narrower).

нет - нем - не́мка	дел - наде́л - заде́л	мел - мял	мя́лка - ме́лко - ме́лочи
бес - бел - бе́лка	сяк - кося́к - бося́к	нем - ням	ре́ки - ре́чка - ря́дом
мял - мя́та - мя́со	вял - завя́л - заве́т	меч - мяч	те́ма - те́сто - те́сно

To make it clear: Two-in-one vowels (at the moment «Я» and «Е») do not affect, and are not affected by, other vowels (e.g.: «А», «О», «Э» or «И») in any way, as two vowels next to each other are always read as two separate sounds. AFTER vowels, «Я» and «Е» sound exactly as they are in the alphabet, with strong and distinctive /й/ sound, e.g.: «ИЯ» in «Росси́я» sounds like /и й а/ at the end.

c) Just read and recognise. Watch out for palatalised consonants (those *before* «E»). These words will sound very much like their English equivalents, but palatalisation makes them sound more Russian.

текст, момéнт, зéбра, метр, арéна, балéт, библиотéка, дирéктор, комéдия, оркéстр, комéта, крем, акадéмия, скетч, батарéйка, камéлия

> **NEW WORDS:**
>
> **МЯ́СО** - *meat*   **МА́СЛО** - *butter*

To differentiate between two similar words, it might help to find some kind of a link or an association in real life. For example, some of my students think that meat is harder to chew than butter, so the word «мясо» with palatalised /м'/ is harder to pronounce. Some link «мясо» to cats who like meat and say "meow", which starts like «мя» in «мясо». Any links will do to help you remember.

Ex. 11 a) Big sort out. Read out all the food items:

стадиóн, банáн, завóд, кинó, я́блоко, торт, стол, окнó, мáсло, вокзáл, квартúра, сáндвич, кáсса, мя́со, лимóн, картúна, тост, мáрка, салáт

> *WORTH REMEMBERING: In addition to not having articles (like "a" and "the"), Russians do not have anything similar to the words "do" or "does" that make questions or negative sentences in English. For example, to ask "Does he eat meat?" we need to do exactly the same as we did before – raise the tone of our voice:* Он ест мясо? *(Remember that this can be translated as "Is he eating meat?" too.)* **To say that we do not eat something, we just need to put «НЕ» in front of the verb:** Я не ем мáсло.

b) Reading for meaning. If you are translating the sentences below, make sure that you phrase your translations properly in English. Find at least three phrases which can be translated only one way.

Тáня ест мя́со? – Да, ест.

Я не ем салáт.

А Кáтя мáсло не ест.

– Кто не ест торт? – Онá не ест.

– Что он ест? – Лимóн. – Лимóн?! – Да.

– Собáка сáндвич не ест? – Да, не ест.

Нáдя ест я́блоко? – Нет.

А тост он ест? – Нет, не ест.

Он не ест мя́со. А онá?

Check that you tried to palatalise consonants before «Я» in the names.

c) Let's try it in Russian. Using the food items from Ex.11a, Google sentences on your mobile like "He/she is eating an apple." Choose an image and say what you see, e.g., «Он/á ест я́блоко.».

If you work in a group, write the words for food items from Ex.11a on slips of paper, put them in a bag and have each person draw one. You need to say that you are eating what you have on the slip. The person next to you has to say the sentence about you and only then about themselves (remember to swap between «ем» and «ест»). Keep going, until everybody has said two sentences. If you have time, you can swap slips and have another round.

d) Now it's your turn. Make blocks of two sentences: the first about you and the second about somebody else (for example, your brother or daughter, if you have one; otherwise use names). Say whether you or somebody else eat meat, salad, butter or "Kit-Kat", e.g., Я <u>ем</u> мясо, а (мой) брат не <u>ест</u>. Remember to choose the correct form of "eating", «ем» or «ест».

When you THINK RUSSIAN, add negative sentences now! Also, when you are at the table you can think of how to say in Russian that you are eating, for example, some toast or an apple, etc. Keep speaking.

Now we have space for just one more new letter in this unit, in order to be able to say "hello" and "thank you" in Russian.

⬤ GROUP III (Funny Shapes) «П п» stands for *p* in *pot*.

And that's it. We can do with something fairly straightforward after our tricky «E» (Did you say *ye* like in *yes*?) and all that tongue activity with palatalisation.

Ex. 12 a) Decoding Cyrillic. Watch your stress. Note that the last word in each string on the left has the same stress pattern as «ко́мната».

капо́т - пото́к - па́тока	по́за - Эзо́п - эпизо́д
поко́й - поко́и - по́ймана	по́яс - пая́л - поясни́л
поёл - поёла - по́едом	по́чта - поча́ток - почита́л
поби́т - пробо́й - про́бовал	па́водок - подво́дник - поводо́к

Check that you spotted the difference between «поко́й» and «поко́и» (with a long «И»).

> **NEW WORDS:** ПО́ЧТА - *post-office, mail, often email*
>
> ПА́ПА (па́па) - Dad

«Э́то мой па́па»

A typical Russian letter box on a door

As strange as it looks, the word «па́па» is masculine (by default). So, we will say: «моя́ ма́ма», but «мой па́па». The word «па́па» came into Russian from French and was initially only used by the aristocracy. Then, in the 20th century it became extremely common in conversational speech and pushed the two original Slavic words out: one into formal speech and the other into slang. Thus, in a dictionary you will find another word for "father", which is formal. There is a formal word for "mother" too.

b) Say it in Russian. Let us see how we can combine a new word, for example, «па́па», with the other Russian words that we have come across. Say the phrases and sentences aloud. Watch the intonation in your questions.

your Mum and your Dad	Is this your Dad? – Yes, it's him.	My Dad eats meat. – And mine doesn't.
my Dad, my daughter and I	How is your Dad? – Great!	My Dad is not a doctor. He is a director.
This is my Mum, and Dad is there.	Is Dad at home? – No, (he isn't).	Dad is at home tomorrow.

You can do this kind of exercise with any new words yourself, aiming to combine them with the words you already know and make various phrases, sentences, questions and answers. It will help your speaking enormously. If you have a chance, try saying things aloud. You can write them as well if you are learning to write.

Tip! It is important to differentiate between «П» and «Л». Some of my students see «Л» as a letter with one "leg" out ("leg" starts with "l" for «Л»). Alternatively, you can note that both sides of «П» are parallel (which starts with the same sound). Some link «П» to the letter pi (π) in maths.

c) Try not to trip up! Make sure that you keep the stress on the same syllable throughout the column (i.e., second on the left, first on the right). Remember to make your «ЛИ» (like in *lit*) sound different from «ЛА» (like in *fall*).

лопа́та - лопа́тка - пала́тка	па́лка - ла́пка - пи́лками
допи́л - поди́ - пола́дил	па́лочка - по́лочка - ла́почка
опла́та - запла́та - зарпла́та	вли́пла - Па́влик - пла́вали
пила́ - лила́ - прили́пла	по́лдник - по́длинно - по́длая

d) Just read and recognise. Read aloud, watching out for the tricky Russian «P». If you are learning to write, you can write these out into three groups: those with «П», those with «P» and those which have both. If you feel that you would possibly be happy to pick up more words, highlight a few which you think might be useful and make sentences with them, noting their stresses.

план, па́спорт, а́рмия, порт, стоп, пирами́да, тра́ктор, старт, спазм, спорт, пило́т, тра́нспорт, капита́н, исто́рия, ко́мпас, парк, компа́кт-диск, при́зма, эско́рт, рэп, олимпиа́да, пара́д, микроско́п, пира́т, аэропо́рт, тапио́ка, рок-н-ро́лл, поэ́т, карп, эскала́тор, па́нда, трампли́н

e) Attention: palatalisation! Spot palatalised consonants, including «П», before «E» and «Я». Note that some words do not have any palatalised consonants.

пе́на - пе́ла - пе́кло   со́пли - сопи́т - сопя́т

па́ста - спе́та - пя́тая   де́ло - поде́лка - плодя́т

пя́тка - тя́пка - тря́пка   ве́тка - заве́т - приве́т

> **NEW WORDS: ПРИВЕ́Т!** - Hello! (*when meeting; informal*)
>
> **СПАСИ́БО** - Thanks, thank you   **ПОКА́!** - Bye! (*informal*)

Check that you tried to bring the tongue closer to the palate to pronounce «В» in «Приве́т» (as it is before «Е»), that your stresses in «Приве́т» and «Пока́» are at the very end, and that «А» in «Пока́» is much longer than weak and unrounded «О».

To make it clear: Russian has some words which you can only use with family and friends, and others which you need for more formal situations or for people older than you. As «Приве́т» and «Пока́» are marked as informal, you can use them to your peers but not to your teacher, for whom you would have formal alternatives, with «До свида́ния» being one of them (formal *hello* is our job in the next unit).

f) What would you say in Russia if:

you meet your friend Ка́тя in the street;   somebody gives you a pencil;

you are phoning your friend Па́вел;   you are a vegetarian;

you are asking how his Dad is;   you are given a box which is not yours;

you are leaving your friend's house;   you are at home tomorrow;

you want to find out whether the building is a post-office;   you are leaving an office.

Check that you tried to palatalise your «В» in «Приве́т».

RUSSIASCOPE: RUSSIAN FIRST NAMES

Some Russian first names will remind you of English names, e.g.: Антóн, Николáй, Áнна, Марúя, Натáлия. *Some names, though, are different – they were used by Russians ages ago and have Slavic roots, e.g.,* Владислáв, Владúмир, Станислáв, Светлáна, Ярослáв. *Parts of these names have meanings – for example, three of them contain* «слав-» *from* «слáва», *translated as "glory".* Владúмир *has part of the verb "to own" (*влади- *) and the word* «мир» *(meaning "world"), while* Светлáна *comes from* «свет» *meaning "light".*

You'll discover, though, that Russians, the same as people in other countries, do not always use full (formal) names – very often they refer to friends and family by short or just familiar versions. Unlike full names which have different endings for males and females, familiar name forms normally have «А» *or* «Я» *at the end, so you cannot tell whether they belong to men or women unless you know the full version. Mind you, in English there is no obvious difference between male and female names anyway. Usually a familiar form contains some part of a full name and you can work out the original. If in doubt, you can always ask* «Это он?» *or* «Это онá?».

How does it sound? As we discovered, names with «Й» at the end are male names. You might also remember that «Й» (like *y* in *employ*) normally follows vowels, e.g., Николáй. As well as «А», «О» or «Э», it can follow «И» (like *ee* in *employee*). This might feel a bit tricky, but in reality we read them as any other Russian letters: one after the other. So, if you happen to see **«ИЙ»** you will need to pronounce TWO sounds: start with a long and effortless «И» (like *ee* in *see*), and then tense your tongue up briefly to finish with a tense and rapid «Й». Have a go: Анатóлий, Витáлий, Дмúтрий, Арсéний, Васúлий, Аркáдий.

Ex. 13 a) What's in a name? Watch out for palatalised consonants *before* «Е» or «Я». Read the full (formal) forms of the first names on your left and mark them as male or female. Then start reading the familiar versions on the right, matching them up with those on the left (they will be the same gender). Finally, read the pairs aloud following the order of the left column.

Note that not all familiar forms start with the same letter as their full versions. Sometimes they start with the next letter or with the next syllable, similar to English "Elizabeth" and "Beth", e.g., Ивáн - Вáня. Occasionally, you might come across really peculiar pairs, something like "William" and "Bill".

Full/formal name	male/fem. (to fill in)	Short/familiar form (to match)	male/fem (matched)
Васи́лий		То́ня	f
Антони́на		Ва́ся	m
Никола́й		А́ня	f
Константи́н		Ва́ня	m
Вале́рия		Ди́ма	m
Ива́н		Ко́стя	m
А́нна		На́стя	f
Влади́мир		Ко́ля	m
Дми́трий		Зи́на	f
Анастаси́я		Бо́ря	m
Зинаи́да		Ле́ра	f
Анато́лий		Воло́дя	m
Бори́с		То́ля	m

ДО СВИДА́НИЯ or ДО ЗА́ВТРА (well, hopefully)

Remember your informal **ПОКА́** which is best saved for your friends, rather than a teacher. Having said that, I am not quite your teacher but more of a guide, who could possibly be a friend . . . So, perhaps we can try **Пока́-пока́.**

Something old, something new (*revision of unit 3*)

As we agreed that I am not your formal teacher but rather a friendly guide, we can perhaps start with **ПРИВЕ́Т**. You can reply to me: Приве́т (as we are on friendly terms), but please remember not to use this to your teacher in class, as it is too informal! We will learn the one you need for that today.

Let's try to remember a few things that we have discovered up to now. We have now had a go at 20 Russian letters! Can you recognise them?

GROUP I (*The Easy*): **Мм, Тт, Кк, Аа, Оо** (*Have you named the last two the Russian way?*)

GROUP II (*The Tricky*): **Сс, Нн, Вв, Рр, Ее** (*like ye in yes*)

GROUP III (*Funny Shapes*): **Ээ, Яя, Лл, Дд, Чч, Бб, Зз, Пп,**

Ии (*like ee in employee*), **Йй** (*like y in employ but tense and rapid*)

? 1.   In the lists above, can you find *six* letters which represent vowel sounds and can carry the stress (two in Group 1, one in Group II and three in Group III)? Make sure you name them the Russian way. Have you included two two-in-one letters?

2.   Is the Russian «Й» a vowel or a consonant?

3.   Can you now read out all the Russian consonants (those which are not vowels), including «Й»?

4.   When do we read «О» as a weak and unrounded sound? Can stressed «О́»-s be "weakened"?

5.   What is more important – to "weaken" the unstressed «О» or to make the stressed vowel long?

Ex. 1 a) Decoding Cyrillic. Read Russian anagrams. In each word note where the stress is and see whether there are any unstressed, unrounded «О»-s. Remember that you cannot "weaken" stressed «О́»-s.

Tip! Find three «Б»-s devoiced to /п/, including those before «К».

ОБИ́Л - ЛИ́БО	БА́НКА - КАБА́Н	СА́МБО - БА́СОМ
СКОБА́ - БО́КСА	БРА́ВО - РАБО́В	КО́РОБ - РО́БКО
РАБО́Т - ТО́РБА	КОРО́БКА - БАРО́ККО	НАБА́ВИЛ - НАБИВА́Л

? 6. Can you name two other consonants that "lose their voice" at the end of Russian words?

b) Try not to trip up! Watch your stress too.

Tip! Remember that to differentiate between «Б» and «В», you are looking for a "bar" in «Б б».

обра́т - оборо́т - отворо́т   бинт - винто́м - би́нтиком - бинтова́л
заба́ва - забия́ка - забива́л   свод - свобо́да - дво́рника - дробови́к
конво́й - боково́й - боево́й   врач - боча́р - бо́чками - бочково́й

c) Jog your memory. Can you remember the meanings of the words below? Read out those words which contain «В» and then those which contain «Б». Make sure that you know what the word means when you read it. If you work with someone else, you could test each other.

рабо́та, заво́д, ванна, брат, приве́т, соба́ка, вокза́л, спаси́бо, за́втра, коро́бка, ви́за, я́блоко, вино

> *Check that you remember that Russians would pronounce the final «Д» in «заво́д» as /т/.*

Remember to mark two or three words which you are not sure about or find tricky. Find them in the previous unit or in the dictionary at the back and go through your routine of learning new words, making sentences at the end. Next time you do your Russian, have another go at them. Revisiting helps us retrieve things we have come across before.

? 7. Which sound is long: that for «И» or the one for «Й»?

8. What is the other difference between «И» and «Й»?

9. Which two sounds does «Я» represent at the start of a word (like in «я́блоко») or after a vowel (like in «Росси́я»)?

Ex. 2 a) Decoding Cyrillic. In each pair of words below, read the first word and then try to read it *back to front* to get the second word. Note the difference in spelling!

МАЙ - ЯМ   КАЙ - ЯК   РАЙ - ЯР   ДАЙ - ЯД

> *Check that you understand that the letter «Й» is not written in front of «А» because Russians use «Я», which represents both of those sounds at the start of a word. You'll need to remember this if you are learning to write.*

b) Try not to trip up! Make sure that you make «Й» and «И» sound different. Note that «О» is strong and long in «мой» and weak and unrounded in «моя́».

мой - моя́ - мой   твой - твоя́ - твои́   ча́ял - ча́йник - ча́йнка   во́ин - война́ - воя́ка
бай - бая́н - бой   за́йка - зая́дло - за́йка   ма́йка - мая́к - маис   до́йка - дойл - дая́рка

10. Which two endings can feminine words have in Russian?

11. Why do the words linked to feminines often have «А» or «Я» at the end?

12. Which form of *my* («мой» or «моя́») is used with masculines?

13. Which Russian word (not a name) that you learnt in Unit 3 has «А» at the end but is masculine?

c) **Reading for meaning.** Find the words for *my/mine* and *your/yours*, say whether they are in a masculine or feminine form and explain why. Remember to raise the tone of your voice at the end of the questions with no question words.

Э́то мой брат. – Он до́ктор? – Нет.

Как твой па́па? Он до́ма?

Приве́т. Как твоя́ соба́ка? – Отли́чно.

Э́то твоя́ коро́бка? – Да, моя́. Спаси́бо.

Что э́то? – А э́то моя́ рабо́та. – Да? Э́то отли́чно.

Э́то твой па́спорт? – Да. – А ви́за? – Ви́за там.

d) **Let's try it in Russian.** Imagine you meet your Russian friend. Try starting a small conversation. 1) Say hello. 2) Ask how their brother/Mum/Dad/daughter are, using the correct form of *your*. (Assume that it's a good day today and everybody is great. If working in pairs, make sure you use «Спаси́бо» when answering.) 3) Ask whether they are at home. Your friend might say yes or no, and that they are at home tomorrow. Have a few goes, taking turns starting the conversation.

Ex. 3 a) Try not to trip up! Make sure you differentiate between «П» (for *p* in *pot*) and Russian «Р» (for *r* in *error*).

по́чка - по́рча - чо́порно

ро́стом - па́стор - про́пасти

по́яс - я́рко - я́ростно

копа́л - капра́л - кора́лл

доро́с - подно́с - допро́с

поро́й - закро́й - запо́й

по́вар - про́бовал - побо́рник

Э́рика - э́пика - экспро́мт

пло́мба - пло́вом - пломби́р

b) **Jog your memory.** Mark the stresses where needed. First find the monosyllabic words (words with *one* vowel) which do not need marking. Read out all the words with «П», then all those with «Р» and finally those which contain both.

карти́на, папа, работа, паспорт, торт, квартира, брат, почта, карта, марка, доктор, коробка;

завтра, спасибо, привет, пока

c) **Question time.** In the first line of the exercise above, mark feminines and masculines in a different way. Think of how you would ask somebody in Russian whether those people or things are theirs (note the tone of your voice). If you work with someone else, you can take turns asking questions and give positive and negative answers (full, shorter or short).

? 14. Why have we called «Я» (like *ya* in *yak*) and «Е» (like *ye* in *yes*) two-in-one letters?

15. What is the difference in pronunciation between «Е» and «Э», when at the start of a word?

> **Check** *that you named* «Е» *the Russian way – like "ye" in "yes".*

Ex. 4 a) Try not to trip up! Watch that your «Я» and «Е» start with a /й/ sound here. Note that the stress patterns are different in different strings.

ям - ем - им - Э́мма	Э́лла - е́ли - и́ли - я́лик
ест - я́сно - Э́тна - и́стина	е́сли - я́сли - исла́м - э́ллипс
пойл - пая́л - пое́л - поэ́т	иди́ - Эди́та - еди́м - ядови́т

? 16. What are the two possible ways of translating «я ем»?

b) Reading for meaning. Read aloud. Choose those phrases which can be translated in two ways.

Я ем сала́т.	Бана́н она́ ест.	Кто ест торт? – Зи́на и Е́ва.
Поли́на я́блоко ест.	Что ест Оста́п? – «Твикс».	Она́ лимо́н ест? – Нет. Она́ ест я́блоко.
Он ест ма́сло? – Да.	Бори́с са́ндвич ест.	А тост Зо́я ест? – Да, ест.

? 17. How do we read two vowels which are next to each other? E.g., ИЯ, АЯ.

18. What if they are the same? E.g., ОО, ЯЯ, ИИ.

19. How would you read «Е» after another vowel, e.g., ОЕ, ЕЕ, ИЕ?

> **Check** *that in the last letter combinations your* «Е» *came out as* /й э/ *every time.*

c) Decoding Cyrillic. Watch your stress too.

Tip! Make sure that you read «Е» *at the end of words! Remember that Russians do not normally skip or omit letters. Also, note that the first sound after* «О» *is going to be* /й/, *even though the last vowel is unstressed and therefore weak and does not need any effort.*

дво́е	молодо́е	ма́лое	ста́рое
тро́е	золото́е	са́мое	кра́сное

> **Check** *that you put only ONE stress in each word above.*

d) Jog your memory. See whether you remember these:

бана́н, я́блоко, торт, ма́сло, са́ндвич, мя́со, лимо́н, тост, сала́т

> *Check* that your «М» in «мя́со» *sounds closer to the palate than in* «ма́сло».

e) Let's try it in Russian. Think of how you would ask in Russian about somebody else eating. This is great fun to do in a group. Let each person in the group have a picture of an item of food or a slip with a Russian word for it. Everybody needs to get up and find somebody to talk to. Introduce yourself and say what you are eating (e.g., Я Ната́лия. Я ем я́блоко.) Once you have both said your bit, change partners. Try to remember other people's names and what foods they had. After you have spoken to at least three people, make a circle and take turns to ask questions about different people in the group (e.g., «Ната́лия ест бана́н? – Нет. Она́ ест я́блоко.» OR «Что ест Дэ́йвид? – Он ест мя́со.» OR «Кто ест мя́со? – Дэ́йвид.») Try to ask different types of questions.

? 20. How do we need to pronounce consonants *before* «Я» or «Е» (e.g.: «Н» in «нет»)?

21. Why are they called palatalised?

22. Do we pronounce a separate /й/ sound if a consonant is *before* «Я» or «Е», for example in «нет» or «мя́со»?

23. Why do we need to learn to palatalise consonants in Russian?

24. What is more important in Russian: to palatalise consonants or to put the stress right?

Ex. 5 a) Let's get this right. In each string below there is at least one palatalised consonant. Before reading a word, check whether there is «Я» or «Е» in it and whether there is a consonant to be palatalised *before* them.

на - не - но	пай - пей - по́йма	де́лал - да́та - дя́тла
бос - бас - бес	ве́тка - ва́тка - Вя́тка	по́чка - пе́чка - па́чка
вал - вял - вол	Бэ́лла - бе́лка - ба́лка	ря́са - ра́ки - ре́ки
рек - рак - рок	мя́со - ма́сло - ме́сто	зе́бра - зя́блик - за́бран

b) Just read and recognise. Sort out the words below into two columns: those with «Э» and those with «Е». Find three words which go in both. Remember to read all the words aloud.

Tip! Note that «Е» *at the start of words and after vowels is read like ye in* **yes**.

аэродро́м, е́вро, эпизо́д, комплиме́нт, эмбрио́н, экспре́сс, Достое́вский, кассе́та, контине́нт, дие́та, аэродина́мика, портре́т, библиоте́ка, эле́ктрик, спортсме́н, дире́ктор, эбони́т, экспе́рт, дискоте́ка

> *Check* that you read «е» as /й э/ in е́вро, Достое́вский and дие́та.

Reading Challenge: Полиэтиле́н

? 25. Do Russians use words like *do* or *does* to make negative sentences?

26. How do we know when to use «нет» or «не»?

27. What do Russians use after «Да» or «Нет» in their answers, for example for *it is, he isn't* etc.?

c) Let's get this right. Give negative answers, full and shorter. E.g., Это сок? – Нет, это не сок. (Or Нет, не сок.) Твой па́па ест мя́со? - Нет, мой па́па не ест мя́со. (Or Нет, не ест.)

Это заво́д?

Это твоя́ ка́рта?

Вокза́л там?

Твой брат ест сала́т?

Это мя́со?

Твоя́ до́чка ест я́блоко?

> **NEW WORD: ВОТ** – *Here you are. Here you go.*

Check that you realise that «Вот» does NOT mean "here".

d) Now it's your turn! Have a mix of pictures (on your mobile) of people, places and things – some that are yours and some that are not. Take turns showing pictures to your partner for them to ask you a question, using «твой»/«твоя́». If the answer is no, give a full negative answer and then introduce your item/person/place, starting with «Вот». E.g., Это твоя́ ко́мната? – Нет, это не моя́ ко́мната. Вот моя́ ко́мната. (Вот. Это моя́ ко́мната.)

Ex. 6 a) Decoding Cyrillic. Make sure that your loud «З» and quiet «С» sound distinctively different.

ро́за - роса́ - заро́с

со́ло - зола́ - засо́л

Си́ма - зима́ - Зоси́ма

изно́с - насо́с - зано́с

расса́да - заса́да - зооса́д

зака́за - сарка́зм - каза́рма

сно́ва - знобит - зазно́ба

зами́нка - слаби́нка - размми́нка

зло - слон - засло́н

> **How does it sound?** Though a lot of Russian consonants sound very similar to English consonants, some combinations of them might be quite unusual for an English speaker, e.g., «ЗД». You need to read these as any other combinations of letters in Russian: one after the other, with *no* gap in between. As we are going to come across «ЗД» fairly often in Russian, we need to start practicing it.

b) Decoding Cyrillic.

здо́рово - здоро́ва   езда́ - поезда́   зда́ний - зда́ние

раздо́р - разда́ча   дрозда́ - борозда́   здра́во - здра́вие

? 28. Why don't we write «А» after «Я»?

29. Is the letter «Й» normally written *after* or *before* a vowel?

30. How would you read «ИЙ»?

c) Big sort out. Underline all male names (with «ИЙ»). Read the list aloud, with one stress in each name.

Мари́я, Никола́й, Ли́дия, Вита́лий, Ли́я, Анато́лий, Викто́рия, Ма́я, Дми́трий, Ната́лия, Васи́лий, Арка́дий, Кла́вдия

> *Check that you read* «ИЙ» *as two sounds: a long and effortless* /и/
> *followed by a tense and rapid* /й/.

? 31. Which letters do most familiar versions of Russian first names have at the end?

32. How can we find out whether they are male or female?

d) What's in a name? Find full versions of the familiar names below among those which you read above. Note that there are more names in the list above, thus some of the familiar forms are not included in the list below. Make sure you read all names aloud, keeping an eye on your palatalised consonants *before* «Я».

Ви́ка, То́ля, Вита́ля, Ли́да, Ди́ма, Ко́ля, Кла́ва, Ва́ся

> *Check that you understand that the choice of* «А» *or* «Я» *at the end of familiar forms does NOT depend on gender of full names – there are phonological reasons behind this.*

Ex. 7 a) Just read and recognise. Big sort out too. Sort out the words below in alphabetical order:

А Б В ... Д Е ...... З И Й К Л М Н О П Р С Т .... Ч .... Э ... Я

акроба́т, по́ни, орби́та, бала́нс, ко́бра, аспири́н, бики́ни, топа́з, э́кспорт, балла́да, лабири́нт, бар, а́либи, поэ́ма, бота́ника, ковбо́й, лаборато́рия, са́мба, комба́йн, про́за, босс, бойко́т, компроми́сс, ро́бот, таба́к, компози́тор, монопо́лия, зоопа́рк

> *Check that you read* «ОО» *in* зоопа́рк *as TWO sounds.*

b) Say it in Russian:

Hello (*on the phone*)	Good-bye.	See you tomorrow. (*Till tomorrow*)
Hello (*when meeting, informal*)	Bye! (*informal*)	Thank you. (*Thanks.*)

UNIT

4

Excuse me. Have you got a pen?

WHAT'S THE PLAN?

► to recognise and read four new Russian letters, including one from Group IV;
► to ask *How are things?* and give a couple of possible answers;
► to say *Sorry* and *Excuse me* in Russian;
► to ask where things are;
► to look at some Russian numbers and find out what James Bond is called in Russian;
► to say in Russian that you have something;
► to find out why a second name is so important in Russia.

GROUP III (Funny Shapes) «Ш» «Ш ш» is similar to *sh* in *shop*

But pronounced a bit *more towards the back* of your mouth and a bit *shorter*.

How does it sound? «Ш» and «Ч» are often called "hushers" in Russia. I think it would be important for you to know that Russian has quite an array of *hushing* sounds. That is why we need to make sure that you pronounce each of them distinctively different from the others when you read. For example, «Ш» has to sound slightly **more towards the back and a bit shorter than** *sh* in *shop*; you might want to curl your tongue a bit like for the English /r/. At the moment, these qualities might feel like mere subtleties, but later on we will have another hushing sound which is also similar to *sh* in *shop* but is pronounced at the front of your mouth; it will be longer too. You might just want to keep this in mind to start getting used to moving your tongue to the back for your /ш/. **Different "hushers" make different words in Russian!**

Ex. 1 a) Decoding Cyrillic. Try moving your tongue back a bit to make /ш/ sound more Russian. Remember that stress is most important.

ваш - ва́ша - кла́виша

шпо́ра - што́ра - што́пором

бро́шка - бло́шка - шабло́н

ша́йка - ша́йба - шайта́н

по́шло - пошла́ - пошли́те

ко́шка - кало́ша - коко́шник

за́мша - зама́шки - замара́шка

ло́шади - ладо́шки - шокола́д

Check that you realised that Russians would pronounce «Д» at the end of «шокола́д» as /т/

NEW WORDS:

ШКО́ЛА - *a school*   **МАШИ́НА** - *a car (a lorry)*
КО́ШКА - *a female cat*   **КАРАНДА́Ш** - *a pencil*
ЧА́ШКА - *a (tea) cup*   **ШОКОЛА́Д** - *a bar of chocolate*

«Это школа»

Check that you remember to "weaken" your «О»-s in «шокола́д».

To make it clear: The Russian word «маши́на» in conversational speech is more of a general term than the English word "car" and applies to a vehicle rather than just a car. That's why a lorry or a van can also be referred to as «маши́на».

b) Reading for meaning. Note the genders of the new words.

Алло́. Это шко́ла? – Да. – А дире́ктор там?

Приве́т. Это твоя́ маши́на? – Да, моя́.

Стакан и ча́шка там. – Спаси́бо.

Это твой каранда́ш? – Нет, не мой.

Твоя́ до́чка шокола́д ест? – Да, ест.

Я не ем шокола́д, а папа мя́со не ест.

Ма́ша не ест шокола́д, она́ ест я́блоко.

Как твоя́ ко́шка? – Отли́чно. Спаси́бо.

c) Let's try it in Russian. Practice your new words in questions and in full negative answers (try suggesting possible alternatives), e.g., Это карандаш? – <u>Нет</u>, это <u>не</u> карандаш. Это термо́метр. Try using «твой» or «твоя́» in your questions too, e.g., Это твоя́ шко́ла? – Нет. Это не моя́ шко́ла. Это банк.

Ex. 2 a) Try not to trip up! Watch that «Ш» (like *sh* in *shop* but ***more*** to the ***back***) makes a very different sound from «Ч» (like *ch* in *child*) – the two hushers need to be distinctive.

ШАР - ЧАР	КА́ЧКА - КА́ШКА	по́рча - па́рочка - парша́
ДА́ША - ДА́ЧА	ПА́ЧКА - ПА́ШКА	кро́шка - ко́рочка - корчма́
НА́ША - НА́ЧАЛ	МО́ЧКА - МО́ШКА	до́чка - ло́дочка - ладо́шка
ША́ЙКА - ЧА́ЙКА	ТО́ЧНО - ТО́ШНО	со́шки - ска́зочки - каза́шки

b) What's in a name? Match the full (formal) first names on the left with their familiar versions on the right. Work out from the full form whether they are male or female.

Full (formal) name	male/female	Familiar version
Ната́лия		Ма́ша
Инноке́нтий		Арка́ша
Мари́я		Ната́ша
Па́вел		Ке́ша
Арка́дий		Па́ша

c) If you are learning to write, try to write English names in Cyrillic. Remember you need to listen to how they sound: Sharon, Charlie, Ashley, Sherlock, Chuck, Sheila, Chelsie, Shaun, Sean

Check that you realised that the last two will look the same in Russian.

How does it sound? We have established by now that the single stress in Russian requires the most of your effort, making the stressed vowel much longer and louder, taking the strength away from other vowels in a word. The most affected so far has been unstressed unrounded «О». Something similar happens with «Е» (like *ye* in *yes*) - ***unstressed «Е» gets "weakened"*** and does not sound as a clear *ye* (or /й э/). In fact, after palatalised consonants away from the stress, it sounds more like /и/. It is good to keep this in mind when you listen to Russians, but when you speak, putting *all* your effort into one stressed syllable will weaken unstressed «Е»-s naturally. Concentrating on pronouncing a good long /и/ in place of an unstressed «Е» might take the effort away from the stressed vowel and create double-stressing, which makes Russian words sound odd. So, *NO* effort on the unstressed «Е»-s.

> **To make it clear:** Stressed or unstressed, «E» indicates palatalisation of the conso-
> nant BEFORE it. It is more important to concentrate on palatalised consonants than on
> unstressed «E», with **stress remaining the top priority**.

Ex. 3 a) Attention: palatalisation! Watch your stress too. Make sure that your stressed «E»-s
are much louder and longer than unstressed ones. Remember – no separate /й/ after consonants.

мел - мелá	дéло - делá	бедá - бéдно	земля́ - зéмли
нем - немá	рéки - рекá	стенá - стéнка	пенáл - пéна
век - векá	сéра - сестрá	кетá - кéта	ветрá - вéтер

b) Just read and recognise. Your priority is still to put only *one* stress per word. Note that in
most of the words in this exercise «E» is *not* stressed, so do not concentrate on it – put the effort
into the vowel which is under the stress!

тóстер, метрó, баскетбóл, áдрес, балери́на, диáметр, лáйнер, бейсбóл, трéнер, обели́ск,
теáтр, манекéн, комментáтор, экзáмен, волейбóл, секрéт, адренали́н, ви́дeo, ресторáн,
дезодорáнт

> **NEW WORDS:** **ИЗВИНИ́ТЕ** - *Excuse me, Sorry*
>
> **КАК ДЕЛÁ?** - *How are things?*

Check that you noticed the stress in «делá»,
and that your «A» is much longer and louder than the weak «E».

> **To make it clear:** Technically, «делá» does not mean "things"; it is better translated as
> "doings", "things you do". You can also translate «Как делá?» as "How are you doing?",
> but keep in mind that «делá» is NOT a verb.

c) How does it work in Russian? Read and try to understand the conversations in the street.

- Привéт. Как делá?
- Отли́чно. Спаси́бо.

- Извини́те. Это ресторáн?
- Да, ресторáн «Эли́та».
- Спаси́бо.

- Извини́те. Это теáтр?
- Нет, не теáтр.
- А что это?
- Это вокзáл. Теáтр там.
- Спаси́бо.

d) Now it's your turn. This is good to do with someone else. On the Internet, find some pictures representing the words below (it is better to key the words in Russian if you can, though it would be OK in English too). Show your partner a picture for them to ask questions to work out what it is. Follow the Step-by-step guide below. Do not give them the answer straightaway – make them work for it! Remember to raise the tone of your voice at the end of the questions. Make sure that you take turns. E.g., Это заво́д? – **Нет**. Это **не** заво́д. – Это кино́? – Нет. Это **не** кино́. – Это вокза́л? – Да. (OR «Да, вокза́л.» OR «Да. Это вокза́л.») Even if the answers sometimes look obvious, this is excellent practice, as not everything will look this obvious when you are in Russia!

заво́д, теа́тр, парк, вокза́л, по́чта, рестора́н, стадио́н, библиоте́ка, кино, метро́, банк

Check your stresses, make sure you put only one in each word.

Step-by-step guide to asking a stranger whether the building in front is the right one.

1. To stop a stranger, say *Excuse me* (**Извини́те**).

2. Ask your question starting with «Это» (Remember to raise the tone of your voice at the end!)

3. Wait for the answer. If it is a *Yes,* say *Thank you* (**Спаси́бо**). If it is a *No,* ask what it is (**Что это?**).

4. Say *Thank you.*

Tip! Before reading the new words check their stresses. There is only one «Е» which is under the stress – the others are weak.

> **NEW WORDS:**
>
> **СЕСТРА́** - *a sister*   **РЕКА́** - *a river*
> **СТЕНА́** - *a wall*   **ТАРЕ́ЛКА** - *a plate (a dish)*

Ex. 4 a) Big sort out. Group the words below into four groups according to their logical links.

брат, река́, ча́шка, ко́мната, па́па, стака́н, окно́, сад, сестра́, таре́лка, до́чка, кварти́ра, стена́

b) Reading for meaning:

Это брат, сестра́ и я. *(on a photo)*
А это кто? – А это моя́ сестра́ Да́ша.
Сестра́ до́ма? – Нет, она́ до́ма за́втра.
Твоя́ сестра́ шокола́д ест? – Нет, не ест.

Что это? – А это река́ Нева́, а это река́ Мо́йка.
Там река́, а мост там. – Спаси́бо. До свида́ния.
Это твоя́ таре́лка и сала́т. – А вода́? – Вода́ там.
Это мой сад. – А стена́ твоя́? – Да, моя́.

c) Let's try it in Russian. Make different sentences (or questions) with new words, using the old familiar words below. It is good to do this with someone else. One person says a random old word, and the other uses it to make a sentence with a new word from the box. If you are learning to write, you might want to write a few phrases down. Make sure you write without looking in the book and only then check what you have written.

это, там, кто, что, как, он, она́, мой/моя́, твой/твоя́, до́ма, ем/ест

🔵 GROUP IV (The Strangers) «Ь ь» - the "soft sign"

The time has come to have a look at the first of some rather peculiar letters of the Russian alphabet.

How does it sound? *The "soft sign" does NOT stand for any sound!* True to its name, it is more of a sign than a letter. Its main job is to indicate that a consonant *before* it needs to be palatalised (or softened), in the same way it would be before «Я» or «Е» – that is, by bringing the tongue closer to the palate and tensing it up slightly. The difference is that this time there is no vowel after the palatalised consonant. The soft sign is normally used at the very end of words (e.g., брать – *to take*) or between two consonants (письмо́ - *a letter from somebody*).

To make it clear: We need to differentiate between the shape of the soft sign «ь» and that of «Б» (like *b* in *bar*). It will still be helpful to look out for the "bar" at the top of «Бб». Hopefully this link will work for you. But whether it does or does not, never call the soft sign «ь» "little b" – it would confuse you. Unlike «Б», you can never have a soft sign («ь») at the start of a word or after a vowel, as it has to have a consonant *before* it, to indicate its palatalisation.

Ex. 5 a) Let's get this right. Try to make the last consonants in each pair sound slightly different by moving the tongue closer to the palate for the one before the soft sign «ь». These are all different words!

КОН - КОНЬ	МАТЬ - МАТ	ТОП - ТОПЬ
ВОН - ВОНЬ	БРАТЬ - БРАТ	БРОС - БРОСЬ
ДАН - ДАНЬ	БИТЬ - БИТ	ШАР - ШАРЬ
РАН - РАНЬ	ПЛОТЬ - ПЛОТ	ЛОМ - ЛОМЬ

Now, thanks to the soft sign, we can try Russian numbers. Before you read the Russian words for numbers, have a look at the stresses, as this is always a priority. Find five monosyllabic words, then one word with the stress at the end, and finally, three with the stress at the front. Note one unstressed «O» and one unstressed «E». Spot six soft signs. There are a lot of palatalised consonants (those BEFORE «Я», «E» and «Ь») in this box. «ЛЬ» in «ноль» is pronounced like *l* in *lit* (NOT like *ll* in *fall*). Whatever you do, make sure that you put only ONE stress! Good luck!

Tip! *Keep in mind that plain and palatalised consonants can make different words in Russian; for example, «брат» means "brother", while «брать» means "to take". So, noting the soft sign in words is important.*

NEW WORDS:

0 - **НОЛЬ**	3 - **ТРИ**	6 -	9 - **ДЕ́ВЯТЬ**
1 - **ОДИ́Н**	4 -	7 - **СЕМЬ**	10 - **ДЕ́СЯТЬ**
2 - **ДВА**	5 - **ПЯТЬ**	8 - **ВО́СЕМЬ**	

As you would imagine, Russians do have words for 4 and 6, but we need to learn a few more things before we can read them.

In Russia, the same shapes are used for numbers as in the West: 1, 2, 3, 4 etc. They are actually called Arabic numerals. Occasionally, you may come across Roman numbers: I II III IV V etc., for example, in numbering book chapters. It is not common, though.

b) Big sort out. Read the lines of numbers ALOUD. In each line, find one number (call it in Russian) which is out of sequence; say what it means in English.

ноль, оди́н, пять, два   во́семь, пять, де́вять, де́сять

семь, три, во́семь, де́вять   оди́н, два, семь, три

c) Let's do it in Russian. These are some local telephone numbers from my Tula telephone book, with no area code.

31 71 35   25 39 81   77 81 82   32 99 57   71 58 29

RUSSIASCOPE: *Russia's international dialling code is "007". (Can you read it in Russian?) So, James Bond's agent number would sound as «ноль - ноль - семь» in Russian. When Russians read out local telephone numbers, though, they normally pair up the digits in them and read them as two-digit (or even three-digit) numbers. You will learn to do that too when you get around to bigger numbers. The area codes are not used that much, as they would be the same for the whole city and do not need to be dialled within it. But make sure you have them to be able to dial from abroad. Russians never mind you using their landline for local calls, as they normally pay a fixed monthly amount which does not depend on* *the number of calls. Calls to other cities or mobiles, though, are horrendously expensive from a land line. If you intend to stay in Russia for an extended period of time, it might be cheaper to get a Russian SIM-card, but check in the shop that your mobile accepts it.*

How does it sound: As you might have realised, the Russian /л/ sound, similar to many other Russian consonants, has two versions: one, like *ll* in *fall*, is a plain consonant (e.g., in «молоко»), while the other, like *l* in *lit*, is a palatalised consonant (e.g.: in «отлично»). The latter often proves to be challenging at the end of words, so try to bring your tongue closer to the palate when you have «ЛЬ», for example in «НОЛЬ». For plain (hard) «Л»-s, it might help to move the middle of the tongue slightly lower and more towards the back, like we did for «Ш». «Л» and «ЛЬ» make different words in Russian.

Ex. 6 a) Let's get this right. You are aiming to make «ЛЬ» and «Л» in each pair sound slightly different.

КОЛ - КОЛЬ	ДАЛЬ - ДАЛ	стол - стольник	мал - мальчик
МОЛ - МОЛЬ	СТАЛЬ - СТАЛ	зол - зольник	пал - пальчик
СТОЛ - СТОЛЬ	БИЛЛЬ - БИЛ	скол - сколько	нал - Нальчик

b) Just read and recognise. You might not have thought that there would be any words with the soft sign which would sound like those in English. Try these. Bringing the tongue closer to the palate for «ЛЬ» will make them sound more Russian. If you want, you can first read out seven monosyllabics which do not have a stress mark over them.

модель, карамель, вальс, мораль, никель, роль, эмаль, скальп, кобальт, стиль, медаль, дрель, бинокль, дизель, тальк, ансамбль, бальзам, эль, пальма, альбом, календарь

***RUSSIASCOPE:* КРЕМЛЬ** *(with the tongue closer to the palate)*

КРЕМЛЬ *(which stands for Kremlin as you might have suspected) is a word for an old Russian fortress or sort of a castle, citadel if you want. You might be surprised to know that the Moscow Kremlin, though being one of the largest and the most elaborate, is not the only one. In fact, a lot of ancient cities in Russia have a* Кремль, *with my home city of Tula being one of them. Here are some others:* Казань, Рязань, Ярославль, Владимир, Пермь, Тобольск. *You can find these on online maps — you need to look in the European part, where Russians developed as an ethnic group.*

«Кремль, Тула»

«Кремль, Москва»

NEW WORD: СКÓЛЬКО – *How much? (How many?)*

Check that you tried to make your «Ль» sound like l in lit with the tongue closer to the palate; that there is NO sound between /л'/ and /к/.

c) **Let's try it in Russian.** As the word for *is* is not used in Russian, and for «+» we often use «И» (for *and*), reading the sums below in conversational Russian might be like this: Оди́н и два - три. (with the pause for the dash). It is good to do it in pairs using «Ско́лько?» and picking the sums in random order. The person answering should not look in the book. Have fun!

2 + 1 = 3	8 + 1 = 9	3 + 2 = 5	7 + 2 = 9	5 + 3 = 8
7 + 1 = 8	9 + 1 = 10	5 + 2 = 7	8 + 2 = 10	7 + 3 = 10

To make it clear: At this stage it is best to avoid using numbers with other words, as in Russian you need a different ending to link them together. At the moment, we have other things to get on with, like mastering the rest of the Cyrillic alphabet.

🔵 *GROUP II* «У у» stands for *oo* in *moon*

How does it sound? It might pay back to put your **lips a bit more forward** to make /у/ distinctively different from /o/. For once, it does not really matter whether «У» is stressed or unstressed; it will sound very similar, but you still must put all the effort on a stressed vowel. As this is one of the Tricky Letters, the most important thing is to watch that you always read «У» the Russian way: as *oo* in *moon*.

Ex. 7 a) Decoding Cyrillic. Note that the stress patterns in the third column are different in different lines. Remember to put your lips forward for «У».

ПОСТ - ПУСТ	КОМ - КИМ - КУМ	туп - тип - тупи́к - типу́н
СОМ - СУМ	ПИЛ - ПУЛ - ПОЛ	пуск - писк - писку́н - пусти́л
ЗОБ - ЗУБ	СТУЛ - СТОЛ - СТИЛЬ	рус - рис - рису́нок - ру́сичи
РОЛЬ - РУЛЬ	НОЛЬ - НУЛЬ - НИЛ	внук - вник - вну́ками - вни́кнут
СÓШКА - СУ́ШКА	ДИ́МА - ДÓМА - ДУ́МА	бу́рка - би́рка - бируш - буера́ки

Check that you spotted one pair where «Б» at the end would be pronounced as /п/.

RUSSIASCOPE: РУБЛЬ *(with the tongue closer to the palate)*

The name of the Russian currency is «РУБЛЬ». After the split of the USSR, inflation in Russia soared for nearly a decade, and Russian money went through devaluation and some other changes. In the last thirty years, at different times, the rouble has been worth anything between £1and 0,01p. Recently it has settled at around 80 roubles to a pound. Now roubles can be bought outside Russia.

NEW WORDS:

СТУЛ - *a chair*   СУ́МКА - *a bag, a handbag (not a plastic bag)*

РУ́ЧКА - *a pen (not a felt pen)*   ПАКЕ́Т - *a plastic bag*

---

b) Say it in Russian. Check the genders of our new words and choose the correct form of *my* and *your* for each of them. Make small phrases with the new words – you can use my suggestions below if you wish.

my desk and my chair;	Your chair is there.	Excuse me. Is this your bag? – Yes, it is.
your pen and your pencil;	This is not my pen.	This is your plastic bag. – Thank you.

c) Let's try it in Russian. An excellent game to play in a group is "Find a person whose . . .". You need to collect an item from each student (make sure you know the Russian word for it; use ру́чка, каранда́ш, су́мка, паке́т, ча́шка, таре́лка, стака́н, коро́бка, вода́, бана́н, са́ндвич etc.). Put all the items in a bag for each student to pull a random item out. Then they have to go round asking everybody whether that item is theirs. It is good to try making full questions and giving fuller answers. E.g.: Это твоя́ ру́чка? – Нет, это не моя́ ру́чка. (Нет, не моя́.0 *OR* – Да, это моя́ ру́чка. (Да, моя́.)

To make it clear: We need to differentiate between the shape of «У» (like *oo* in *moon*) and that of «Ч» (like *ch* in *child*). Note that «У» is slanting, while «Ч» is strictly vertical. These two shapes should not cause you any trouble when you read, as «У» is a vowel while «Ч» is a consonant. Just keep an eye on them when you write.

---

d) Try not to trip up! Keep an eye on «Ш» (like *sh* in *shop* but *more* to the *back*) and «Ч» (like *ch* in *child*) too.

ум - чум - шум	ту́ша - ту́ча - уша́т	шу́ба - чубу́к - чуваша́
у́шки - ту́чки - ту́шки	часть - у́часть - уша́ст	у́дочка - чуда́к - учуди́л
ру́чка - шту́чка - шу́точка	чу́мка - чу́шка - чума́зая	пу́шка - пучо́к - пошути́л

How does it sound? I agree that our new word below looks a bit of a mouthful. I will give you a few tips to make it manageable. To start with, you do not need to say the first «В» here (it occasionally happens in large consonant clusters in Russian), so we will put it in brackets: **здра́(в)ствуйте**. Then, to make it easier, we can split the whole word into three parts: здра́(в)-ствуй-те. If you practice those three parts separately you will get used to saying them fairly soon. When you start putting them together, try to remember to put only ONE stress at the front by making «А» long - здра́(в)-ствуй-те. I hope you do not regret not having this in your first lesson.

NEW WORD:

ЗДРА́ВСТВУЙТЕ - *Hello (formal, official)*

Most Russians are not formal people, but you might have noticed that there are formal and informal forms of names and some words. Our language reflects the tradition of respecting elders and the powerful by using different, more respectful forms of ordinary words. In modern Russia these forms are normally used with people you do not know well and in all formal situations, like interviews, official meetings, customs control etc. As you might not know many people in Russia, «Здра́(в)ствуйте» might be a good one to use to start with. You can also come across «Здра́вствуй», which is halfway between «Приве́т» and «Здра́вствуйте». It can be used, for example, in an office environment to a colleague of the same age with whom you have worked for a while, or a schoolteacher might use «Здра́вствуй» to a pupil. Note that you should always use «Здра́вствуйте» to a teacher.

Ex. 8 a) Say it in Russian:

Hello *(on the phone)*.	How is your Dad?	Good-bye.	Thank you.
Hello *(to a friend)*.	How is your sister?	Bye-bye *(informal)*.	Excuse me.
Hello *(formal)*.	How are things?	See you tomorrow.	Great. (*Excellent.*)

NEW PHRASE:

О́ЧЕНЬ - *very*

О́ЧЕНЬ ПРИЯ́ТНО. - *(Very pleasant)* = *Pleased to meet you.*

---

b) Let's try it in Russian. Think of how you would say *Hello* to a Russian you meet at break time or at a party, and how you would introduce yourself and reply to their introduction. If you work with someone else, try a couple of initial exchanges with a new friend to get something like this:

- Здра́(в)ствуйте.

- Здра́(в)ствуйте.

- Я Наташа.

- А я Дэйвид.

- О́чень прия́тно.

We will expand this in our next unit, but for now try practicing this, with different people if you can.

c) Just read and recognise. And big sort out too. Read out all the words where «У» is stressed, then where «И» is stressed and finally, words with other stressed vowels (where «У» is unstressed). Make sure that «У» sounds like *oo* in *moon* every time, with the lips more forward.

суп, тури́ст, купо́н, авто́бус, букле́т, сувени́р, бамбу́к, туале́т, аква́риум, музе́й, ка́ктус, проду́кт, тайм-а́ут, ви́рус, докуме́нт, шо́у, карикату́ра, силуэ́т, лимузи́н, табу́, дуэ́т, культу́ра, университе́т, мину́та, кузи́на

To make it clear: The word «кузи́на» refers only to a female cousin; for a male cousin we need «кузе́н», where /з/ is not palatalised – this sometimes happens in foreign borrowings. Russians understand these words, and though the Slavic versions are preferred, for us the borrowings might be a good way out for the time being.

If you feel you would like to learn more words, you can pick a few which you think are useful from those in the "Just read and recognise" section and add them to your new words, noting their spelling and stress. E.g., тури́ст, туале́т, сувени́р, музе́й or университе́т.

WORTH REMEMBERING: It might sound incredible, but to speak about having something, Russians do NOT normally use the verb "have". The verb which you can find for it in a dictionary is restricted to legal or scientific texts. For everyday conversations, Russians have a special phrase «**У МЕНЯ́ ЕСТЬ . . .** » *(Did you read «У» like oo in "moon"?) Literally, it translates as "By me is (owned) . . .". As you can see, there are no words for "I" or "have" in it at all. E.g.,* «У меня́ есть соба́ка.» *means "I have a dog." (though literally «у» means "by", «меня́» is a form of "me" and finally «есть» is that very word for "is" which Russians almost never use!) But when we see* «У меня́ есть . . .» *we will always translate it as "I have . . ."*

«Есть» in «У меня́ есть . . .» and «ест» in «Он/а́ ест» are two different words. «Т» in «У меня́ есть . . .», as you might have noticed, is followed by the soft sign («Ь»), which indicates that it should be palatalised. But do not worry about confusing them – languages are amazing at balancing things up. In conversational speech, «есть» normally only appears in special contexts, like our new "having" phrase «У меня́ есть . . .», where it is accompanied by «У» (which does not appear in phrases about eating).

How does it sound? It might be worth having a little go at saying «**меня́**» correctly as as not to confuse it with other similar words in the future. The stress is at the end, which makes «Е» weak. Both consonants are palatalised.

Ex. 9 a) Reading for meaning. Make sure you read «У» as *oo* in *moon* every time you see it.

У меня́ есть ру́чка.

А у меня́ марка есть.

У меня́ есть брат и сестра́.

У меня́ есть сок. – А у меня́ есть вода́.

У меня́ есть бана́н. – А у меня́ я́блоко есть.

Чай у меня́ есть.– А молоко́? – Спаси́бо. У меня́ есть лимо́н.

b) Let's try it in Russian. Say in Russian that you have the following things:

a glass, a cup, a pencil, an apple, (*some*) water, a bag, a passport, a job, (*some*) milk, a room, a dish, a pen, a chair

Tip! You need to "train" yourself NOT to start with «Я» whenever you would want to say "I have" in Russian. Try to pause for a second and remind yourself that the first thing you need to say is «У», like oo in moon.

WORTH REMEMBERING: To say "You have . . .", Russians use the same pattern as they do for "I have . . .". So, we need to produce "By YOU is (owned) . . ." by changing "me" for "you". Thus, we will start with «У» (like oo in moon) which means "by"; then we will change «меня́» (which is a form of "me") for «ВАС», which is a form of "you"; and finally say «есть». So having done all that, we get «У вас есть . . .» which would translate as "You have . . .".

c) Reading for meaning. These are all statements, *not* questions.

У вас есть карта, а у меня́ есть а́тлас.

У меня́ есть ру́чка, а у вас каранда́ш есть.

У меня́ есть су́мка. – А у меня́ паке́т есть.

У вас соба́ка есть, а у меня́ есть ко́шка.

I hope that you remember that to ask a question in Russian, we DO NOT change the word order – we just raise the tone of the voice. It is exactly the same for the "You have . . ." construction.

Ex. 10 a) Reading for meaning. Remember to raise the tone of your voice at the end of the questions when reading.

Tip! Keep in mind that the word order in Russian is quite loose, and words can easily change places in a sentence (often to add some emphasis). Note that you still need to phrase your translations properly in English.

У вас есть мя́со? – Да, мя́со есть.   У вас есть до́ктор? – Да.   Ко́мната есть у вас? – Извини́те. Нет.

А вода́ у вас есть? – Извини́те, нет.   А у вас сестра́ есть? – Нет.   У вас есть стул? – Да, есть. Спаси́бо.

Check that you remember that «Извини́те» means "Sorry" as well as "Excuse me".

Remember that when you speak, it is better to stick to the standard word order, e.g., У вас есть . . . ? *or* У меня́ есть. . . . It makes it easier to follow, for both you and your listeners. Just keep in mind that native Russians are not necessarily going to do it.

b) Let's try it in Russian. Think of how you would ask in a Russian shop or a cafe whether they have the things below. You might want to start with «Извини́те». Here the tone of your voice is better raised on «есть».

(some) tea, a stamp, *(some)* soup, an apple, a glass, a pen, *(some)* meat, a table, *(some)* water, *(some)* salad, a chair, a plastic bag, *(some)* milk, a job, (a bar of) chocolate, a box, a pencil, *(some)* butter, a cup

Do you remember that «Да» or «Нет» are good polite answers in Russian, and we do not need the extensions like "(Yes), I have." or "(No), I haven't."? As far as giving a full answer goes, at the moment it is safer to give only full positive answers, because to make this having construction negative we need to know a few more things. Let's say that for now in Russian "It is better to have it than not to have it". It might be an excellent practice, if you have not got something, to try finding an alternative (if there is one). E.g., У вас есть сестра́? – Нет, но у меня́ есть кузи́на.

> **NEW WORD: HO -** *but*

c) Reading for meaning:

У вас есть сок? – Нет, но есть лимона́д.   У вас есть дом? – Нет, но у меня́ кварти́ра есть.

А суп у вас есть? – Нет, но есть сала́т.   А у вас а́тлас есть? – Нет, но у меня́ есть ка́рта.

А чай есть у вас? – Да. – Оди́н. Спаси́бо.   А су́мка у вас есть? – Извини́те, нет, но вот паке́т.

У вас вино́ есть? – Нет, но бу́дет* за́втра.   Извини́те, у вас есть ру́чка? – Нет, но вот каранда́ш.

* бу́дет – *will be (= there will be)*

Check that you remember that «Вот» is used when presenting or giving something

d) How does it work in Russian? Read conversations in a shop and in a café (one at a time). Keep track of what you are reading. If you work with someone else, you might read these in parts. Highlight the phrases which you would need to do the shopping in Russia.

– Здра́вствуйте.	– Здра́вствуйте.
– Здра́вствуйте.	– Здра́вствуйте.
– У вас есть молоко́?	– У вас есть сок?
– Да, есть.	– Извини́те. Нет.
– Оди́н литр.	– А пепси-ко́ла или лимона́д?
– Вот молоко́.	– Есть лимона́д.
– Спаси́бо. Ско́лько это?	– Отли́чно. Оди́н стака́н.
– 10 рубле́й.	– Мину́тку*. *(after a minute)* Вот.
– Спаси́бо.	– Спаси́бо.
	* Мину́тку – *(here) Just a minute.*

You might have noticed that "please" is missing from these conversations – it will be one of our first jobs in Unit 5.

Also, the prices here and in the next few units do not match real prices in Russia – we need bigger numbers for that. If you are going to Russia tomorrow, writing prices on a little notepad will do the job. I have even seen people bargaining using a notepad (which is «блокно́т» in Russian).

Finally, you will notice that the word «рубль» has different endings after different numbers. In Russian, numbers require case agreements. That is why I have advised you not to use numbers with nouns at this stage. If you use the word «рубль» as it is, Russians will understand you, but grammatically it might not be correct.

e) Now it's your turn. Pick one of the conversations above and try to think what you would say to buy milk in a Russian shop or a drink in a Russian café. It is great to act these out with a partner. It might pay to have a good look at the conversation before you decide that you are ready to do it without reading. You can have a couple of goes playing different parts and "buying" different things.

🔵 GROUP III «Гг» stands for *g* in *golf*

Now we can read the Russian name for *England*: **А́НГЛИЯ** *(Did you do one stress at the front?).* In fact, we can name all parts of Great Britain in Russian too: А́нглия, Уэ́льс, Шотла́ндия, Се́верная Ирла́ндия. Do you remember the Russian word for Russia? "Great Britain" in Russian is one word which is made of two parts: **Великобрита́ния.**

Ex. 11 a) Decoding Cyrillic. Before you start, try finding two words with a devoiced «Д», one line with the soft signs «Ь» and one with palatalised /н/-s. Also, keep an eye on unstressed «О»-s that are scattered throughout.

ногá - дугá - рогá	гай - гáйка - гáйками	гать - ругáть - построгáть
погóн - загóн - вагóн	год - гóрод - гóродом	дрýга - подрýга - попугáй
шагú - шагáл - шугáл	нéга - гáснет - гнéвная	глас - соглáсно - голосá
Егóр - багóр - бугóр	блáга - влáга - глáвное	гимн - гимнáзия - магазúн
галýн - чугýн - драгýн	гýсто - глýпо - пýгало	ягода - угóда - угадáл

RUSSIASCOPE: **ГЛÁСНОСТЬ И ПЕРЕСТРÓЙКА**

You might have heard these two words in English. They refer to political developments in the second half of the 80s that instigated crucial changes in the Soviet Union and are considered a turning point in modern Russian history. ГЛÁСНОСТЬ (Glasnost) literally means "Openness" and was a policy that called for increased transparency in government activities in the USSR. Introduced by the Soviet leader Mikhail Gorbachev, ГЛÁСНОСТЬ is often paired with ПЕРЕСТРÓЙКА (Perestroika), the literal meaning of which is "reconstructing" or "rebuilding", referring to the restructuring of the Soviet political and economic system. Perestroika is often argued to be a cause of the dissolution of the Soviet Union and the end of the Cold War.

How does it sound? «Г» is one more consonant which, like «в», «д» and «б», is devoiced at the end of words. (Remember «Смирнóв» and «сад»?) When word-final, Russians pronounce «Г» as /к/. E.g.: «друг» (Russian for *friend*) will sound like /д р у к/. It is important to keep this in mind when you listen to Russians. Have a go at saying these as Russians would: маг - шаг - враг, миг - стриг - бриг, мог - рог - стог, слуг - плуг - друг.

NEW WORDS:

ДРУГ - *a friend (normally male)*

ПОДРÝГА - *a female friend, but not a girlfriend!*

ГДЕ? - *Where?*

МАГАЗИ́Н - *a shop*

КНИ́ГА - *a book (to read, not to write in!)*

ТЕТРÁДЬ - *a book for writing*

Check that you realise that «г» would sound different in «друг» and in «подрýга»;
that in тетрáдь there are two palatalised consonants, the first and the last;
that both of them would actually sound the same, as «ДЬ» is devoiced at the end of
the word to /т'/.

«Это мой друг Олéг.»

«А это моя подрýга Óльга.»

Check *that you realise that «О» in «Олéг» and «Óльга» would sound different because of the stress.*
that Russians would read «Олéг» with /к/ at the end, like in «друг».

b) Reading for meaning:

Это моя́ подрýга Гáля, а это мой друг Гриша.

У вас Вот кни́га «Войнá и мир»? – Да, есть. Вот. Извини́те. А где магази́н «Рýсский сувени́р»?. Это не магази́н, это пóчта. Магази́н там.

Это твоя́ кни́га? – Нет, не моя́. – А карта твоя́? – Да.

Есть у меня́ друг Гри́ша. – Извините, а где он? – Там.

Приве́т, а твоя́ сестра́ где? – Онá дóма. – А это кто?

А тетрáдь у вас есть? – Извини́те, нет. Но есть блокнóт.*

_____

* блокнóт – *a small notepad*

c) Let's try it in Russian.
Read each sentence below and then turn it into a question. Make sure that you stick to the most straightforward word order in your question and change your intonation. E.g.: У меня́ сестра́ есть. *(I have a sister.)* – А у вас есть сестра́? *(Do you have a sister?)*.

У меня́ есть рýчка.

Есть у меня́ друг.

У меня́ сýмка есть.

Тетрáдь у меня́ есть.

У меня́ есть кни́га.

У меня́ водá есть.

d) Question time.
Think of how you would ask a stranger in Russian where things or people are. (Do you remember the Russian word for *Excuse me*?) Ask in Russian where the following are. E.g.: моя́ кóмната - Извини́те. (А) где моя́ кóмната? (You do not have to use «А», but Russians tend to.)

карандáш, магази́н «Сувени́р», моя́ сестра́, завóд «Штамп», марка, моя́ кни́га, Кремль, твоя́ сýмка, твой друг Ми́ша, моя́ чáшка, вокзáл, твоя́ тарéлка, рекá Москвá, мой стул, тетрáдь, подрýга Лéна, моя́ корóбка, пакéт

Ex. 12 a) Attention: palatalisation! Before reading a string, find and underline palatalised «Г»-s (those BEFORE «Е», «Я» or the soft sign «Ь»). Then read the string aloud. Keep in mind that in this exercise all consonants before «Е» are going to be palatalised, but you need to underline only the softened «Г»-s.

гóнка - Гéна - нéга	бегá - бегемóт - бéгал	где - гудéл - дугé
гель - голь - гáлька	газéта - егозá - гéтто	гóре - герóй - погрéй
Гéра - грéку - грéки	гепáрд - Пелагéя - пéгий	влáге - вогнáл - головé

Check that you noticed your unstressed «Е»-s.

Though we classed «Г» as a Group III letter, it can occasionally play a little trick on you, particularly in words which remind you of similar English words. It is all due to the fact that in English the letter which produces /g/ (like in *golf*) can also be read in a different way (like in *George*). In Russian, though, you normally read «Г» as *g* in *golf*! Compare: гитáра - *guitar* and агéнт - *agent*.

b) Just read and recognise. Make sure that you read «Г» as *g* in *golf* everywhere. If there is a word that you do not recognise, you can check it on an online translator.

магнúт, грýппа, зигзáг, аллергúя, галóп, магнóлия, тáнго, гель, сигарéта, генерáл, гимнáстика, гороскóп, интрúга, грипп, гéйзер, áнгел, Гермáния, галерéя, грамм, регнóн, вигвáм, бригáда, геомéтрия, эмигрáнт, генерáтор, галáктика, ангóра, энергия, сигнáл, коллéга, эгоúст, гарáнтия

c) Let's try it in Russian. Read Russian names below and say in Russian whether they would be «друг» or «подрýга». You can add твой /твоя́, if you wish.

Галúна, Гéрман, Евгéний, Óльга, Геннáдий, Григóрий, Евгéния, Ангелúна, Геóргий, Олéг

Check your stress in Олéг.

NEW WORD: ИЛИ - or

Ex. 13 a) Reading for meaning:

Это магазúн или пóчта? – Магазúн. Пóчта там.
У вас есть рýчка или карандáш? – У меня́ - рýчка.

Сок или лимонáд? – Сок. Спасúбо.
Это твоя́ кнúга или моя́? – Твоя́.

Check that you understand that questions with «или» cannot be answered with «Да» or «Нет».

b) Question time. Practice asking questions with the word «ИЛИ». It is good to do this in pairs. Try using different structures: У вас есть, это, твой/я (мой/я́), он/а ест. Make use of «Извинúте» and «Спасúбо». You can start with the pairs below:

сок : водá	рýчка : карандáш	я́блоко : банáн	теáтр : кинó
таксú : твоя́ машúна	стакáн : чáшка	сестрá : подрýга	собáка : кóшка

c) Now it's your turn. Answer the following questions about yourself in Russian. If you work with someone else, take turns asking and answering questions. Remember not to use «Да» or «Нет» to answer questions with «или».

У вас есть брат?

А друг или подру́га у вас есть?

А у вас соба́ка есть?

У вас есть су́мка или паке́т?

А маши́на есть у вас?

У вас дом есть? А сад?

RUSSIASCOPE: PATRONYMICS

*So far we have had a look at Russian first names and surnames. As for the middle names, unlike in England where parents can choose as many of those as they wish, in Russia people have only one second name. It is not chosen either, as it comes from the father's first name. It is called the patronymic (from Greek "patēr" for "father"). Both boys and girls have patronymics, but the endings are different. For example, my father's first name was «Влади́мир», so my patronymic is «Влади́мир**овна**» (try to manage one stress in this!). My brother's patronymic, though, is «Влади́мир**ович**» (still one stress). In Old Russian it would have meant "Vladimir's daughter/son". Girls can take their husband's surname when they marry, but they keep their patronymic for life. So, all children born to the same father inherit his first name.*

Patronymics are not optional and are very important in Russia. Together with the full (formal) form of the first name they make up the formal way of address (with no surname!) For example, my pupils at school called me «Ната́лия Влади́мировна», which is the equivalent of "Mrs. Parker" in Britain. People use the full first name together with the patronymic to address a doctor, a teacher, a lawyer, their boss, an elderly neighbour or even colleagues at work. Patronymics are not used with family, friends, children or teenagers. Younger adults in modern Russia, influenced by the Western use of first names, tend not to use patronymics with each other, even in formal situations. Often they try to compromise by using the formal form of their first name on its own.

Patronymics always follow full (formal) versions of first names – e.g., I am Ната́лия Влади́мировна, and cannot swap these round or use «Ната́ша» with my patronymic. As far as surnames go, they can be placed at the very front or at the very end but never in between a first name and a patronymic, e.g., Ната́лия Влади́мировна Па́ркер or Па́ркер Ната́лия Влади́мировна.

Tip! Some patronymics end in «-евна»/«-евич» (instead of the standard «-овна»/«-ович»). In these you might have two vowels next to each other. Make sure you read them both, one after the other, e.g., ае, ее, ие (where «е» is like "ye" in "yes").

91

Ex. 14 a) Watch your stress! Make sure that you keep one stress in both father's first name and his child's patronymic.

Антóн - Антóнович	Алексáндр - Алексáндровна	Вúктор - Вúкторович
Борúс - Борúсович	Николáй - Николáевна	Дмúтрий - Дмúтриевна
Сергéй - Сергéевич	Алексéй - Алексéевна	Úгорь - Úгоревич

b) What's in a name? Look at the list of children on the left. Identify their patronymics and find their fathers in the right column, with some of the children having the same fathers. Make sure you read all names aloud and try to put ONE stress only.

Children	*Fathers*
Антóн Валентúнович	Николáй Алексéевич
Андрéй Николáевич	Сергéй Дмúтриевич
Óльга Вúкторовна	Валентúн Ивáнович
Яна Валентúновна	Константúн Егóрович
Галúна Алексáндровна	Алексáндр Петрóвич
Олéг Сергéевич	Вúктор Геóргиевич
Валентúна Николáевна	
Елéна Константúновна	
Пáвел Вúкторович	

c) How does it work in Russian. Read and understand the conversations below. Choose a suitable title for each of them: «Друг» or «Рабóта».

1)
– Здрáвствуйте.
– Здрáвствуйте. А кто секретáрь?
– Галúна Вúкторовна.
– Извинúте. А где онá?
– Онá там.
– Спасúбо.

– Здрáвствуйте, Галúна Вúкторовна.
Я Геннáдий.
– Óчень приятно, Геннáдий. Здрáвствуйте.
– У вас есть рабóта для меня*?

– Да. Вот.
– Спасúбо.

2)
– Привéт, Грúша.
– Привéт, Антóн. Как делá?
– Отлúчно. Спасúбо.
– Извинú*. А твой папа Ивáн Алексéевич
или Ивáн Алексáндрович?
– Ивáн Алексéевич.
– Спасúбо.

– Здрáвствуйте, Ивáн Алексéевич.
– Здрáвствуй, Грúша

---

* Извинú - *familiar version of* «Извинúте».

---

* для меня - *for me*

d) What would you say in Russian if:

you walk into an office;

somebody gives you something;

you want to ask how things are;

you stop a stranger;

somebody introduces themself;

you need to ask where she is;

somebody asks you how you are;

you want to introduce yourself;

you need to ask whether they have something;

you need to say sorry to a friend.

Check your answers in the two conversations above.

e) If you are learning to write, try to think how Russians would write the names below. Remember to listen to the sounds. Note that English "e" in the middle of these words will appear as «e» in Russian.

Coventry, America, Preston, Glastonbury, Shropshire, Alaska, Glasgow, Oregon, Exeter, Cheshire, Arizona

Check that you wrote "Glastonbury" as «Гластонбери» and that you did NOT write «Е» at the end of «Чешир».

Until I say hello to you at the start of the next unit, THINK RUSSIAN. You can ask questions with «или» and «Где?», as well as using «Извини/те». Having just learned our "having construction", try to imagine how you would ask for something in a Russian shop, and what they might say to you, or how you could say that you have a friend or a brother or a sister. You can look for numbers around you too. Keep peddling.

For now, though, it might be time to say good-bye. If it is late and you are going to bed, we can say **СПОКÓЙНОЙ НÓЧИ** which stands for *Good night*, but literally means "calm/peaceful night". Russians use it only when they are going to bed, NOT when they are leaving a house.

So, if you are going to bed, Спокóйной нóчи. Otherwise, До свидáния.

Something old, something new (*revision of unit 4*)

Привéт. Как делá? *(One stress only? Have you put it at the end?)* Do you think you can answer this? **Отлично** is an *excellent* answer (if pun works across languages). At the start of each unit from now on we will be looking at other ways of answering this question, so that you have a few options to fit different situations. Today it is going to be **Устáл/а** (with «У» like *oo* in *moon*), which means *(I am) tired*. You have probably worked it out that «а» at the end is for ladies. «Устáл/а» can be used as a question too – just remember to put the tone of your voice up. You can ask me «Устáла?». The answer is likely to be «Да, устáла.», as I often work late. What would you say about yourself?

1. Do you remember the other *hello* – Здрá(в)ствуйте *(*with only ONE stress at the front)?
2. Why have we put (в) in brackets?
3. When do Russians use «здрáвствуйте»? Do you remember *Hello* to be used on the phone?
4. What is the difference between «здрáвствуйте» and «здрáвствуй»?

If you are not sure whether to use Привéт or Здрáвствуйте, start with Здрáвствуйте and, if you are an adult, then you can see what people use to greet you. For example, if somebody says Привéт to you, you can say Привéт back, and if I say Здрáвствуйте, you need to reply with Здрáвствуйте too. Always use Здрáвствуйте to a teacher, a doctor or an official, for example, a customs officer.

Let's have a go (the dotted line is your part):

- Привéт. - ....   - Как делá? - ....

- ....   - Здрáвствуйте.

- ....   - Устáл/а.

Our first job is to recap the things we have learnt so far. And we have done a fair bit!

GROUP I (*The Easy*): **Мм, Тт, Кк, Аа, Оо**

GROUP II (*The Tricky*): **Сс, Нн, Вв, Рр, Ее** (*like . . . in . . .*), **Уу** (*like oo in moon*)

GROUP III (*Funny Shapes*): **Ээ, Яя, Лл, Дд, Чч, Бб, Зз, Пп, Шш, Гг**

Ии (*like ... in ....*), **Йй** (*like ... in .... but tense and rapid*),

GROUP IV (The Strangers): **Ьь** (*the soft sign*)

Find your new letters in the alphabet: А Б В Г Д Е ... З И Й К Л М Н О П Р С Т У ... Ч Ш ....Ь Э ... Я

5. Can you pick out seven vowels in the list above? Have you named them the Russian way?

6. What is the difference in pronunciation between «У» and «О»?

7. Does «У» sound very different when it is away from the stress?

Ex. 1 a) Decoding Cyrillic. Keep an eye on «У» and «И». It might be better to read slowly but correctly.

Tip! When pronouncing «У», *try to put your lips forward a bit more than you do in English, to make it different from* «О». *Make sure that your* /л/ *in* «лу» *sounds like* **ll** *in* **fall** *(with tongue low and back), but that* /л'/ *in* «ли» *is like* **l** *in* **lit**.

кли́ка - кули́к - луку́м - кли́кнула

пи́ли - пу́ли - пилу́ - лупи́ли

гру́за - грузи́н - грози́т - Гру́зия

гру́ша - Гри́ша - игру́шка - руба́шки

ту́я - Ли́я - струя́ - ста́туя

пойди́ - пойду́ - уйди́ - подойду́

у́гол - у́гли - иглу́ - и́глами

Ура́н - Ира́н - руи́на - Украи́на

Check that in «Украи́на» *your* «И́» *is longer than your* «А».

8. How would Russians pronounce «Г» at the end of words (e.g., друг)?

9. Can you name the other three consonants you know that get devoiced at the end?

b) Try not to trip up! Read Russian anagrams aloud, watching your stress. Find three words with a devoiced consonant at the end.

гу́сли - слу́ги

заго́н - газо́н

го́род - до́рог

го́рка - каго́р

до́лго - го́лод

ша́пка - Па́шка

мно́го - го́мон

баго́р - горба́

ру́чка - чу́рка

гра́дина - гарди́на

ши́шка - ша́шки

рагу́ - уга́р

c) Jog your memory. Mark the stress *where needed.* Read aloud and try to remember what each word means. Mark those that you can't remember and check them out.

друг, завод, привет, магазин, коробка, где, сумка, работа, музе́й, отлично, книга, Кремль, вокзал, яблоко, извини́те, стул, библиоте́ка, собака, ручка, завтра, рестора́н, вот, подру́га, уста́л/а, пакет, виза, теа́тр, вода, здравствуйте

Check that you remember that the final «Д» *in* «заво́д» *sounds like* /т/ *in Russian.*

> **To make it clear:** You might remember from the last unit that the word for *Excuse me* or *Sorry* (Извини́те) also has an informal version «Извини́», which is used with family, friends and children.

d) Question time. Ask where the following are. If you can't remember the word or need to check the stress, you can peep into section C on page 95. Start your questions with «Извини́те», unless you have «твой»/«твоя́», then you need to use the informal «Извини́». If you work in pairs, you can give two types of answers: «Вот.» about things and «Там.» about people and places. E.g.: Извини́те, где я́блоко? – Вот. OR Извини́. Где твоя́ сестра́? – Там.

a pen, your book, my friend Victor, a shop, your chair, water, the factory, your friend Natasha, a library, a plastic bag, your box, the station, my bag, the Kremlin, a stamp, a museum, your dog, my passport, your visa

e) Try not to trip up! Let's not forget about our tense and rapid «Й». Make sure you still differentiate between «У» and long «И».

дай - дуй - ра́дий	ста́йка - стро́йка - стру́йка	уе́ду - пое́ду - прие́ду
кий - куй - Кай	зно́йная - та́йная - бу́йная	ей - пей - бей
буй - бай - Бийск	бо́йкий - я́ркий - ру́сский	сане́й - музе́й - Андре́й

*Check you read «ИЙ» as TWO sounds: a long and effortless /и/ and
then a tense and rapid /й/;
that in the last two strings the consonants before «ей» are palatalised
and are NOT followed by a separate /й/.*

? 10. Does the *soft sign* «Ь» stand for any particular sound? What is its main purpose?

11. Where can you normally find the soft sign within words?

12. What other letters can indicate the palatalisation of consonants in Russian?

13. What is more important in Russian: to palatalise or to devoice consonants?

Ex. 2 a) Decoding Cyrillic. Watch out for the soft sign to make sure that you bring your tongue closer to your palate for the consonant *before* it.

Tip! Keep in mind that Russian palatalised «Ль» needs to sound like *l* in *lit* (closer to the palate), which is different from plain «Л» for *l* in **fall** (with your tongue low and back).

путь - пут	га́лка - га́лька	ел - ель - е́льник	сколь - скол
пусть - пуст	гу́лко - гу́лька	мел - мель - ме́льник	у́голь - у́гол
лунь - лун	по́лка - по́лька	стал - сталь - стально́й	уголькѝ - уголкѝ

14. Name one number between zero and ten with the stress at the end.

15. What are the TWO ways of translating «Ско́лько»?

b) Jog your memory. Note that we will learn words for 4 and 6 in Unit 5.

ноль, оди́н, два, три, . . ., пять, . . ., семь, во́семь, де́вять, де́сять

c) Big sort out. Put the numbers below in the correct order starting with zero – try not to look at the line above. Then call the even numbers out, then the odd numbers. Try counting backwards, missing 4 and 6.

три, во́семь, два, ноль, де́сять, оди́н, пять, де́вять, семь

d) Let's try it in Russian. Similarly to how we did sums in Russian in Unit 4, we are going to try simple subtractions in Russian using «ми́нус» for *minus*, e.g.: Де́сять ми́нус два - во́семь. It is good to do this with somebody else asking questions with «Ско́лько». E.g., Сколько десять ми́нус два? - Во́семь.

e) Try not to trip up! Spot palatalised consonants – there is at least one in each line. You might want to underline them first, before reading each string. Note the unstressed «О»-s too.

Tip! Remember that «Е» and «Я» also indicate palatalisation of the consonant BEFORE them, like in «нет» or «мя́со».

погóн - погóня - огóнь   по́ступь - сту́пе - до́ступ
гостя́м - погóст - гостéй   гóрка - гóрько - гря́дка
отгу́л - гуля́л - прогу́лка   воск - вéско - Ва́ська
голубóй - голубéл - голуба́я   зóрко - зóрька - рéзок

16. Do you remember the difference between the two Russian "hushers" that we have had: «Ш» and «Ч»?

17. Why might it be helpful to pronounce «Ш» at the back of your mouth and to make it short?

Ex. 3 a) Try not to trip up! Keep an eye on «Ш» and «Ч». Note that the stress patterns vary in the last column.

ко́чка - ко́шка   шасть - часть   чу́рка - шку́рка - Шу́рочка
су́чка - су́шка   пала́ш - пала́ч   Па́шка - по́чка - ша́почка
пéчка - пéшка   пушóк - пучóк   чува́ш - внуша́л - внуча́та
ча́рка - ша́ркал   ушла́ - учла́   рушни́к - ручни́к - башма́чник

b) Spot the difference! These are all real words. In every word there is at least one letter changed or added to make the following word.

у́тка - шу́тка - чу́шка - ту́шка - ту́чка - ту́чки - шту́чки - шу́точки

c) Jog your memory. Mark the stresses where needed. Make sure you know what the words mean. Finally, read out all the words containing «Ш» and then those with «Ч».

ко́шка, до́чка, ру́чка, Ли́дочка, каранда́ш, шокола́д, чай, Шотла́ндия, ча́шка, маши́на, «О́чень прия́тно», да́ча, Ната́ша, отли́чно, Чайко́вский, шко́ла, «Споко́йной но́чи»

> **Check** that you remember that, though the phrase «Споко́йной но́чи» stands for "Good night", the word «споко́йной» does NOT mean "good"

d) Question time. Using the word «и́ли» (for *or*), make questions by finding alternatives for the words below. E.g.: chair – Э́то твой стул и́ли мой? OR sister – Э́то твоя́ сестра́ и́ли твоя́ кузи́на?

If you are working in pairs, remember that you cannot answer these questions with «Да» or «Нет». You can use different types of sentences.

a pen, a friend, an apple, a school, a copybook, a shop, water, a car, chocolate, a cat, a dacha, a bag.

18. What happens with «О» and «Е» if they are not stressed?

19. What is more important: to palatalise consonants before «Е» or to "weaken" unstressed «Е»-s?

Ex. 4 a) Watch your stress! Make sure that you lengthen the correct vowel and palatalise the consonants before «Е».

мел - мела́ - ме́лко
те́сно - тесна́ - те́сто
де́ло - дела́ - де́лать
свет - светло́ - све́чка
бе́гать - бега́ - бе́гал

песо́к - пе́сня - песо́чком
река́ - ре́ки - речна́я
сестра́ - се́стрин - сестри́чка
Герма́ния - Ге́рман - меге́ра
дерза́й - де́рзок - дерзи́ла

b) Big sort out. Before reading, highlight the words where «Е» is stressed (including mono-syllabics). Then circle five words where you would start «Е» with a /й/ sound. Now read all the words in order, keeping an eye on palatalised consonants and noting weak unstressed «Е»-s. Make sure you know what the words mean.

«Как дела́?», ем, метро́, бале́т, рестора́н, е́вро, теа́тр, сестра́, Достое́вский, река́, музе́й, извини́те, ест, университе́т, дие́та, стена́, библиоте́ка

20. What does «У» in «У меня́ есть . . . » mean literally?

*Check that you read «У» like **oo** in **moon** and «Е» in «есть» like **ye** in **yes** here.*

21. Is there a Russian verb for *have* in «У меня́ есть . . . »?

22. Is there a word for *I* in this phrase? How is «меня́» translated into English?

23. What is the actual meaning of «есть» in «У меня́ есть . . . »?

24. How should we translate «У меня́ есть . . . » into English when we read?

Ex. 5 a) Fancy a challenge? Read what different people say on the left. They come from *two* different families. Work out who belongs to which family. Fill in the names on the right to make correct statements. It might help to draw two little family trees.

Tip! Both children and adults use familiar versions of names to speak about their family members. For example, my daughter might refer to me as «мама Ната́ша». She does not use this form to address me, though.

"Dmitriy's family"

"Valentin's family"

Я́на: У меня́ есть брат Анто́н.

Ли́да: У меня́ есть папа Ди́ма.

Светла́на: У меня́ есть до́чка Ли́дочка.

О́льга Ви́кторовна: У меня́ есть до́чка Я́на.

Анто́н: У меня́ есть папа Ва́ля.

Дени́с: У меня́ есть мама Све́та.

Дми́трий: У меня́ есть до́чка.................

Анто́н: У меня́ есть сестра́.................

Ли́да: У меня́ есть брат....................

Я́на: У меня́ есть мама.....................

Валенти́н Ива́нович: У меня́ есть до́чка.............

Дени́с: У меня́ есть сестра́.......................

b) Now it's your turn. Think of your friends and family. Say in Russian that you have the members that you know Russian words for. Use their names. If you are learning in a group, you can do an exercise which somebody starts (e.g, У меня́ есть сестра́ Ка́тя.), then other people say similar phrases about their family or friends (e.g., А у меня́ есть сестра́ Мэ́ри.). Note that if you have the same relation with the same name, you need to use «И» instead of «А», even at the start (e.g., И у меня́ есть сестра́ Ка́тя), but that does not happen very often. If you have not got the same family member, you need to give an alternative (e.g.: А у меня есть подру́га Га́бриэл.) Enjoy speaking Russian!

Reading Challenge: Вермишёль

? 25. What does «вас» mean in «У вас есть . . . »?

26. What English phrase is the equivalent of «У вас есть . . . » ?

27. What do we need to do to turn it into a question?

28. When do Russians say «Вот»?

c) Find a person who. . . Think of how you would ask in Russian whether a person has something. In a group you can play a game where your purpose is to find people who have certain things or people (see my list below) and record their names. Remember to raise the tone of your voice at the end of your questions. The winner is the one with most names.

Tip! Remember that you do not know how to make full negative answers with «У меня есть» – try giving alternatives using «НО» (for "but") instead. E.g., У вас есть сестра? – Нет, но у меня есть кузина/подруга.

an apple, a sister, *(some)* water, a garden, a brother, a cat, a copybook, a plastic bag, a pen, a stamp, a dog, a daughter, *(some)* tea, a pencil, a book, a map, a car

Ex. 6 a) What's in a name? These are full (formal) versions. Put ONE stress only and watch out for «Е»-s, stressed or unstressed, after consonants or at the beginnings of words.

Tip! Make sure that all the names starting with «Е» have a /й/ sound at the front (like ye in yes).

Елéна, Андрéй, Светлáна, Екатерúна, Алексéй, Елизавéта, Арсéний, Алексáндр, Валентúна

b) Big sort out. In the list of names above find a correct full name for each of the familiar versions below. Note that you have fewer diminutive names.

Свéта, Лúза, Вáля, Лéна, Кáтя, Сáша

> **Check** *that the full name you have found for* «Сáша» *has* «са» *in it.*

? 29. What is a patronymic?

30. Why are patronymics so important in Russia?

31. Which form of the name does the patronymic follow: full or diminutive?

c) What's in a name? Relying on patronymics, *sort out* the family relationships of the people below: father (1), mother (2), sons (3, 4, 5) and a daughter (6). The sons appear in order from the oldest to the youngest. Read all the names aloud, putting ONE stress in each word.

Стру́гов Ива́н Дми́триевич (. . . . .)

Стру́гова Мари́я И́горевна (. . . . .)

Стру́гов Алекса́ндр Дми́триевич (. . . .)

Стру́гов Дми́трий Ви́кторович (. . . . .)

Стру́гова Е́ва Дми́триевна (. . . .)

Стру́гов Илья́ Дми́триевич (. . . . .)

d) What would you say in Russia when:

you stop a stranger to ask something;

someone says «Здра́вствуйте»;

you have got a visa;

you are tired;

you are going to bed;

you would like to know how much something is;

you give something to somebody;

you are sorry;

someone asks you «Как дела́?»;

you need to know where a railway station is.

5

Say "please"

▶   to recognise and use two new Russian letters (one of them being from Group IV);

▶   to learn more words with your 26 Russian letters;

▶   to say *Please* in Russian;

▶   to learn how to buy something in a Russian shop;

▶   to find out what "babushka" actually means in Russian;

▶   to return questions in Russian;

▶   to attempt a conversation with a person you have just met.

GROUP III (Funny Shapes) «Жж»

«Жж» **stands for *s* in *pleasure*** but is pronounced ***more at the back*** of your mouth, which makes it sound harder.

> **How does it sound:** There are a couple of hitches with reading this letter correctly. First of all, you need to make sure that you do not read it as the English "j" – Russians hear "j" as *two* sounds: /д/ and /ж/. So, all English names starting with "J" in English will start with «Д» in Russian: Джо, Джоа́нна, Джэйн, Джа́стин, Джу́лия, Джойс, Джулиа́н etc. So, «Ж» is only for *s* in *pleasure* but **pronounced more at the back**. Try not slip into dental /з/ (for *z* in *zebra*) either.
>
> It is also very important to distinguish it from /ш/. Though both /ж/ and /ш/ are pronounced at the back of your mouth with the middle of the tongue low, /ж/ is much more voiced, sort of **louder than /ш/**.

Ex. 1 a) Decoding Cyrillic. As always, watch your stress and note unstressed weak «O»-s.

ЖАР - ЖОР   КÓЖА - КРÁЖА   ЖНУТ - ЖМУТ - ЖМÝРКИ
ЖУК - ЖУЙ   СÁЖА - СТÝЖА   ВÁЖНО - НÉЖНО - МÓЖНО

рожóк - кружóк - пирожóк   слýжба - дрýжба - жáлоба   ýжас - ужáсно - ужáсник
пожáр - пожáрник - поражáть   жуть - жýтко - жýткая   жáло - ужáлит - пожáловать
ажýр - абажýр - кожурá   жаль - ждал - жáдное   жáлуй - пожáлуй - пожáлуйста

Check that you spotted four soft signs.

NEW WORDS:

ПОЖÁЛУЙСТА - *Please*

МÓЖНО - *Is it OK/possible? May I? Can I (have)?*

Tip! Don't worry about pronouncing «Й» in «пожáлу(й)ста» – Russians don't. It will make saying "Please" easier. Make sure you put only ONE stress in it, with all the effort on «ЖА» and no effort on the «У» or the front «О». Have a go: пожáлу(й)ста

«Мóжно» is a brilliant word – it is a sentence in one word! It is very polite and can be used as a question and as an answer. One thing you should never do is use «Я» with it. E.g., Мóжно чай? (Is it possible to have some tea? = Can I have some tea?) – Да, мóжно. (Yes, it's possible. = Yes, you can.) Note that «мóжно» is associated with being allowed or a possibility, rather than "having". That is still «У вас есть . . . ?».

b) Say it in Russian. Make sure that your «Ж» is loud and that your tongue is at the back of your mouth.

Yes. Please.   Do you have a pen? May I?   You can have some butter. Here you are.
No. Thank you.   One glass, please.   Can I have some tea? – Milk or lemon? – Milk, please.
Can I have a pencil?   Can I have my passport   Do you have a banana? Can I have one, please?

WORTH REMEMBERING: Russian «ПОЖÁЛУЙСТА» has THREE meanings!

*1)   The first one matches the English "**please**", e.g.,* Чай, пожáлуйста.

*2)   It is also used as a reply to «Спасúбо» and can be translated as "**You are welcome**" or "Don't mention it". (Keep in mind that technically «пожáлуйста» does not mean "welcome" or "mention".) E.g.:* Спасúбо. – Пожáлуйста.

3) *Russians also use* «пожа́луйста» **when they give you something.** *It often comes with the word* «Вот» *(for "Here you are" or "Here you go"), e.g.,* Вот, пожа́луйста. *In these phrases* «пожа́луйста» *is not translated into English in any particular way. If you think about it, Russians use* «пожа́луйста» *three times more than people use "please" in English, not because they are more polite, but because it has two other meanings. Try to read this conversation for meaning:* - Мо́жно чай, пожа́луйста? - Вот, пожа́луйста. - Спаси́бо. - Пожа́луйста. *Note that "Thank you" is always* «Спаси́бо».

c) Let's try it in Russian. Think how you would ask for things in a Russian shop or a café using «мо́жно» and what answers you might hear. If you can work with someone else, try mini-conversations, with one person trying to place an order or asking for things over the counter. The other can say either «Да. Вот, пожа́луйста» *OR* «Нет. Извини́те». E.g.:, Мо́жно чай, (пожа́луйста)? – Да. Вот, пожа́луйста. – А молоко́ мо́жно? – Нет. Извини́те. Try to keep track of what you (or your customer) can and can't have. Once you are comfortable with this, you can extend your conversation by using «Спаси́бо» to get «Пожалуйста» as a reply.

NEW WORDS: ДЕ́НЬГИ - *money*

Ex. 2 a) How does it work in Russian?

In a shop	*In a cafe*
– Здра́вствуйте.	– Мо́жно чай, пожа́луйста?
– Здра́вствуйте.	– Да, коне́чно. Оди́н?
– У вас есть мя́со?	– Нет. Три, пожа́луйста.
– Да, есть.	– Молоко́?
– Мо́жно 1 килограмм, пожа́луйста.	– Нет, спаси́бо.
– Да, коне́чно*.	– Лимо́н?
– Это ско́лько?	– Да, пожа́луйста.
– 8 рубле́й, пожа́луйста.	– А сколько это?
– Вот де́ньги.	– 9 рублей, пожа́луйста.
– Вот мя́со, пожа́луйста.	– Вот. У меня́ есть 10 рубле́й.
– Спаси́бо.	– Спаси́бо. Вот, пожа́луйста, рубль и чай.
– Пожа́луйста.	– Спаси́бо.
– До свида́ния.	– Пожа́луйста.
– До свида́ния.	

* коне́чно – *of course, certainly*

RUSSIASCOPE: ЛИТР ИЛИ ПЙНТА

Russia is completely metric, and people do not understand pints, inches or miles at all, though there are words for them in Russian dictionaries. In Russian shops, get ready for «килогра́мм» *and* «литр», *and to speak about distances you would need* «метр» *and* «киломе́тр».

---

b) Jog your memory or find it in the conversations above. Keep your «Ж» voiced and back.

Hello. (*in a shop*)	Please.	No. Thanks.	You are welcome/Not at all.
Do you have. . . ?	Thank you.	Yes, please.	Good-bye.
Can I have . . .?	Here you are.	How much is it?	Here is the money.

To make it clear: As you can see, there are a few ways to ask for things in a shop:

1) You can name the item and say «пожа́луйста» (E.g., Сок, пожа́луйста).

2) You can say «Мо́жно» (E.g., Мо́жно сок?). «Пожа́луйста» can be used with it as well.

3) If you are not sure if they have got your item, you can ask «У вас есть . . . ?» (E.g., У вас есть сок?). No «пожа́луйста» here, as it is not normally used with questions

---

c) Step-by-step guide. Let's go shopping in Russia! Remember that if you do not say anything at all, you are still most likely to walk out of that shop with what you wanted! Everything you say would be a bonus. If you want to learn to hold a conversation in Russian, have a few goes following the plan below, and then try without looking in the book. Great to practice with someone else.

1. Say *hello*, using the formal version (**Здравствуйте**).

2. You can start with «**У вас есть**» or «**Мо́жно**». Today you are buying мя́со/молоко́/вино́/каранда́ш.

3. Say the *amount* you need (1 килогра́мм / 1 литр / 1 стака́н / оди́н). Use «**Мо́жно**» or «**пожа́луйста**» or both.

4. Ask how much it is (**Ско́лько?**) and try to catch the price.

5. Think of what you can say when you *give the money*. (Relax – if you forget to say «**Вот**» they will still be happy to have your money.)

6. *Thank* the person serving you (**Спаси́бо.**) and say good-bye (**До свида́ния.**).

RUSSIASCOPE: «Пожа́луйста» *has a stem similar to an old word* «пожа́ловать», *which in Old Russian had two meanings: 1) to grant and 2) to arrive (to sort of grant one's presence). The first meaning gave us* «пожа́луйста», *while the second became a popular greeting* «Добро́ пожа́ловать!» *which means "Welcome!" (something like 'kindly arrive'). Please note that* «Добро́ пожа́ловать!» *is a fixed phrase and is best used as it is, without putting it inside other sentences or linking it to other words. It is NEVER used as an answer to* «Спаси́бо».

Ex. 3 a) Try not to trip up! Note that both «Ж» and «Ш» are pronounced at the back, but «Ж» is distinctively louder than «Ш», more voiced in linguistic terms. Note that the stress patterns change within columns.

ЖАР - ШАР   стежо́к - стишо́к
СА́ЖА - СА́ША   пирожо́к - порошо́к
ЖА́РИТЬ - ША́РИТЬ   ра́дужно - раду́шно
ТУЖУ́ - ТУШУ́   мо́жно - мошна́

How does it sound? This is all about hushing sounds, «Ч», «Ш» and «Ж», which sometimes behave differently from the rest of the consonants. For example, most of them **cannot be palatalised** – they are as they are. This means that the letter «Ч» makes the sound of /ч/ (like *ch* in *child*), whether it is before «Е» or not. Similarly, the sound for the letter «Ш» is ALWAYS going to be harder than *sh* in *shop* and /Ж/ harder than *s* in *pleasure,* and they are NOT palatalised if followed by «Е». The letter **«Е» loses its /й/ sound after "hushers"** and sounds just like /э/ without influencing /ч/, /ш/ or /ж/ at all. So, «чек» sounds like /ч э к/, «шесть» sounds like /ш э с т'/ (Russian for "six") and «то́же» - like /т о́ ж э/ (Russian for "also"). "Hushers" in Russian do not necessarily follow general rules, so we need to know our "hushers"!

b) Decoding Cyrillic:

чек - чем - чей   же - жест - же́нин   душе́ - ва́ше - на́ше
шесть - шерсть - ше́стеро   честь - шесть - жесть   драже́ - да́же - то́же

NEW WORD: ТО́ЖЕ - *too, also, as well*

«Га́ля – то́же моя́ подру́га.»

> **WORTH REMEMBERING:** *Russians use* «тóже» *a lot. It is particularly handy when saying* **"ME TOO"**. *One thing you need to watch is which form of "me" you are using (*«я» *or* «У меня»*). It needs to be the same as in the phrase to which you respond using* «тóже». *E.g.,* **Я** студéнт. – **Я** тóже. OR **У меня** есть пакéт. – **У меня** тóже. *You can make fuller sentences if you wish, e.g.,* У меня тóже есть пакéт.

c) **Let's try it in Russian.** Respond to the phrases below using the right form of *"Me too"*. This is great to do in pairs. Make sure your «Ж» is loud and at the back.

Я дóма.	У меня есть книга.	Я устáла.
У меня есть сестрá.	Я инженéр.	Я ем салáт.
Я ем мя́со.	У меня есть тетрáдь.	У меня есть друг.

> **How does it sound?** We also need to differentiate between «Ж» and «З». While both of them are loud (voiced) sounds, when we say «З» we press our tongue to the front teeth (like *z* in *zebra*) while to say «Ж» you start with *s* in *pleasure* and then move your tongue towards the back of your mouth to make it harder.

Ex. 4 a) Try not to trip up!

РÓЗА - РÓЖА	ЛÓЖА - ЛОЗÁ	наказáл - накажý	лежáть - лизáть
ЛÝЗА - ЛÝЖА	КÓЖА - КОЗÁ	доказáл - докажý	держáть - дерзáть
МÝЗА - МÝЖА	МÁЖУТ - МАЗÝТ	показáл - покажý	жевáть - зевáть

> *Check that you noticed that in the last column the last* «З» *would be palatalised, while* «Ж» *wouldn't.*

b) **Just read and recognise.** First, mark the words with «Ж» in some way and then read the list aloud.

журнáл, вокзáл, тóже, пижáма, зáвтра, журналúст, завóд, вáза, бáнджо, пожáлуйста, виза, казинó, желé, мóжно, инженéр, транзúт, дизáйн, желатúн, магазúн, жасмúн, мéнеджер

> **How does it sound?** Similar to «Д» in «сад» and «Г» in «друг», at the end of words Russians pronounce «Ж» like /ш/. For example, багáж (for *baggage* or *luggage*) will sound more like /б а г á ш/. Try to sound like a Russian, devoicing the final «Ж» to /ш/: гарáж, мирáж, вояж, беж, коллéдж, массáж, престúж, Эрмитáж.

NEW WORDS:

МУЖ - *husband*   ЖЕНА́ - *wife*

***Check** that you realise that «ж» in «муж» is devoiced to /ш/ and the stress in «жена́» is at the end.*

c) What would you say in Russia if you needed to:

introduce your husband/wife;

ask somebody how their wife/husband is;

say that you have a wife/husband;

ask whether their wife/husband eats chocolate;

ask whether this is their wife/husband;

say that your wife/husband is tired;

ask whether they have a wife/husband;

say that your wife/husband does not eat meat;

ask somebody where their wife/husband is;

say that your wife/husband is at home.

***Check** that your «жена́» had the stress at the end.*

d) If you are learning to write, try to write the English names below in Russian. Make sure you sound the name first and spot where you would need to write «Дж» and where «Г» is required. Remember it is the sound, *not* the English letter that will help you.

*Tip! There are a few different ways of **writing «Ж»**: 1) Most common is a handwritten ж, when you can make two vertical semicircles and put a cross in the middle. 2) Some of my students prefer to put semi-circles horizontally: Ж. 3) Some like a "quick way" when you write an X and put a vertical line through the middle. Choose the one which appeals to you and stick with it. It is not like it can be confused with any other letter, is it?*

Jim, John, Gordon, Jack, Gina, Joy, Gale, George, Jude, Gloria, Giles, Jozy, Judith, Josh, Gwen, Julia, Jean, Jill

***Check** that "ia" at the end came out as «ИЯ» in Russian.*

Let's have some more words with our "hushers".

> **NEW WORDS:** БА́БУШКА - *grandmother, grandma*
>
> ДЕ́ДУШКА - *grandfather, grandpa*
>
> МА́ЛЬЧИК - *a young boy, a little lad*

__Check__ that the stress is at the front in all the words (like in «ко́мната»)
and that you only have ONE in each word; that «Д» in де́душка and
«Л» in ма́льчик are palatalised, that is, your tongue moves up and to the front.

To make it clear: «Де́душка», the same as «па́па», has «А» at the end but it is masculine by its meaning. So, we would need to say: **Мой** де́душка до́ма. OR Это **твой** де́душка?

RUSSIASCOPE: БА́БУШКА

Ба́бушка *in Russian is not only a relative – it is a way of life. Most Russian women like being a* ба́бушка. Ба́бушка *is a matronly figure, kind and wise, the head of the household. Traditionally children were raised by a* ба́бушка, *and a lot of them still are. Quite often Russians can address an elderly lady as* Ба́бушка, *and it is normally accepted as a sign of respect. Similarly, any elderly gentlemen can be called* де́душка. *Often a familiar version of their name is attached to it. For example, my Grandma, called* Анастаси́я Андре́евна, *was known in the village as* ба́бушка На́стя. *Note that this word in Russia is NOT used for Russian dolls. (We will learn the word for them later.)*

«Это моя́ ба́бушка На́стя»

Ex. 5 a) Question time. Turn the following phrases into questions. Remember that you do NOT need to change the word order but might need to change some words. E.g., Это **мой** брат. – Это **твой** брат? Watch the tone of your voice. If you work with someone else, you can practice giving negative answers. If comfortable, try using «ИЛИ» (for *or*) too.

Это моя́ ба́бушка.	Мой де́душка уста́л.	Мой муж там.
Еле́на Константи́новна дома.	Ма́льчик шокола́д ест.	Это магази́н «Ру́сская кни́га».
Моя́ сестра́ ест мя́со.	Это мой друг Андре́й.	Моя́ жена́ уста́ла.

__Check__ that you know that Russians would pronounce «друг» as /д р у к/ and «муж» as /м у ш/,
and that the stress in «ба́бушка», «де́душка» and «ма́льчик» is at the front.

Now look at the same sentences above and think which words can be replaced with «Как?», «Где?», «Кто?» and «Что?» to make different questions (to which these sentences would be answers). E.g., Это моя бабушка. – Это кто? Remember to change «мой/моя» for «твой/твоя» if needed. Make sure that you use each of the question words at least once. If working in pairs, remember that you cannot use «Да» or «Нет» to answer these questions.

Tip! You can change the word order and put the question word first or leave it as it is. E.g.: Это кто? *OR* Кто это?

«Кто» *always is used as masculine, so to ask "Who is tired?" we need* «Кто устал?», *even if the answer is* «Она́ уста́ла».

GROUP IV (The Strangers) «Ы»

Ы ы We came across one letter from this group in the last unit, the soft sign «ь», but the soft sign is more of a sign than a letter. This one is a proper letter which stands for a particular sound. The shape does not seem to be a problem, though I guess it looks a bit like a soft sign with a stick on the right, but there is no stick-like letter (like "I") in Russian. Some of my students call it "sixty-one", which makes it easier to identify.

As far as the sound goes – hold on tight! Do you remember that Russian does not have sounds for *th* or *w*? – English does not have a sound like /ы/. This does not mean that you cannot say it. It only means you are not used to saying it. We will learn it the same way as I learnt to say *th* and *w* in English. I will explain what to do with your lips, teeth, and tongue, and you will follow this step-by-step guide to make this sound correctly.

> **How does it sound?** To read «Ы» - 1) Close your *teeth*. 2) Move your *tongue to the back* of your mouth. 3) Put your lips into a *"smile"* and say /i/. As your teeth are still closed, you will end up with a somewhat Wallis-and-Grommet expression – and the correct sound for «Ы»! At no time should your lips go forward – keep smiling with your teeth closed. I know it looks and sounds strange. Is this why we called this group *The Strangers*? You might not be confident to start with, but with practice you will get used to our Strangers and they might become your friends. Ready. Steady. Go! – Teeth together, tongue to the back and smile - Ы-Ы-Ы-Ы-Ы.

Ex. 6 a) Decoding Cyrillic. Note that you do not need to put too much effort into «Ы» when it is away from the stress. So, smile – there is a first time for everything. Good luck!

Tip! Watch your stress in the last three columns, as well as weak unrounded «О»*-s.*

МЫ	СЫТ - СЫН - СЫР	кот - коты́	кос - ко́сы	мыл - мы́ла
ТЫ	МЫЛ - МЫС - МЫТЬ	нос - носы́	рос - ро́сы	сыр - сы́ра
ВЫ	ПЫЛ - НЫЛ - СТЫЛ	суп - супы́	мат - ма́ты	дым - ды́ма

> **How does it sound?** We need to make a distinctive difference between /ы/ and /и/. The main trick is in the position of your tongue: /и/ is made at the front of your mouth, close to the palate, while **/ы/ is at the very back**, away from the roof of your mouth. There is one more important issue with these two. As «И» brings the tongue closer to the palate, the consonants *before* «И» are palatalised (the same as before «Я» or «Е»), e.g., ми́шка (an affectionate word for a "bear", a teddy-bear). **«Ы», on the contrary, does not affect pronunciation of consonants** at all, e.g.: мы́шка (meaning "a mouse"). We did not concentrate on this before as it was not essential – most consonants before /и/ get palatalised naturally, because of where it is. Now that you have learnt about /ы/, you need to watch where your tongue is.

b) Attention: palatalisation! Remember our three steps to make «Ы» and make sure your lips are "smiling".

МЫЛ - МИЛ	БИТ - БЫТ	Ми́ла - мы́ла	лыса́ - лиса́
БЫЛ - БИЛ	БИТЬ - БЫТЬ	Ди́ма - ды́ма	высо́к - висо́к
ВЫЛ - ВИЛ	ВИТЬ - ВЫТЬ	си́то - сы́то	слыла́ - слила́
ПЫЛ - ПИЛ	НИТЬ - НЫТЬ	ми́шка - мы́шка	пыта́л - пита́л

> **To make it clear:** There are no words in Russian that start with «Ы». It is often found in the middle of words and many times at the end, as it often makes our plurals.

> **NEW WORD:** ГО́РОД – *city, town*

Check which «О» is stronger and how you read the final «Д».

c) Big sort out. Read the names of some Russian cities and rivers. Finding them on maps might be fun. If working with someone else, you can take turns picking a random name for the other one to find in the list and say whether it is го́род or река́. E.g., Сы́зрань – это го́род.

го́род Ты́нда, река́ Колыма́, го́род Чебокса́ры, го́род Ры́бинск, го́род Кызы́л, река́ Ирты́ш, го́род Сы́зрань, го́род На́бережные Челны́, река́ Вы́чегда, го́род Ана́дырь

NEW WORDS:

СЫН - *son*	**ЯЗЫ́К** - *language*
СЫР - *cheese*	**ру́сский язы́к** - *Russian language*
МУ́ЗЫКА - *music*	**англи́йский язы́к** - *English language*

RUSSIASCOPE: Similar to how English speakers say "cheese" when their picture is taken, Russians say «СЫР» when looking at a camera. Do we have funny smiles?

Ex. 7 a) Reading for meaning:

Это мой сын Же́ня, а это моя́ дочка Са́ша.

У меня́ есть жена́ и сын. – А у меня́ есть дочка.

Мой сын не ест мя́со. – Мой то́же.

Вот вино́ и сыр. – Спаси́бо. Ско́лько это?

Мо́жно сыр? Один килогра́мм, пожа́луйста.

Я ем сыр, а мой муж сыр не ест.

Как твой англи́йский? – Отли́чно. Спаси́бо.

У вас есть кни́га «Ру́сский язы́к»? – Извини́те, нет.

Check that you have spotted TWO differences between the pronunciation of the name «Же́ня» (short for Евге́ний or Евге́ния) and the word «жена́».

b) Now it's your turn. Think how you would ask a Russian about their family, friends, pets etc., employing «У вас есть . . . ?». Remember to use your new words. If you work with somebody else, have a conversation about each other. Try to be as truthful as possible – you will remember things better if they are relevant. It is *very* important that you take turns asking and answering questions. You might want to return questions using a shortened version «А у вас?», similar to *And you?* in English. E.g., У вас есть сын? – Нет, но у меня́ есть брат. А у вас? – У меня́ то́же есть брат. А у вас есть сестра́? – Да, есть. А у вас? Enjoy using your Russian.

The word «ру́сский» is also used to speak about somebody being Russian, e.g.: Он ру́сский (note «Она́ ру́сск**ая**»). The word for an Englishman, though, needs a different "bit" attached to the stem of «А́нглия» – we have «англича́нин» for him. As you would imagine, the female version has to have an «А» at the end – «англича́нка». Languages or nationalities do NOT start with a capital in Russian! We will be speaking about different nationalities in a couple of units, but the small table below will be our start.

Country	Language	Nationality
Росси́я	ру́сский язы́к	ру́сский/ру́сская
А́нглия	англи́йский язы́к	англича́нин/англича́нка

c) Let's try it in Russian. Say whether the following people are English or Russian, using male and female forms.

Анна Па́влова, Влади́мир Пу́тин, Гари Ли́некер, Лев Толсто́й, Джéссика Э́нис, Уи́нстон Чéрчиль, Мари́я Шара́пова, Ма́ргарет Тэ́тчер

d) Now it's your turn. Are there Russians or English among your friend and family? Speak about them. Otherwise, find some celebrities to speak about.

> *WORTH REMEMBERING: This is all about "YOU", Russian words for "you" to be more exact. Yes, there are a few. Similar to how in English you can have "I" and "me", both referring to the same person in different types of sentences, Russians have a few forms for "you". We already know one of them - «вас» in «У вас есть . . . ?». This is not the dictionary form, though. If we compare this phrase to «У меня́ есть . . . », the word «меня́» (meaning "me" if you remember) technically is a form of «я» (meaning "I"), which IS the dictionary form. What we need is a dictionary form of «вас», which is «ВЫ».*

Ex. 8 a) Reading for meaning. In each line underline a form of *you* («ВЫ» or «ВАС»), and determine why one is used rather than the other.

Алло́. Андрéй Никола́евич? Вы где? – Я до́ма.

У вас есть де́ньги? Мо́жно рубль?

Извини́те. Вы Елéна Ви́кторовна? – Нет. Она́ там.

Здра́вствуйте. Я Ната́лия Влади́мировна. А вы?

У вас су́мка или пакéт есть? – Да. Вот, пожа́луйста.

Вы мой до́ктор? – Да. Я Валенти́н Ива́нович. – Óчень прия́тно.

b) What would you say in Russia if you needed to ask somebody:

whether they are Russian;

whether they have a pen;

who they are;

whether they are a doctor;

where they are;

whether they have (any) money.

c) How does it work in Russian? Read this conversation that I witnessed when I worked as an interpreter in Russia during one of our company's corporate events.

— Здра́вствуйте.

— Здра́вствуйте.

— Я Джон Па́ркер. А вы?

— А я Олéг Сергéевич Ивано́в, но мо́жно* Олéг.

— Óчень прия́тно. Вы инженéр?

— Да, а вы?

— А я то́же инженéр.

— Извини́те, а вы англича́нин, да?

- Да, но моя жена́ - ру́сская. *(Calls his wife)* Это моя́ жена́, Жа́нна. Жанна, это Оле́г.
- О́чень прия́тно. У меня́ тоже есть жена́, и сын. А у вас есть сын или дочка?
- У меня́ тоже есть оди́н сын. Он студе́нт.
- А мой сын - программи́ст.

---

* Мо́жно *(here)*- You can call me/ it's possible/it's OK

d) Jog your memory or find in the conversation above:

I have	you *(two forms)*	but	and *(two forms)*	I am sorry
you have	And you? *(two forms)*	or	also/too	Nice to meet you

e) Let's try it in Russian. If you work with someone else, you can try acting out this conversation in Russian. If you are learning on your own, read the first line but cover the rest of the conversation by a sheet of paper. Think of your answer, say it aloud, then check it and move to the next line. Try speaking for Оле́г and then for Джон.

> **WORTH REMEMBERING: "AND YOU?"** *is a very convenient way to keep the conversation going. There is one thing to keep in mind, though. In the same way that when saying "Me too", you had to choose between «я» and «У меня́ есть» to return a question using "And you?", we need to look at the original question and use the same form with «А» in front and the tone of your voice raised. E.g.,* **У вас** *есть брат? – Да.* **А у вас?** *OR Вы инжене́р? – Нет.* **А вы?**

f) Step-by-step guide to starting a conversation with a stranger. Imagine that you are invited to some kind of event in Russia (you never know . . .). Think of how you would try to start a conversation with the person standing next to you. You might not know in Russian all the words that you would say in English, but you definitely can say a couple of things.

1. Start by saying *hello.* «**Здра́вствуйте**» is a good choice when you don't know people.

2. *Introduce* yourself. At the moment this is a good way: **Я** .... **А вы?**

3. Don't forget to say «**О́чень прия́тно.**» when others introduce themselves.

4. Say that you are *not Russian* (or that you are English, if you are English and if you remember the word).

5. If you know the Russian word for your job, try that, e.g., **Я инжене́р**/до́ктор/студе́нт. А вы?

6. People like talking about families. Find out about brothers or sisters or perhaps a Russian friend – you would need «**У вас есть . . .**». (Note that if you are returning a question like this, you would need «А у вас?»)

When you have a conversation in a foreign language, you need to make sure that you take turns asking and answering questions, so it does not turn into an interrogation where only one person asks questions and the other only answers. Give each other time to ask the next question. There is one important rule – you cannot use any English

Let's have a break from different Russian YOUs and do something else. It might be good to fill the gaps in our numbers, don't you think?

> **NEW WORDS:** ШЕСТЬ - *six (6)*
>
> ЧЕТЫ́РЕ - *four (4)*

> *Check that you understand that none of the «Е»-s would need a /й/*
> *sound as they are after consonants;*
> *but in «шесть», «Е» will sound like /э/ as it is stressed, while in*
> *«четы́ре» both «Е»-s are more like /и/, as they are unstressed;*
> *that «Ш» and «Ч» remain unchanged, as they are hushers.*

Ex. 9 a) Jog your memory. Try to remember all the numbers from zero to ten. Now say the number following those below. If you like a challenge, have a second go, saying the one before.

четы́ре, оди́н, де́вять, шесть, три, семь, пять, два, во́семь, ноль.

b) Let's try it in Russian. Here are some adverts from some Tula companies. Have a go at reading their names (the words in the largest print) and one of their telephone numbers. If you work with someone else, you can pick a number in random order for the other one to find the company and read the name.

Well, having had our break, we might need to get back to our Russian YOUs.

RUSSIASCOPE: ВЫ ИЛИ ТЫ

«ВЫ» *is a polite form of "you", to address somebody whom you would say* «Здра́вствуйте» *to, somebody like a teacher, an official or an older person.* «ВЫ» *goes very well with* «Извини́те» *and the use of patronymics. As you might have guessed, Russians have another word for "you" which is informal and would go with* «Приве́т». *This word is* «**ТЫ**». *It is used among family and friends, to children and teenagers or people whom you know well enough to use familiar versions of their names. Note that to their own grandma and grandpa, children use* «**ТЫ**», *as they are classed as family, and familiar forms of the names are used with them. E.g.,* Ба́бушка, ты уста́ла? – Нет, спаси́бо, Ли́дочка. *(Check your stress.)*

Russians would normally address a person they have just met with «ВЫ», *so you are safer with this one. It might be worth noting though, that* «ВЫ» *is never used towards children and rarely towards young teenagers.*

Ex. 10 a) Let's try it in Russian. Choose whether you would use «ТЫ» or «ВЫ» to the following people:

дире́ктор, твоя́ сестра́, тури́ст, Андре́й Никола́евич, сын, до́ктор, твой де́душка, Ли́дочка, ру́сский друг, не твоя́ ба́бушка, ма́льчик Са́ша, жена́/муж

NEW WORDS:

ТЫ ЕШЬ - *You eat/You are eating*

Check that your «ЕШЬ» *starts with a* /й/ *sound.*

To make it clear: Remember that our "hushers" («Ч», «Ш» and «Ж» so far) are always read in the same way, not depending on what letters are around. So, «Ш» and «ШЬ» sound exactly the same, short and at the back. The soft sign here has a different purpose. Just as «-А» links the words related to feminines, «-ШЬ» links the verb to «ТЫ».

---

b) Reading for meaning. Keep an eye on when you are going to translate «Ты ешь» as *You eat* and when as *You are eating*.

Ты ешь мя́со? – Да. Я ем, но муж не ест.

Что ешь? – Мандари́н. – Мо́жно? – Вот, пожа́луйста.

Ты шокола́д ешь? – Нет, не ем, но моя́ сестра́ ест.

Я ем сыр. А ты ешь? – Да, я то́же ем.

Что ты ешь? – Суп. А ты? – Сала́т.

Алло́. – Алло́. – Ты ешь? – Да, извини́.

Check that you remember that «извини́» *is an informal version of* «извини́те».

c) Find the person who doesn't eat meat, cheese, salad, butter, chocolate, soup. Using our new phrase «Ты ешь?», think how you would ask somebody whether they eat something. If you can do it in a group, each person goes round asking others and jotting down their names and the food they do not eat. When asked, try to give different types of answers. After everybody has finished (or when you all have had enough), say in Russian who does not eat those foods (E.g., Джон не ест сыр.). You need to use only *one* name per phrase and take turns. If you are on your own, make questions first and then speak about the people you know. Make sure you use correct forms of *eat* (ем/ешь/ест).

d) Question time. Imagine that you are hosting a Russian boy (e.g., мальчик Саша) – you can find an image of my young village friend on p. 241. Think how you would ask him whether he is Саша or Паша; whether he eats meat; whether he is Russian; where he is *(on the phone for example)*; whether he eats chocolate; whether he is tired.

WORTH REMEMBERING: If we think logically, «ТЫ», similar to «Я» and «ВЫ», should have a different form to make an informal version of "You have . . . ", shouldn't it? And it does – it is «ТЕБЯ», which is a form of «ТЫ» after «У». «У тебя есть . . . » also means "You have . . . ", the same as «У вас есть . . . », but it is only used with people to whom you can use «ТЫ» (let's call them ТЫ-people). E.g., Ваня, у тебя есть ручка? but Иван Сергеевич, у вас есть ручка?

So, technically Russians have two YOUs in the dictionary (formal «ВЫ» and informal «ТЫ»), and then each of them has one more form to make the "You have . . ." phrases («ВАС» and «ТЕБЯ»).

English	Russian Dictionary Form	Russian Second Form, used in "having" constructions (after «У»)
I > me	**Я**	**(У) МЕНЯ**
you	**ВЫ** *(formal)*	**(У) ВАС** *(formal)*
you	**ТЫ** *(informal)*	**(У) ТЕБЯ** *(informal)*

Check that you read «тебя» *with the stress at the end and a vowel between the palatalised* /т'/ *and the palatalised* /б'/ *(like **b** in **bar**).*

Ex. 11 a) Reading for meaning. In each line, underline a form of *you* («ТЫ» or «ТЕБЯ»). Make sure you understand why they are used that way.

Маша, у тебя есть пакёт? – Да. Вот, пожалуйста.

Алло, Галя. Ты дома? – Да. – Я тоже.

Дима, извини. У тебя карта есть? Можно?

Оля, ты ешь сыр? – Нет, извини, не ем.

А бабушка у тебя есть? – Да. – У меня тоже.

Володя, ты устал? – Нет. Спасибо, дедушка.

Check that both «бабушка» *and* «дедушка» *have the stress at the front.*

b) Let's try it in Russian. Let's go back to that imaginary ру́сский ма́льчик Са́ша whom you are hosting. You can now think about how to ask him whether he has a brother or a sister, his own room, a pet, a friend etc. If you work with someone else, you can take turns asking questions and see who is the last to think of a relevant word. (In this exercise, you do not need to give answers.)

To make it clear: Some of my students seem to sometimes confuse our new word «ТЕБЯ́» (in «У **тебя́** есть») and **твоя́** (for *your/s*). You probably see why. So, we need to make sure that you pronounce them differently. In «ТЕБЯ́», «Б» (like *b* in *bar*) is separated from «Т» by the letter «Е», thus is palatalised - /т' и б' а́/, while in «твоя́», «В» (like *v* in *van*) follows «Т» with no gap /т в а й а́/. Note that «Б» in «ТЕБЯ́» is also palatalised before «Я» - /т' и б' а́/ (with no /й/ sound, unlike in твоя́ - /т в а й а́/). So, in «ТЕБЯ́», we have two palatalised consonants with a vowel in between, while in «твоя́» there are two hard consonants with no gap. Can you hear now how different they are? Have a go slowly: твоя́ - ТЕБЯ́.

---

c) Reading for meaning. Make sure that you read and translate «твой»/«твоя́» and «тебя́» correctly.

У тебя́ есть жена́? – Да, есть. – Твоя́ жена́ медсестра́*, да? – Нет. Она до́ктор.

А де́душка у тебя́ есть? Да? – Да. – Как твой де́душка? – Отли́чно. Спаси́бо.

Это твоя́ жена́? – Нет. Это моя́ сестра́. – О́чень прия́тно. А у тебя́ есть жена́? – Да. Она дома.

У тебя́ сын или до́чка есть? – У меня́ есть до́чка. – Твоя́ до́чка студе́нтка? – Да, студе́нтка.

А муж у тебя́ есть? – Да, но это мой брат. – А где твой муж? – Там.

---

* медсестра́ - *nurse*

d) Let's get this right. Fill in the blanks with a correct word: «ты», «вы», «тебя́» or «вас». Watch out for other words around to help you decide whether the situation is formal or informal.

Алло. На́стя? .... дома? – Да.   Ва́ня, ... уста́л? – Нет, спаси́бо, ба́бушка. А ты?

Здра́вствуйте. У .... есть сыр?   Андре́й Никола́евич, ... дома за́втра? – Нет.

Извини́. У .... есть ру́чка?   Извини́те, у .... есть молоко́? – Да. Вот, пожа́луйста.

Приве́т .... ешь суп? – Да, ем.   На́стя, у .... есть газе́та «Вре́мя»*? – Да. – Мо́жно?

---

* вре́мя - *time*

e) Now it's your turn. Imagine that you are at a party and different people (for example, an old friend and somebody you've just met) ask you different questions. Answer each question below; speak about yourself as truthfully as possible, to remember things better. Then turn the question back, using correct version of *And you?* Note that you now have four forms to choose from. If you work with someone else, you can take turns asking questions and answering them, following your answers by the right form of *And you?*

Вы журналист?

У вас есть собáка?

А сыр ты ешь?

У тебя друг есть?

А у вас есть книга «Рýсский язы́к»?

Ты устáл/а?

Вы медсестрá?

У тебя есть тетрáдь?

Алло. Ты дома?

I think you worked extremely hard in this unit, getting to grips with Russian "hushers", with different meanings of «пожáлуйста» and shopping in Russian. And what about «Ы» (?!) and all those forms of YOU? That's in addition to all the new words that we have done. So, it might be time to say «До свидáния» or «Спокóйной ночи».

Tonight, I am also going to wish you **Good luck - УДÁЧИ!** This word is always positive in Russian – for "bad luck" there is a different word. So, keep positive, keep thinking Russian and keep peddling – you will get there. Удáчи!

Something old, something new (*revision of unit 5*)

Здра́вствуйте. Как дела́? I am not going to go formal with you all of a sudden – we will just practice the formal greeting today, as you might need to use it with Russians who have not become your friends yet. What would your answer be: «Отли́чно» или «Уста́л/а»? Quite often, Russians respond with «**Норма́льно**» *(with «н» at the front and «но» at the end, two weak «О»-s and palatalised /л/ like in* **lit** *before the soft sign)*, which can be translated as *As normal* or *Fine*. Do not take it on board, though, using it for English *normally*, as it is not going to work – «Норма́льно» is only used as a reply to «Как дела́?».

Today we will also see how to return the «Как дела́?» question. So, let's remember how we returned questions in Unit 5.

1. How would you translate: «А вы?», «А ты?», «А у вас?» and «А у тебя?»?

2. Where do you need to look to choose the correct form for *And you?*?

As Russians prefer using *And you?* to ask how things are in return, rather than repeating «Как дела́?», we need to know the structure of «Как дела́?» to choose the right form – and it is not obvious.

> **WORTH REMEMBERING:** «Как дела́?» *is actually a shortened version of the full sentence* «**Как у вас дела́?**» *(which literally stands for "How* <u>do you have</u> *your things?"). This means that to return this question, we need the* «у вас» *option. The conversation might look something like this:* Здра́вствуйте. Как (у вас) дела́? – Отли́чно. Спаси́бо. А у вас? – Норма́льно. *In case you need to go informal, you would need* «у тебя» *instead. E.g.,* Приве́т. Как (у тебя) дела́? – Отли́чно. **А у тебя?** – Норма́льно.

Let's try! I am going back to my usual informal self and will say «Приве́т. Как дела́?». Choose your answer and the form of *And you?* to match my question. Make sure you say it aloud. What if somebody says: «Здра́вствуйте. Как (у вас) дела́?»? What would you answer then?

Now that we have said our greetings, we need to have a look at where we are with our Russian letters. Our letter groups are gradually filling up. Check that you know how to read all the letters listed below. If in doubt, have a quick skip back to previous units. Make sure you name all the letters the Russian way.

GROUP I (*The Easy*): Мм, Тт, Кк, Аа, Оо

GROUP II (*The Tricky*): Сс, Нн, Вв, Рр, Ее (*like . . . in . . .*), Уу (*like oo in **moon***)

GROUP III (*Funny Shapes*): Ээ, Яя, Лл, Дд, Ии, Йй, Бб, Зз, Пп, Гг, Чч, Шш, Жж *(like s in **pleasure but more to the back**)*

GROUP IV (*The Strangers*): Ьь *(the soft sign),* Ыы *(1) teeth together, 2) tongue to the back, 3) lips into a smile and say "i". We will have a good go at this one again today.)*

Have you realised that you now know as many letters in Russian as you do in English? Here they are in alphabetical order:

А Б В Г Д Е … Ж З И Й К Л М Н О П Р С Т У … … … Ч Ш … … Ы Ь Э … Я

(?) 3. Can you name the three hushing sounds that we have had so far?

4. What is the difference between «Ш» and «Ж», and what do they have in common?

5. Do you remember how to differentiate between «Ж» and «З»? What is similar about them?

Ex. 1 a) Try not to trip up! Watch your "hushers" and your «З».

шу́тка - жу́тко - чу́тко	шаль - жаль - зна́ли
да́ча - Да́ша - да́же	поча́л - пожа́л - позва́л
жа́рко - ча́рка - ша́ркал	зача́ть - зажа́ть - зашла́
ча́йка - ша́йка - лужа́йка	жабо́ - забо́р - шабло́н

b) Let's try it in Russian. Very much like people in England say *Yes, please* or *No, thank you* when they are offered something, in Russia people use «Да, пожа́луйста» or «Нет. Спаси́бо». Think which one you would need if you are offered: tea, juice, wine, meat, an apple, some milk, some butter, a big gateau, some soup, some salad etc. If you work with someone else, one of you can "offer" an item by raising the tone of their voice (e.g., «Я́блоко?») and the other would need to accept (Да, пожа́луйста) or refuse (Нет. Спаси́бо). Remember to take turns.

(?) 6. In how many situations do Russians use «пожа́луйста»?

7. How can you ask for things in a shop in Russia (try to remember a couple of different options)?

8. What does «ВОТ» mean? Does it mean *here*?

c) Let's get this right. Imagine you are buying a big gateau in a cake shop in Russia. Think about the words that you would use. Write them in the conversation below or just say your phrases. You can do it from memory or choose from the list underneath the conversation. It might be good to read this in parts with somebody else. Try to have a go at both parts.

– ....

– Здра́вствуйте.

– .... торт?

– Да. Оди́н?

– Оди́н, ... Ско́лько это?

– 8 рубле́й.

–...............................

– Вот торт, пожалуйста.

–...............................

– Пожа́луйста.

–...............................

– До свида́ния.

Вот де́ньги, мо́жно, пожа́луйста, до свида́ния, спаси́бо, здра́вствуйте

d) Now it's your turn. Think of what you would need to say in a Russian shop to buy cheese/ meat (1 kilo), juice (1 glass), chocolate (two). Great to do with someone else. Do this without looking in the book.

> ***Check*** *that you remember that any numbers after one are best used on their own for now.*

9. Do we need to palatalise «Ч», «Ш» or «Ж» if they happen to be before «Е»?

10. How do we read «Е» after "hushers", e.g.: то́же?

Ex. 2 a) Decoding Cyrillic. Watch your "hushers" and your «Е».

Tip! «Е» *after hushing sounds under the stress will sound as a very clear /э/, while away from the stress it will be weak. Thus, make sure that you know where your stress is! Keep your tongue at the back for* «Ж» *and* «Ш».

желто́к - шесто́к - чесно́к	зашепта́л - ше́пчет	че́стно - че́рви - челове́к
шесто́й - честно́й - жено́й	нажела́ть - же́сти	жезл - же́стом - железня́к
мече́ть - манже́т - планше́т	почему́ - че́ком	ше́я - ше́йка - шевели́ть

b) Jog your memory. Underline all the words with «Ж». Read the list aloud, making sure that you read «Ж» and «Ш» distinctively. Watch your stress, particularly if it is not marked. Check that you remember what the words mean. If you are learning to write, write out the words with «Ш» and those with «Ж» into different columns.

школа, мо́жно, каранда́ш, ба́бушка, пожа́луйста, жена́, шесть, маши́на, инжене́р, ча́шка, журнали́ст, де́душка, то́же, шокола́д.

> **To make it clear:** The word **ТО́ЖЕ** can also mean *either* or *neither* in Russian. E.g., Я не уста́ла. – Я то́же не уста́л/а. (*I am not tired either.*). Thus, we can use «то́же» to say *Me neither*. Russians often add «нет» after «то́же», e.g.: Я не уста́ла. – Я то́же нет.

c) Let's try it in Russian. Below I have written a few sentences about myself and my friends and family. You need to think what you can say about yourself to respond to my statements. Note that these are *not* questions – you just need to say something on the same topic. It can be positive or negative. E.g., Я не ем шокола́д. – Я то́же нет. OR У меня́ есть друг. – У меня́ то́же есть друг. OR А у меня́ есть подру́га. So, you and I will have some sort of conversation.

Я Ната́лия.	У меня́ есть муж.	Я не ем мя́со.
У меня́ есть брат.	Он англича́нин.	Моя́ до́чка ест шокола́д.
Я ру́сская.	У меня́ есть до́чка.	У меня́ есть маши́на.

d) Watch your stress and unstressed «О»-s. Also, make sure that you read «Г» as *g* in *golf* and «Ж» as *s* in *pleasure*.

бо́ги - божо́к	рожо́к - рога́	са́га - сажа́л
дру́га - дружо́к	пирожо́к - пирога́	бе́гал - бежа́л
дви́гал - движо́к	бережо́к - берега́	до́рого - дорожа́л

11. How do Russians pronounce «Г» at the end of words (e.g., in «друг»)?

12. What happens to «Ж» at the end (e.g., in «муж»)?

e) Jog your memory. Read aloud, keeping your eye on «Г» and «Ж».

муж, подру́га, кни́га, жена́, друг, журна́л, магази́н, англича́нин, гара́ж, инжене́р, мо́жно, колле́дж, го́род, где, пожа́луйста, де́ньги, журнали́ст, англича́нка

Check that you realised that Russians will read «ж» in «гара́ж» as /ш/.

RUSSIASCOPE: Гара́ж *in Russian means a place where a car is kept, not where it is fixed. That would be «Автосе́рвис».*

f) Now it's your turn. Think of at least *two* sentences about half a dozen people you know. Start with «У меня́ есть. . . .» and then think of another sentence about them, for example, about their occupation, or what they eat or don't eat, or whether they are at home or will be at home tomorrow; say their name if you run out of options. If you work with someone else, try to exchange statements about yourselves and your people, like you did with me earlier. Make sure that you take turns and remember – no English!

Reading Challenge: Рождество́

(This actually means "Christmas") Make sure that you have one stress on the last «О», which is the longest vowel here.

? 13. Why did we call Group IV *The Strangers*?

14. What was the first letter of this group called? Why?

15. Do you remember the *three* things you need to do to read «Ы» correctly?

16. Name one thing you should never do when pronouncing /ы/.

Ex. 3 a) Decoding Cyrillic. Move your tongue back for your «Ы» and keep smiling!

бык - рык - стык	кады́к - балы́к - башлы́к	мал - малы́ш - малы́шка
ры́ба - ды́ба - глы́ба	нары́в - наплы́в - надры́в	глуп - глупы́ш - глупы́шка
сыр - сы́ро - сы́рость	добы́л - добы́ча - ды́бом	бар - бары́ш - бары́шник

Check that you spotted a line with devoiced «В»-s

b) Try not to trip up! Make sure you spot the soft sign (Ь) and differentiate it from «Ы». Remember that consonants before «Ы» are NOT palatalised. Watch your stress – not all «Ы»-s are stressed.

мать - ма́ты	дань - даны́	свить - сви́ты	тронь - тро́ны
дать - да́ты	шарь - шары́	слить - сли́ты	рань - ра́ны

c) Big sort out. Spot the numbers among the other words below. You can underline them first and then read them out loud, keeping in your head what number it is. Watch the stresses – they might help you.

семь, воск, четве́рг, пять, ови́н, де́сять, пя́тка, во́лос, два, жесть, дева́ть, во́семь, оди́н, десяти́на, три, се́мя, шесть, де́вять, четы́ре, дава́й, трико́

d) Let's try it in Russian. Count in Russian from one to ten and back. Then say the even numbers and then the odd.

? 17. What do we need to watch to make the difference between /ы/ and /и/?

18. How do we read consonants before «И»?

Ex. 4 a) Attention: Palatalisation.

ты́на - ти́на	пи́ли - пы́ли	крыт - Крит
ны́не - Ни́не	Ли́ка - лы́ка	ты́кать - ти́кать

b) Jog your memory.

сын, язы́к, му́зыка, ру́сский язы́к, сыр, англи́йский язы́к, четы́ре.

? 19. Can we use the word «англи́йский» to speak about an English man? What do we use?

20. Can we call a Russian person «ру́сский»?

21. When do we use «ру́сская»? Do you remember the word for an English woman?

c) Big sort out. Highlight (or underline) the words with «Ы» and then read all the words in order, paying attention to where your tongue is. Make sure that you know what the words mean.

кни́га, сын, язы́к, Росси́я, спаси́бо, англи́йский, му́зыка, кино́, оди́н, буты́лка, сыр, англича́нин, вино́, А́нглия, макаро́ны, ру́сский, кварти́ра, четы́ре, англича́нка, стадио́н, ви́за

d) What would you say in Russia if you want to:

say that you are not Russian;

ask where the university is;

ask someone whether they have a copybook;

say that your friend is a student;

say that you have a pen;

say that you don't want something;

ask for some tea;

give money to a shop assistant;

say that you have a (plastic) bag;

say that you don't eat cheese.

? 22. What is the difference between «ТЫ» and «ВЫ»?

23. Whom do Russians always address with «ТЫ»?

24. In which situations do you need to use «ВЫ»?

25. Which form, «ТЫ» or «ВЫ», do Russian children use with their own grandmas? Why?

Ex. 5 a) Let's get this right. Choose whether you would use «ТЫ» or «ВЫ» to the following people:

Еле́на Константи́новна, твой сын, журнали́ст, твоя́ ба́бушка, ма́льчик Ва́ня, не твой де́душка, секрета́рь, На́стя, твоя́ ру́сская подру́га, ме́неджер, англича́нин.

> *Check that your* «Еле́на» *started with a* /й/ *sound.*

? 26. When do we need «ТЕБЯ́» and «ВАС»?

27. What do Russians do with «У тебя́ есть» to turn it into a question?

28. Which of these («У тебя́ есть . . . ?» or «У вас есть . . . ?») would you use in a shop?

29. When would you use «У тебя́ есть . . . »?

> *Check that you read* «тебя́» *correctly, with a vowel between* «т» *and*
> «б» *(like "b" in "bar") and with both consonants palatalised.*

b) Let's get this right. Fill in the gaps with «ты», «вы», «тебя» or «вас».

Извините. У .... есть сыр?

Мальчик, ... Коля или Костя?

Здравствуйте .... директор?

Женя, а у .... есть машина завтра?

Привет. Как дела? – Отлично. А у .... ?

.... устала, Лизочка? – Нет, бабушка.

Паспорт, пожалуйста. А виза у .... есть?

Я Наталия Владимировна. А .... ?

Здравствуйте. Как у вас дела? – Нормально. А у .... ?

Извини, у .... сок или лимонад есть? – Вот сок.

c) Let's get this right. Turn the formal phrases below into the informal version, for example, to ask мальчик Саша.

У Вас есть сыр?

Извините. Вы – студент?

Вы завтра дома? – Да. – До свидания.

Здравствуйте. Как у вас дела?

Алло. Ольга Викторовна? Вы где?

Андрей Николаевич, паспорт у вас есть?

? 30. How do we read «ШЬ» in «ешь»?

31. Why do Russians put the soft sign at the end of «ешь», if «Ш» is read the same?

32. What are the two ways of translating «ты ешь»?

d) Let's try it in Russian. It's good to do this in a group. Ask the person on your right whether they eat meat/cheese/salad/chocolate/soup/butter. After they have answered your question, they ask the person on *their* right using another food item from the list. Listen to the answers and try to remember what the person next to you eats/doesn't eat. When you have finished, start the second round, where you have to say what the person on your right eats/doesn't eat (using «ОН/А ЕСТ» instead of the forms you used in the first round). If you work on your own, you can imagine asking your friends and family and then talking about them using a different form of the verb.

It's important to listen in the class to what the other people say in Russian, as it will help you get used to listening to Russians. Do you know that there are four skills in language: reading, speaking, listening and writing. You need to practice those which are important to you, and it might be all of them.

6

Where are you?

WHAT'S THE PLAN?

▶ to recognise and use two new Russian letters;
▶ to learn more words with your 26 Russian letters;
▶ to say *That's OK.* in Russian;
▶ to say where people and things are;
▶ to have a go at adding "bits" to the end of familiar Russian words and see what some of them do;
▶ to have a go at saying where you are today and tomorrow;
▶ to identify some plural forms in Russian;
▶ to find out a little bit about cities and the countryside in Russia.

GROUP II (The Tricky) «X x»

We did not have any letters from the Tricky group in the last unit. Well, this is the last of them.

How does it sound? «Xx» is made in the same place in your mouth as English /k/ but is pronounced in a totally different way – rather than exploding like /k/, **it flows**, without any stops or interruptions. Some textbooks compare Russian /x/ to Scottish *ch* in *loch*, which I think might be taking it too far. On the other hand, sometimes the flowing nature of Russian /x/ is likened to that of English *h* in *hen*. Though this is true to an extent, the air flow of Russian /x/ is considerably stronger, in addition to being produced in a different place. As you know, English /h/ is so light that people sometimes do not pronounce it. But Russian /x/ should be distinctively heard. Try to find some middle ground between those two suggestions. And of course, we need to read the letter «X» wherever it is written.

Ex.1 a) Let's get this right. Make sure you differentiate between «K» and «X».

сок - сох	ход - код	ко́лко - хо́лка	блох - блок
сук - сух	хит - кит	ве́ко - ве́ха	худа́ - куда́

To make it clear: *When you write in Russian, you DO NOT NEED this shape «X» if you hear /k s/. E.g.,* ТЕКСТ, КОНТЕ́КСТ, ТЕКСТИ́ЛЬ, БОКС, ТОКСИ́Н, МИ́КСЕР

b) Decoding Cyrillic. Watch your stress too. See how comfortable you feel with the Russian /x/. If you find it easy, skip the first three lines of word pairs below and go straight to the word strings underneath them. If you feel you need to practice it, take it steady, but take breaks too – you will get there.

ХАМ – МАХ	ХОЛСТ – СОХ	ТИ́ХО - ТИХА́	ГЛУ́ХИ - ГЛУХА́
ХИЛ – ЛИХ	ХОЛМ – МОХ	СУ́ХО - СУХА́	БЛО́ХИ - БЛОХА́
ХУД – ДУХ	ХРАП – ПРАХ	СНО́ХИ - СНОХА́	ПЛО́ХО - ПЛОХА́

хлам - хлор - хлыст	их - ины́х - литы́х	шах - хоро́ш - хорошо́	запа́х - Заха́р - са́хар
хват - хвост - хво́я	стих - стихи́ - стихи́я	лох - лопу́х - лопуха́	захо́д - похо́д - вы́ход
мех - смех - грех	е́хать - уе́хать - нае́хать	э́хо - эпо́ха - эхоло́т	хлеба́л - хлеба́ть - хле́ба

Check that you spotted at least three devoiced «Д»-s; that «Е» started with /й/ after a vowel and at the start of a word.

NEW WORDS:

ХОРОШО́ - *good, well, well done!*   СА́ХАР - *sugar*
ПЛО́ХО - *bad*   ХЛЕБ - *bread*
О́ЧЕНЬ - *very*   ВЫ́ХОД - *exit, way out*

Check that you understand that Russians would devoice the last «Б» in «хлеб» and the last «Д» in «вы́ход», that the first two «О»-s in «хорошо́» are weak and unrounded.

> **RUSSIASCOPE:** *The word for "entrance" in Russian, which is «**ВХОД**», looks a bit similar to «**ВЫХОД**». So, if you are looking to get out, look for «Ы». When you pronounce these two correctly they will sound very different too, as in «вход» «О» is stressed and strong; while in «выход», «О» is weak and «Ы» is strong. (Note that «В» in «вход» does not sound distinctive, as it is before voiceless «Х», similar to «Б» in «коробка» – just catch your lip).*

c) Reading for meaning:

У вас есть хлеб? – Да. Вот, пожа́луйста. – Спаси́бо.

Мо́жно сахар? – Вот. – Спаси́бо. – Пожа́луйста.

Извини́те, пожа́луйста. А вы́ход где? – Там.

Ты что ешь? – Хлеб и сыр. – А ты? – А я суп ем.

– Приве́т, Михаи́л. Как дела́?

– О́чень хорошо́! А у тебя́?

– Тоже хорошо́. А как твой сын?

– Непло́хо. Спаси́бо. А твой?

– Норма́льно.

d) Big sort out. Read and translate the little phrases below and sort them out in order from the worst to the best.

Tip! Quite often Russians attach the «не» to the word linked to it, e.g., непло́хо. Did I mention that Russians like attaching bits to words? Watch that your stresses stay in place when you add "bits".

непло́хо, хорошо́, не о́чень пло́хо, о́чень хорошо́, нехорошо́, пло́хо, не о́чень хорошо́, о́чень пло́хо

e) Let's try it in Russian. Think of a conversation that you might have at breakfast in a Russian hotel, when you need to ask for milk and sugar for your tea and to find out where the bread or cheese is. Great to do with someone else. If you have time, you can have a go at a «Как дела?» conversation too, trying different answers.

Ex. 2 a) Try not to trip up! We need to differentiate between the two Tricky letters: «Х» and «Н».

ХАМ - НАМ	На́та - ха́та	пи́хта - пи́нта
ХОР - НОР	пла́на - пла́ха	бу́хта - бу́нта
СОХ - СОН	ве́на - ве́ха	во́рох - во́рон
КРАХ - КРАН	ме́на - ме́ха	меховой - меновой

b) Just read and recognise:

хот-дог, сахари́н, Хе́льсинки, меха́ник, хулига́н, хоккей, психоло́гия, хо́бби, хара́ктер, архитекту́ра, Бухаре́ст, психотерапи́я, хи́ппи, механи́зм, олига́рх, те́хника, орхиде́я, хамелео́н

Today we are going to have a look at how to say in Russian that things or people are in certain places, rather than relying on «там» all the time – for example, in London, in a bag, in a shop etc.

> **NEW WORD: В** - *in, to*

As you see, Russian «В» stands for both *in* and *to* – Russians have a different way of distinguishing between the two functions. Can you work it out if I give you these two phrases: в Омск *(to Omsk)* – в Омске *(in Omsk)*?

> ***WORTH REMEMBERING***: *To say that **somebody or something is in some place**, for example, in London, you will need «В» in front of «Лóндон», as well as «Е» attached to the end of the place. E.g.: **в** Лóндон**е** - **in** London. This works for most places.*

> **To make it clear:** Remember to read «Е» at the end of places. As always, «Е» would indicate that the consonant before is palatalised. What is most important, though, is to keep the stress in place, e.g., Нóвгород – в Нóвгороде. Remember that if «Е» is away from the stress, it does not need too much effort – but you still need to read it.

Ex.3 a) Reading for meaning. Translate each small phrase you read. The names with «Е» at the end will appear without it in English. E.g. в Óмск**е** – in Omsk_.

Tip! As «В» is such a small word and does not have a vowel, it does not have its own stress. When we speak, it often attaches itself to the next word. If the name of the place starts with a voiceless consonant, (e.g.: «К», «С» or «Х»), «В» would get devoiced too, like in «вход».

в Иркýтск - в Иркýтске	в Ростóве - в Ростóв	в Магадáне	в Мадрѝде
в Смолéнск - в Смолéнске	в Сарáтове - в Сарáтов	в Ворóнеже	в Берлѝне
в Норѝльск - в Норѝльске	в Тамбóве - в Тамбóв	в Хабáровске	в Вашингтóне

> *Check that you remember that Russians read «В» at the end as ff in Smirnoff, but before «Е» it goes back to normal /в/, but palatalised.*

b) Big sort out. In the list below, underline those phrases where «В» is translated as *in* and then read the list in order, translating each phrase. Make sure you read «Е» at the end (if you have «Е»).

в банк, в Лóндоне, в пáрке, в магазѝн, в коллéдж, в клáссе, в университéт, в ресторáне, в теáтре

> **NEW WORDS: ДЕРЕ́ВНЯ** - *a village, (often) countryside*

Check that all three consonants in your «дере́вня» are palatalised
and that the first «E» is weak;

RUSSIASCOPE: *Before the start of the 20th century, Russia was mainly a rural country, with only 8% of its people living in towns and cities. So, it is logical that the Russian language has only one word for an urban settlement – го́род, thus not making a difference between "a town" and "a city" and referring to both giant industrial centres and small provincial towns. Го́род Ту́ла, where I come from, has a population of around 500,000 people, which is more than that of Liverpool or Edinburgh, but it is only the 37th largest Russian city, with the rest of the region not even reaching a million people. Large Russian cities are absolutely up-to-date, with modern fashion, music, technology, business etc. The countryside (дере́вня), on the contrary, is developing very slowly and therefore struggles to attract people, though mobile phones, computers and Sky Television are gradually getting there too. In the past, two types of "village" were differentiated: село́ was a village with a church, normally larger than дере́вня, which did not have one. During the 1917 Revolution a lot of churches were destroyed by the Bolsheviks; that is why it is hardly surprising that in modern Russia, the word «дере́вня» is used for most rural settlements. The word «село́» is preserved in some historical names.*

c) Reading for meaning:

Это го́род Санкт-Петербу́рг, а это река́ Нева́.

А в го́роде Ту́ле – река́ Упа́. А это мост.

Одо́ев – это го́род или дере́вня? – Го́род.

А Апу́хтино – это дере́вня? – Да, дере́вня.

Я завтра в го́роде. А ты где? – Я дома.

У меня́ есть карта. Где твоя́ дере́вня? – Вот.

Check that you realise that in Russian the actual names normally
follow the words го́род, дере́вня, река́.

RUSSIASCOPE: *The word «ГО́РОД» in Old Russian had a form of «град». So, the former name of St.Petersburg, Ленингра́д, is translated as "Lenin's city". The World War II famous Сталингра́д actually stands for "Stalin's city". (After Stalin's death it was named Волгогра́д – the city on the Volga River). You can find both «град» and «го́род» as part of the names of quite a number of Russian cities (watch your stress): Но́вгород, Бе́лгород, Павлогра́д, Калинингра́д, Зеленогра́д, among others.*

> **WORTH REMEMBERING:** *Some small Russian words with only one vowel in them* **(monosyllabics)** *often behave differently and sometimes even have a different ending, e.g.,* **САД – В САДУ́** *(in the garden). They are normally words which do not sound like English words – they are of Old Russian origin. Words like «парк» or «банк» (which are similar to English) go with the general rule, e.g., в па́рке, в ба́нке. There are not very many words like «сад», so we will be learning these as we go.*

Ex.4 a) Let's get this right. Put «В» in front of the words below and add the ending, keeping the one stress exactly where it was. Find one word which needs «У» at the end (instead of the normal «Е»), as well as shifting the stress. Keep track of what it is that you are saying.

*Tip! The word that we have learnt for "at home" (до́ма) is a thing of its own. It does not need anything before it or any changes at the end. However, you might come across the other phrase «в до́м**е**», which stands for "in a/the house" (as opposed to the outside). It does not necessarily refer to your own house.*

класс, го́род, магази́н, Манче́стер, сад, рестора́н, Ки́ев, колле́дж, банк, По́ртсмут, университе́т, дом, теа́тр, Росто́в, аэропо́рт, парк

> *Check that you said «в саду́» with the stress at the end.*

b) Reading for meaning. As well as understanding what you are reading, try to remember the information too – after all, we normally need to do that in real life.

Твоя́ сестра́ до́ма? – Нет. Она́ в колле́дже.   Мо́жно хлеб? – Да, но извини́: хлеб в паке́те.

А твой сын где? – В го́роде Ку́рске.   Извини́те. Что э́то в стака́не? Вино́? – Нет, сок.

Ба́бушка в до́ме? – Нет, она́ в саду́.   У тебя́ ру́чка есть? – Да, в столе́. – Спаси́бо.

> *Check that you understand that «в столе́» means "inside the desk" (in a drawer);*
> *that you noticed that the stress in «в столе́» is at the very end.*

c) Let's try it in Russian. Try answering the following questions in Russian without looking at the exercise above – you can check if you forget the information, but answer without reading. Speaking and reading are different language skills!

Tip! In this exercise you do NOT need words like «мой»/«твой», as Russians do not use them as much as English speakers.

Кто в Ку́рске?   Ба́бушка в саду́ или в до́ме?   Сестра́ до́ма?

Где хлеб?   Что в стака́не?   В столе́ ру́чка или каранда́ш?

Have you realised that in the last exercise you got the information in Russian, understood the question about it in Russian and then answered it in Russian? How good is that?!

d) Now it's your turn. Make a list of about five people you know and a separate list of where they are, in a different order (!). If you have time to write all the names in Russian, that would be great, but if you are not learning to write, are pressed for time or do not have all the letters that you need yet, you can leave them in English. Make phrases in Russian about each person. If you work with someone else, swap lists and ask questions that require «Да»/«Нет» answers to find out where your partner's people are. Remember to swap as soon as you get a «Да». E.g.: 1) Джéнни – в Манчéстере? – Нет. 2) Джéнни в Брúстоле? – Да, онá в Брúстоле.

Tip! Foreign place names which do not end in a consonant or an «А» do not take any endings in Russian. I guess that since they cannot be classed as masculine or feminine, they do not fit into the Russian grammar system. E.g., Глáзго – в Глáзго.

> **WORTH REMEMBERING**: *If a place has a vowel at the end (e.g.:* Москвá, дерéвня, окнó), *then this vowel is replaced by «Е». So, instead of adding «Е» to the end of a word as we did with masculine places, in words with a vowel (e.g., feminines) we need to **drop this vowel first**. E.g.,* **Москвá - в Москвé**, дерéвня - в дерéвне, окнó - в окнé. *Make sure that you **keep the stress** where it was – if the stress needs to move, the books and dictionaries will tell you (e.g.:* в столé). *Your main job is to keep it!*

Ex. 5 a) Reading for meaning. Read each phrase aloud, pronouncing all the «Е»-s and translate it (find three words where «Е» is stressed at the end). For each phrase give the dictionary form of the word (with a vowel at the end – «А»/«Я»/«О»). E.g.: в Москвé *(in Moscow)* – Москвá *(Moscow)*. You will have one word which has «О» and another one which has «Я» at the end.

в вáнне	в квартúре	в кóмнате	в тарéлке	в дерéвне
в чáшке	в рекé	в окнé	в сýмке	в Москвé
в шкóле	в библиотéке	в кнúге	в корóбке	в Канáде

> *Check that you understand that «в тарéлке» translates as "in a/the dish" and that «в дерéвне» can be translated as "in a/the village" and as "in the country".*

b) Let's try it in Russian. Let's imagine that this is a list of students with their summer placements. Say in Russian who is where this summer. You would need «В» in front of each place and «Е» at the end. Remember to drop the vowels at the end (if you have them). Make sure you do it all aloud.

Яна Сорóкина - Тобóльск   Марúя Раéвская - Челя́бинск   Зинаúда Губéнко - Лиепáя

Николáй Шýхов - Элистá   Таúсия Чернóва - Калýга   Глеб Лúсин - Пáвловск

Валенти́на Ры́бникова - Я́лта   Генна́дий Пульно́в - Бо́лдино   Па́вел Ермола́ев - Алу́шта

Алекса́ндр Жда́нов - Сара́тов   Оле́г Су́рский - Санкт-Петербу́рг   Ири́на Бобро́ва - Хаба́ровск

To make it clear: «Губе́нко» is a surname of Ukrainian origin. Ukrainian names do not necessarily have «А» or «Я» at the end like Russian female surnames normally do.

WORTH REMEMBERING: As with foreign names, some words which came into Russian from other languages (which cannot be classed as masculines or feminines) do not always adapt well. This means they do not change their endings when all others do. You need to make note of these. E.g., **В КИНО́, В МЕТРО́.**

---

c) Let's get this right. Fill in the correct endings *where needed*. It might help to translate your sentence into English first, then to look at which word means a place (here it would have «В» in front) and finally see which ending you need, if at all. Keep an eye on masculine and feminine words too. E.g., Каранда́ш_ в коро́бк**е**. Коро́бк**а** в столе́.

Карт... в книг.... Кни́г... в класс....   Тетра́дь.... в паке́т...., а паке́т.... в шко́л......

Ручк.... в стол...́. Стол... в ко́мнат....   Сын.... в университе́т...., в Москв...́.

Алло. Я дома....., а сестра́ в кин......   Моя́ су́мк.... в маши́н..., а журна́л... в су́мк....

Check that you remember that «до́ма» *does not need* «В» *at the front or* «Е» *at the end.*

d) Find a person who. . . . Think of someone who is at a university, works in a bank, is in a flat at the moment, has grandparents (or one of them) in the country or a son in a school, has a friend in Moscow, keeps money in the car or water in the bag. If you work in a group, ask different people to find those whom you need. You do not need verbs yet, e.g., У вас есть ба́бушка в дере́вне? or Вы – в кварти́ре или в до́ме? Remember to raise the tone of your voice when asking and make sure that you have «В» at the front and «Е» at the end of each place.

Ⓕ *GROUP III (Funny Shapes)* «Ф ф» «Ф ф» stands for *f* in *foot*

And that is it. No ifs, ands, or buts – just /ф/ like *f* in *foot*. Russian even has *foot* in one English word which has been borrowed by a lot of languages around the world – ФУТБО́Л *(Watch the stress!)*. Note that «футбо́л» is the name of the game, not the word for a ball (which is «мяч»).

Ex. 6 a) Just read and recognise. Big sort out too. Sort out the words below into four groups: 1) words with one vowel (monosyllabics); 2) words with the stress at the front; 3) words with the stress on the last vowel; 4) those which are left over. If you feel comfortable with your stress, you can just have a go at reading these aloud as they are or sort out just the first line (this might be an option if you have not got time, too).

лифт, фонта́н, о́фис, алфави́т, фра́за, суфле́, фильм, фина́л, фотогра́фия, тари́ф, телефо́н, амфи́бия, факт, файл, катастро́фа, фа́ктор, фина́нсы, А́фрика, дельфи́н, фи́ниш, фаза́н, эпи́граф, филосо́фия, гольф, фигу́ра, гра́фика, сейф, платфо́рма, комфо́рт, сафа́ри, флами́нго, флаг

> *Check that you remember that Russians would read* «Г» *in* «флаг» *like in* «друг».

How does it sound? You might remember that in some **borrowed words** (which came to Russian from other languages), consonants before «Е» are not palatalised, like in **кузе́н** /к у з э́ н/. Here are a couple of others: «**кафе́**» read as /к а ф э́/ (watch your stress too!), and «**те́ннис**» is pronounced as /т э н и с/.

NEW WORDS:

КАФЕ́ - *café (Watch your stress!)*   ТЕЛЕФО́Н - *telephone*
О́ФИС - *office (Watch your stress!)*   ФАМИ́ЛИЯ - *surname (a family name, NOT a family)*
ФРУ́КТЫ - *fruit*   ФОТОАППАРА́Т - *camera (not a camcorder)*

RUSSIASCOPE: The word «телефо́н» *applies to both landlines and mobiles, but Russians also use colloquial* «моби́льник» *for mobiles.* «Телефо́н» *can mean a telephone number, e.g.,* У вас есть телефо́н? *or* Мо́жно но́мер?

> *Check that you realise that when you put* «В» *in front of* «кафе́», *nothing would change at the end:* в кафе́.

b) What would you say in Russia if you needed to ask somebody:

where their office is;	whether their surname is "Ivanov";	whether they have fruit;
whether this is their camera;	whether the phone is in the office;	whether this is a café or a restaurant;
whether they eat fruit;	whether they eat fruit;	whether they are in the office tomorrow

You might have realised that we have a small gap in our group of formal and informal forms, with a few forms for *you* but only one stem for *your/s* - твой/твоя́. If you are to have a guess whether it is formal or informal, what would you say? I am quite sure that you would say *informal*. I guess it starts with «Т», the same as «ты» and «тебя́» (which we had for the informal *you*). Good logic. What we have left is a formal word for *your/s*. Here it is.

> **NEW WORD: ВА́Ш/А** – *your/s (formal)*

I would imagine that you have worked out that «А» is for when *your/s* refers to a feminine noun, e.g.: ва́ша ча́шка.

c) **Let's get this right.** Use «ваш/а» with the following words. You can imagine that you are at a party in Russia and you are asking somebody that you have just met whether the following things and people are theirs:

pen, book, friend (*male*), camera, wife, glass, telephone, bag, job, office, friend (*female*), chair, surname, cup, husband, plate, car, table, tea

How does it sound? There is a small peculiarity in pronunciation of some words in Russian which is worth noting to help your communication. In between certain vowels, «Г» sounds like /в/, for example, **СЕГО́ДНЯ** reads as се/в/о́дня (meaning *today*), and **НИЧЕГО́** is pronounced as ниче/в/о́ (which means *nothing*). At this stage, you might just want to remember these two words, though there will be other cases, especially at the end of words. To start with, I will be underlining the funny sounding «Г» for you, but eventually you need to get used to reading the two new words correctly by yourself.

> **NEW WORDS:**
>
> **СЕГО́ДНЯ** - *today*   **НИЧЕГО́** - *nothing*

Ex. 7 a) Reading for meaning. Keep an eye on the funny sounding «Г».

Муж и я дома сего́дня, а сын в университе́те.

У вас хлеб есть? - Извини́те, сего́дня нет.

Что у тебя́ в су́мке? - Ничего́.

У вас есть журна́л или газе́та? - Сего́дня ничего́ нет.

b) Let's try it in Russian. First, we will practice «сегодня». Here is Dmitry's family whom we met in Unit 5, with his parents, who are all living together. Look at the list of people and, by using the form of their name and their age, work out who they are to each other (you do not need to read the ages). Then think of where they could be today – there could be a few possible options. Кто где сегодня? If you work on your own, make full sentences about each person. E.g., Галина Викторовна - бабушка и мама. Сегодня она в магазине. (or Она в магазине сегодня. or Она сегодня в магазине.) Make sure you use «сегодня» every time you speak about a place. If you are working with someone else, take turns asking questions (e.g.: Где Галина Викторовна сегодня? or Галина Викторовна сегодня в магазине?) and giving answers (Сегодня она в магазине. or Нет. Она сегодня в офисе.).

Family	Age (just for reference; matched)	Relations (to match)	Where are they today? (locations to match)
Александр	25	жена и мама	офис
Светлана Борисовна	30	бабушка (и мама тоже)	школа
Лидочка	11	сын	университет
Михаил Никифорович	65	брат, студент	садик (nursery, playschool)
Денис	3	муж, папа (и сын тоже)	сад в деревне
Галина Викторовна	60	дочка	магазин
Дмитрий Михайлович	33	дедушка (и папа тоже)	дома

Check that «школа» lost its last vowel before getting «Е»;
that «сад» had a different ending;
that «дома» did NOT have «В» in front and did not change at all.

c) Reading for meaning.

Как дела? – Ничего.

Извините, пожалуйста. – Ничего.

Женя, ты ничего? – Ничего-ничего. Спасибо.

Андрей Николаевич, вот моя работа. Это ничего?
– Хорошо. Спасибо.

> **To make it clear:** In conversations, Russians occasionally repeat some words two or three times, perhaps for some kind of emphasis. So you can often hear «Да-да-да», «Нет-нет» or «Ничего́-ничего́».

> НО́ВАЯ ФРА́ЗА: **Я ра́д/а** - *I am glad.*

Check that you realise that Russians would devoice «Д» in «рад»
but pronounce it as /д /in the feminine form with «А» at the end.

Ex. 8 a) Reading for meaning. Read the conversation between two former classmates from Tula, Оле́г and О́льга (whom we met on p. 89), who suddenly bumped into each other and are trying to catch up. Try to keep track of what each of them is saying about themselves.

Check that you remember that «О» in «Оле́г» and «О́льга» sound
different because of the stress;
that Russians would read «Оле́г» with /к/ at the end, like in «друг».

Оле́г:	Приве́т, О́ля!
О́льга:	Оле́г! Приве́т! Как я ра́да!
Оле́г:	Я то́же о́чень рад. Как дела́?
О́льга:	О́чень хорошо́. Спаси́бо. А у тебя́?
Оле́г:	Ничего́. Я в о́фисе, в фи́рме, а жена́ в шко́ле. А ты где?
О́льга:	А я в Москве́. У меня́ там есть магази́н.
	А как твоя́ до́чка? Она́ в шко́ле?
Оле́г:	Нет. Она́ студе́нтка в университе́те.
	А твой сын где? Он то́же в университе́те?
О́льга:	Нет. Он в колле́дже.
Оле́г:	То́же в Москве́?
О́льга:	Да. Извини́ - у меня́ сего́дня нет вре́мя*. Вот мой телефо́н.
Оле́г:	Спаси́бо. До свида́ния.
О́льга:	Пока́-пока́.

* вре́мя – *time (to be grammatically correct we need to say «нет вре́мени», but because this is such an odd form, not all Russians use it correctly; you might need to learn it for an exam, though)*

b) Jog your memory or find in the text:

How are you?	Where are you?	in an office	in Moscow	It's OK/It's fine.
And you?	How is your daughter?	in a firm	in a college	I have got a shop.
How glad I am!	Where is your son?	at school	at the university	Here is my number.
(= Glad to see you!)				

c) Let's try it in Russian. Decide who you are going to be: Олég or Óльга. Remember what they can say about themselves and their families. Try to say at least three sentences as if you were one of them. Keep in mind that we have not done verbs yet – they are on our to-do-list for the next unit – but Олég and Óльга have managed quite successfully without them. Remember you need to speak, NOT read! Do not try to remember everything exactly – construct your own phrases on the basis of the information that you have, because that is what we do when we speak.

If you are working with someone else, you can do it as a conversation. To start with, one of you can read their part from the book while the other could try to do it without looking. (Remember to swap.) Then both of you can put the book away and have another go. It does not matter if you forget something, as long as you manage to keep the conversation going.

d) Now it's your turn. Think of what you can say about yourself and your people. Can you make three sentences, like you did for Олég or Óльга? Do NOT start with an English sentence – start with Russian words that you know and build your sentences using what you have. Remember that you are NOT translating from English – you are speaking Russian, which is a different skill. If you are learning to write, you can write it down.

If you have a chance to work with someone else, have a go at a conversation about yourselves. Be as truthful as possible. Also, as you might not know that many Russian people to be on familiar terms with, try formal forms – «ты» would turn into «вы», «тебя» into «вас», «твой/я» into «ваш/а»; watch other words too.

Ex. 9 a) Try not to trip up! Find at least one palatalised /ф'/ (the one before «Е»/«Я»/«И») in each line. Watch your stress too.

граф - графы́ - графи́ть	шарф - ша́рфик - шка́фчики	зефи́р - фуже́р - фуражо́м
ши́фер - шифо́н - шифро́ван	ва́фля - ва́фель - ка́феля	хали́ф - факи́р - фехтова́л
ко́фе - кафе́ - кофе́йник	ту́фель - ту́фли - ту́фельки	тафта́ - торфя́ник - торфяно́й

Check that you palatalised /ф/ in «ко́фе», but not in «кафе́».

NEW WORDS: **КÓФЕ** - *coffee*

КОНФÉТЫ - *individual sweets*

(chocolates, candies)

Check that you palatalised /ф/ in both words;
that you remember that a bar of chocolate is «шокола́д».

Can I just remind you that, when you are learning words, it helps to look away from the book and envisage the words in your head, then look back paying attention to how they are spelt and where the stress is (stick to the same order). Finally, make little sentences using new words together with old words, and perhaps write them down (without looking in the book), if you are learning to write.

WORTH REMEMBERING: *Watching what is at the end of Russian words is extremely important. We have already discovered that «Е» at the end makes all the difference between being there or only going there. One more example is «Ы». «**Ы**» at the end of Russian words means that they are **PLURAL**, that is, there are more than one of them. E.g., «конфéты» means there are a few chocolates/sweets (say in a box or in a bag). One single chocolate will be «конфéта». This is singular and matches the dictionary form. Note that «фрýкты» in Russian is a plural form – there is also «фрукт», which means a single piece of fruit, for example, a banana or an apple (though it does not mean "a piece of" one of those).*

How does it sound: It might feel challenging to say «Ы» so often, but we get used to doing things very quickly if we do them every day. So, let's practice and make lots of plurals. To start with, remember the three things that you need to do to say «Ы» correctly: 1) teeth; 2) tongue; 3) lips. No rush. On the other hand, since in most words you need to **keep the stress where it was, «Ы» ends up being unstressed** a lot of the time. Thus, make sure that you do not put too much effort in it – just move your tongue to the back a bit. It is extremely important not to add a second stress, so learn to make your «Ы» unimportant. Ready. Steady. Go.

---

b) Reading for meaning. Make sure that you read «Ы» at the end and translate the words as plural into English (it's important to get the form right as well as the actual meaning of the word). You also need to give a dictionary form for each word. (Keep an eye on masculines and feminines.) Keep the same stress in singular.

конфéты	шкóлы	вокзáлы	кóмнаты	телефóны
пакéты	фрýкты	завóды	óфисы	ресторáны
машúны	вáнны	картúны	вы́ходы	магазúны

To make it clear: I need to remind you that to be grammatically correct you CANNOT use this plural form with numbers. We need a different "identifier" for words to be linked to numbers. At the moment, numbers are best used on their own, e.g., Мóжно чай? Три, пожáлуйста.

RUSSIASCOPE: *In most Russian food shops, along with boxes of chocolates, you can find individually wrapped «конфéты» which are often sold by weight. They are made in Russia and are normally not very expensive. For a party Russians can easily buy a kilo of these.*

Ex. 10 a) Reading for meaning. Keep track of what you are reading.

В магазѝне

– Здрáвствуйте.

– Здрáвствуйте. У вас есть конфеты «Фаворѝт»?

– Извинѝте, сегóдня нет.

– Ну[1], ничегó. А «Маска» или «Халвá в шоколáде»?

– «Маска» есть сегóдня, а «Халвá в шоколáде» дет[2] бу́ зáвтра.

– Хорошó. А скóлько «Мáска»?

– Шесть рублéй килогрáмм.

– Отлѝчно. Можно килогрáмм, пожалуйста.

– Конéчно[3]. Пакéт?

– Нет, спасѝбо. У меня́ есть су́мка. Вот дéньги.

– Извинѝте, касса там.

– *(comes back from the till)* Вот чек[4].

– Хорошó. Вот вáша «Маска».

– Спасѝбо.

– Пожáлуйста. До свидáния.

– До свидáния.

[1] Ну – *Oh! Well!*

[2] бу́дет – *will be*

[3] конéчно – *certainly, of course*

[4] чек – *a receipt (since the 1930s, Russian banks have never developed a system of cheque books for individual accounts)*

b) Jog your memory or find in the text. Highlight those which you had to check in the conversations – these are the ones for you to work with.

today	It's OK.	Do you have. . . ?	The till is there.
tomorrow	Sorry.	Can I have. . . ?	No, thank you.
We haven't got any today.	Good.	How much. . . ?	You are welcome.

c) Let's get this right. Have another look at the conversation above, then choose the correct answer from those below without referring back to the conversation. When you have finished, check your answers.

1) *What does the customer want:*

- a bar of chocolate

- some chocolates

- a box of chocolates

2) *Which chocolates do they have today:*

- «Фаворит»

- « Маска»

- «Халва́ в шокола́де»

3) *How much do the chocolates cost:*

- 4 рубля́

- 6 рубле́й

- 8 рубле́й

4) *Does the customer want a plastic bag:*

- Yes, he does. He hasn't got a bag.

- No, he doesn't. He has got a plastic bag.

- No, he doesn't. He has got an ordinary bag.

d) If you are learning to write, have a go at writing the following English names in Cyrillic. Remember to listen to the sounds.

Frank, Hannah, Philip, Frances, Harvey, Sophia, Josephine, Hilary, Fay, Felix, Humphrey, Fiona, Geoffrey, Phoebe, Hope, Ralph

Check *that your Russian versions of Geoffrey and Josephine started with «Дж»;*
that Felix finished with «кс».

Do you remember the funny sounding «Г» that sounds like /в/ in «сего́дня» and «ничего́»? My farewell today will have two funny «Г»-s in it – **ВСЕГО́ ХОРО́ШЕГО!** Or, All the best! Keep thinking Russian – every time you see an "exit" sign or put sugar in, when you eat fruit or chocolates – think where things are and how you would say it.

144

Something old, something new (*revision of unit 6*)

Today YOU can start our greetings. Shall we go back to informal, as we agreed?

— .... *(Say hello and ask how things are.)*

— Хорошо́. Спаси́бо. А у тебя́? *(This is my reply.)*

— .... *(Choose your answer and say Thank you.)*

1. Do you remember the full version of «Как дела́?»
2. Why do we use «А у тебя́?» to return this question but not «А ты?»
3. Can you do the formal version of the conversation above?
4. Try to remember some other answers to «Как дела́?».

Ex.1 a) Say it in Russian:

Good. Tired *(about yourself)*. Bad. Not good. Great. Not bad too. Not very good. Fine. Very good.

> *RUSSIASCOPE*: *When answering* «Как дела́?», *Russians might be quite honest and not necessarily very diplomatic. So, do not be surprised to hear* «Пло́хо.» *or even* «О́чень пло́хо.» *when you ask* «Как дела́?».

GROUP I (The Easy): Мм, Тт, Кк, Аа, Оо

GROUP II (The Tricky): Сс, Нн, Вв, Рр, Ее, Уу *(like . . . in . . .)*, Хх *(like k but flowing)*

GROUP III (Funny Shapes): Ээ, Яя, Лл, Дд, Ии, Йй, Бб, Зз, Пп, Гг, Чч, Шш, Жж *(like . . . in . . .)*, Фф

GROUP IV (The Strangers): Ьь, Ыы *(1) teeth . . ., 2) tongue . . ., 3) lips into a . . . and say "".)*

Find the two new letters from Unit 6 in the alphabet below and see which part of the alphabet they belong to:

А Б В Г Д Е . . . Ж З И Й К Л М Н О П Р С Т У Ф Х . . . Ч Ш . . . . . . Ы Ь Э . . . Я.
We have five left!

? 5. Can you remember the three hushing sounds we have come across? Can you find them in the alphabet above?

6. Where in your mouth is Russian /x/ made? What is the main difference between /к/ and /х/?

b) Try not to trip up! Though «X» is not classed as a husher, its shape is sometimes confused with that of our hushing «Ж». Try to make your /ж/ loud and your /х/ distinctive and strong but steady and quiet.

ЖÓРА - ХÓРА	МЕХÁ - МЕЖÁ
МÚЖА - МÚХА	НАХÁЛ - НАЖÁЛ
ЖÁТА - ХÁТА	ХОККÉЙ - ЖОКÉЙ
КРÁЖА - КРÁХА	ПАХÁТЬ - ПОЖÁТЬ
СТРÁЖИ - СТРÁХИ	МАХÓР - МАЖÓР

c) Jog your memory. Read aloud, keeping an eye on «Ж» and «Х».

женá, хорошó, муж, гарáж, вы́ход, мóжно, тóже, плóхо, сáхар, журнáл, вход, пожáлуйста, хлеб

> **Check** *that you have noticed devoiced consonants at the end of words, including «Ж»;*
> *that you remember that Russians would pronounce «В» in «вход» as /ф/.*

d) Let's try it in Russian. Imagine you are going shopping in Russia. In the table below there is a list of what you need to buy with prices listed by them (keep in mind that they are not real) and the quantities you need. As you can see all of the items, you *do not need* to check whether they have them, thus no need to say «У вас есть . . . ?». 1. Ask for an item (using «мóжно»). 2. Say how many you need (using «пожáлуйста»). 3. Work out how much you need to pay and say it in Russian (using «вот»). If you work in pairs, your partner then works out the total, while you can ask «Скóлько?» and say «Вот дéньги». They might offer you a bag – then you decide whether to agree or to refuse. They might get really adventurous and say that they haven't got something – what would you say?

Tip! Note that below the word «рубль» has different endings. It is possibly not your priority to memorise them at this stage. This is just to remind you that Russian words need different bits to link to numbers.

What are you buying?	How much does one item cost?	How many items?	How many Roubles would you need?
чай	3 рубля	3	? рублéй
кóфе	4 рубля	2	? рублéй
карандаш	1 рубль	5	? рублéй
журнáл	5 рублéй	2	? рублéй
хлеб	2.10	1	2.10
шоколад	3 рубля	2	? рублéй

Ex.2 a) Spot the difference! In every word there is at least one letter added to make the following word. Read the words ALOUD, one after another. Watch your stress!

у́хо - ухо́д - уходи́ - уходи́л - уходи́ла - уходи́лась - прохуди́лась

b) Try not to trip up! Read Russian anagrams. As well as reading a tricky «Х» correctly, keep an eye on hushing sounds. Watch your stress too!

ХЛОП - ПЛОХ	ФО́РТО - ОФО́РТ	ХОРО́Ш - ШО́РОХ	ШАРФ - ФАРШ
ЗАХА́Р - ХАЗА́Р	ДУ́ХА - ХУДА́	ЧИХА́Л - ЛИХА́Ч	ВЫ́ХОД - ВЫ́ДОХ
ХВАЛА́ - ХАЛВА́	КА́ФЕЛЬ - КЕФА́ЛЬ	ШАЛФЕ́Й - ШЛЕ́ЙФА	СМЕ́ХА - СХЕ́МА

c) Jog your memory. Mark the stress in words with «Х» (unless they are monosyllabic).

телефо́н, о́фис, хорошо, сахар, ра́д/а, фотоаппара́т, очень, плохо, фру́кты, выход, фами́лия, хлеб

> *Check that you remember that* «фами́лия» *translates as "surname, family name" but NOT "family".*

d) What would you say in Russia if you need to ask somebody:

where there is a telephone;

whether the exit is there;

whether they (*informal*) eat fruit;

whether this is good;

whether they (*formal*) have (*some*) bread;

whether this is their camera (*informal*);

whether they have an office (*informal*);

whether you can have (*some*) sugar;

whether they are glad/happy (*informal, feminine*);

whether their surname is Ivanov or Smirnov (*formal*)

7. What is the difference between «твой»/«твоя́» and «ваш/а»?

8. When do you need «а» at the end of «ва́ша» *(watch your stress)*?

Ex.3 a) Let's try it in Russian. Below are statements of different people. Think how you could ask follow-up questions about the same thing or person. You need to watch whether you need «твой»/«твоя́» or «ваш/а». E.g.: Секрета́рь: У меня́ есть календа́рь. – You: Это <u>ваш</u> календа́рь?

Ли́дочка: А у меня́ есть собака.	....дома??
Студе́нт: У меня́ есть книга «Ру́сский язы́к».	Это..?
Ма́льчик: У меня́ есть де́душка.	Это..?
Такси́ст: У меня́ есть машина.	А где...?
Ваш брат: У меня́ есть друг.	А где...?
Ба́бушка (не ва́ша): У меня́ есть сад.	А где...?
Ва́ша подруга: У меня́ есть сумка.	А где...?

Дени́с: У меня́ есть па́па Ди́ма.

Алексе́й Серге́евич: У меня́ есть жена́.

.... там?

.... до́ма?

Check *that you agreed* «де́душка» *and* «па́па» *as masculine:*
твой де́душка, твой па́па.

9. How do we need to read «Ф» if it is before «Е»?

10. Can you remember a couple of words where ordinary consonants (e.g., «т» or «ф») are not palatalised before «Е»? What kind of words are they?

b) Just read and recognise. Try to spot the words where Russians palatalise their «Ф».

буфе́т, фестива́ль, фи́зика, фейерве́рк, саксофо́н, эффе́кт, профессиона́л, фреска, конфли́кт, рефере́ндум, сфе́ра, фолькло́р, профе́ссор, геогра́фия, кофеи́н, рефо́рма, профе́ссия, атмосфе́ра, физиотерапи́я, хорео́граф, сертифика́т, трансфе́р, ро́стбиф, про́филь, диктофо́н, фиста́шки

11. Try to remember the TWO differences in pronouncing «ко́фе» and «кафе́». Which of them means *coffee*?

c) Jog your memory. Mark the stresses first, then find two words with the palatalized /ф/. Read aloud.

кофе, телефон, фамилия, фрукты, кафе, конфеты, фотоаппарат, офис

d) Question time. Think of what questions could have been asked to get the answers below. Keep in mind that the questions with «кто», «что», «где» or «или» cannot be answered using «Да» or «Нет». E.g., Это ва́ша рабо́та? – Да, моя́. BUT: Что это? – Это конфе́ты.

– .... ? – Это ваш сахар.

– .... ? – Нет. Это не вы́ход. Вы́ход там.

– .... ? – Он ест мя́со.

– .... ? – Извини́те, нет. Но есть ко́фе.

– .... ? – Непло́хо, но о́чень уста́ла.

– .... ? – Это фотоаппара́т.

– .... ? – Да. Это моя́ фами́лия.

– .... ? – Нет, не ем. Я ем фру́кты.

– .... ? – В о́фисе.

– .... ? – Да. Вот, пожа́луйста.

e) Find a person who. . . Think how you would ask different people whether they have something, either in a formal or in an informal way, depending on who the person is. Look at the two lists below: the first is people, and the other is things that they may have. This is great fun to do as a group. The words for all of the people can go into one hat/bag and all of the items into another. Do not show each other the slips that you pulled out, as your purpose is to find out who people are and what they have. The person or their position will determine whether you use formal or informal forms, e.g., Ты ма́льчик? or Вы ме́неджер? Then you need to ask what they have got (again, remember to choose an appropriate form). Use the lists below to make your questions. If you have not got a «Да» after a couple of goes, ask specific questions like «Кто вы?» or «Что у вас/тебя́ есть?».

ме́неджер, ва́ша ру́сская подру́га, ма́льчик Са́ша, не ва́ша ба́бушка, Ли́дочка, такси́ст, ваш де́душка, Анастаси́я Андре́евна, ва́ша жена́/ваш муж, тури́ст, ваш ру́сский друг

телефо́н, конфе́ты, ру́чка, ко́фе, фотоаппара́т, хлеб, кни́га «Ру́сский язы́к», де́ньги, фру́кты, тетра́дь, са́хар

13. What is the difference between «в Ло́ндон» and «в Ло́ндоне»?

14. What do we normally do – keep the stress or move it? When do we need to move it?

15. How do you say in Russian *in the garden*? Where is the stress?

16. Do you remember one more monosyllabic where you need to move the stress when adding «Е»?

17. How do we translate «в столе́»?

Ex.5 a) Say it in Russian.

to the bank – in the bank
to the office – in the office

in the shop – to the shop
in Rostov – to Rostov

to the garden – in the garden
in the city – to the city

Check that you remembered two differences between pronouncing «В»
in «Росто́в» and in «в Росто́ве».
(Think about the difference between being final and not final,
as well as the effect of «Е».)

18. What do we need to do with a vowel (e.g., «А», «Я», «О») at the end before adding «Е», for example, in «Москва́»?

19. Which words do not change at all when «В» is placed in front of them?

20. Do we need «В» in front of «до́ма»? What does «в до́ме» mean?

b) Let's get this right. Read each phrase, translate it (make sure you say *in* in English) and give the dictionary form of the word. E.g., в ба́нке - *in a/the bank* – банк. Note your feminines.

в па́рке	в до́ме	в кни́ге	в столе́	в библиоте́ке	в о́фисе
в Москве́	в ко́мнате	в таре́лке	в дере́вне	в кино́	в кафе́
в шко́ле	в магази́не	в саду́	в ва́нне	в университе́те	в су́мке

c) Let's get this right. Match the people on the left to what they would say or ask on the right. Read aloud.

КТО И ГДЕ?	WHAT WOULD THEY SAY?
Анто́н - студе́нт.	У вас есть хлеб?
Ли́дочка и подру́га - в саду́.	Мо́жно ко́фе? Оди́н са́хар, пожа́луйста.
О́льга - в магази́не.	Я в коле́дже, а не в университе́те.
Яна - вегетариа́нка.	У тебя́ есть конфе́ты или шокола́д?
Оле́г - инжене́р.	Я о́чень ра́да, что у меня́ есть сад.
Све́та - в кафе́.	Я не ем мя́со. Я ем сыр.
Анастаси́я Андре́евна - в дере́вне.	Сего́дня я в о́фисе, а за́втра до́ма.

(?) 21. How would Russians read «Г» in «ниче<u>г</u>о́» and «сего́дня»?

22. What is the direct translation of «ниче<u>г</u>о́»?

23. How would we translate «ничего́» as a reply to «Как дела́?» or «Извини́те»?

d) Say it in Russian. Look at the list of places where Дми́трий is today and tomorrow. Make sentences about him in Russian, using «сего́дня» and «за́втра». Remember your «В» in front and «Е» at the end (unless you get «сад»).

сего́дня:	о́фис	шко́ла	кафе́
за́втра:	магази́н	дере́вня	сад

> **NEW WORD: ПОТО́М** - *then, afterwards*

e) Now it's your turn. Choose a couple of places where you are going to be today and tomorrow, using Russian words you know or names of places. Make sentences about yourself. Try using «пото́м». If you work with someone else, have a short conversation about where you are on these two days. Decide whether you are going to be on familiar terms or go formal. Also, think whether you can use «то́же» or one of the versions of *And you?*. One condition – no English.

? 24. Name the three things you need to do to read «Ы» correctly.

25. Do you remember the TWO main differences between /ы/ and /и/?

Ex.6 a) Decoding Cyrillic. Make sure your /ы/ is at the back of your mouth and /и/ is at the front. Remember that consonants are palatalised before «И» and stay as they are before «Ы».

сыч - ча́сик - часы́   фи́рма - фы́ркал - порфи́ры   пыж - пижо́н - пы́шками

тишь - штык - штыки́   гры́жа - ри́га - рыга́ли   зы́чно - кизи́л - Зы́кина

хрыч - хрип - вихры́   ды́лда - ло́дырь - иди́ллия   вы́шка - вихо́р - вы́вихом

жми - жмых - нажми́   бич - бы́том - обы́чно   чу́мы - мыча́л - ми́чману

Check that you remember that Russians would read «ж» in
«пыж» as in «муж».

b) What's in a name? Read the names of some Russian cities (aloud). Watch out for «Х» and «Ж», as well as for «Ы» and «Ь» (the soft sign).

Хаба́ровск, На́льчик, Жито́мир, Сыктывка́р, Фру́нзе, Арха́нгельск, Сахали́н, Севасто́поль, Иже́вск, А́страхань, Салеха́рд, Уфа́, Нори́льск, Махачкала́, Гро́зный, Нижнева́ртовск, Ухта́, Ста́врополь, Воро́неж, Ахту́бинск

c) Big sort out. In the list below, underline the words with «Ы» and then read the list as it is, making sure that «Ы» and «И» sound different. If you are learning to write, sort out the words into two columns: those with «Ы» and others with «И». Highlight those that are challenging, in order to come back to them later.

сын, кварти́ра, сыр, ру́сский, библиоте́ка, язы́к, макаро́ны, кни́га, англи́йский, четы́ре, му́зыка, оди́н, Росси́я, университе́т, буты́лка, карти́на, конфе́ты

d) Decoding Cyrillic. Remember that *two vowels* are read as two vowels, e.g.: «ЫЕ».

ко́сы - косы́е   не́мы - немы́е   си́ние - си́зые

бо́сы - босы́е   сле́пы - слепы́е   ле́тние - ле́вые

Check that you read «Е» at the end as /йэ/ or ye in yes, as it is after a vowel.

? 26. What does «Ы» at the end of Russian words indicate?

27. How many stresses should you put in a word in the plural?

Ex.7 a) Let's get this right. Put «Ы» at the end of the words below to make their plural. Remember to take «А» off first, if you have it. Note that the stress in this exercise should be the same in plural and in singular, which is why it might be best to pronounce both forms.

конфе́та	вы́ход	кварти́ра	рестора́н	вокза́л	фру́кт
шко́ла	бана́н	ко́мната	фотоаппара́т	о́фис	карти́на
паке́т	магази́н	стака́н	ка́рта	маши́на	телефо́н

b) Reading for meaning. Read this exercise slowly and make sure that all the endings are correct, including «Е». When translating, watch out that your plurals come out as plurals in English.

У вас есть бана́ны сего́дня?   Карти́ны в коро́бке, а коро́бка в ко́мнате.

Фру́кты в паке́те, в маши́не.   Заво́ды в го́роде, а фе́рмы в дере́вне.

Докуме́нты и карты́ в о́фисе.   Студе́нты в Москве́ или в Санкт-Петербу́рге сего́дня?

c) Find a person who has fruit on the table, has documents in a bag, has chocolates/sweets, eats bananas, has pictures in the room/house, has more than one mobile, keeps plastic bags in the car. This is great to do in a group – the winner is the person with the most names on their list.

Work or play?

WHAT'S THE PLAN?

- ▶ to recognise and use two new Russian letters (the last two vowels!);
- ▶ to learn more words with your Russian letters;
- ▶ to identify and start using verbs in Russian;
- ▶ to say whether you work and where you work in Russian;
- ▶ to read lots of Russian words for various sports;
- ▶ to say a few sentences about your hobbies and things you like;
- ▶ to know the difference between the Soviet Union and Russia.

As today we are going to speak about where people work and spend their free time, we are going to start with places. In English there are a few small words that can indicate location, for example *in*, *on*, *at* etc. (e.g., *in* a shop, *on* a farm, *at* school). In Russian we have a few of those too. Now that you can handle «В» (for *in*), we can have a look at one more word out of this group of prepositions.

> **NEW WORD: НА** - *on, on top of*

If you had a go at guessing, what happens at the end of places in Russian when we put «на» in front, what would you say? I hope you know the answer.

> **WORTH REMEMBERING:** *When we put «НА» in front of a place,* **the place needs «Е» at the end***, e.g.,* на коробк**е** (*on top of the box*). *Compare to* «в коробк**е**» (*in the box*). *Note that «Е» can be crucial for understanding, as its absence might give*

a different meaning to the whole phrase, similar to the situation with «B». For example, «на стул_» (with no «E») would mean "on<u>to</u> the chair", while «на сту́ле» – on the chair.

Check that you understand that the stress stays the same with and without «E», unless you know that it should move.

Ex.1 a) Reading for meaning. Keep an eye on translating «B» and «HA» correctly and try not to lose your «E» at the end.

Tip! Quite often Russians use the word «окно́» to mean "windowsill". Thus, «на окне́» would translate as "on a/the windowsill".

в кни́ге, в ва́зе, на сту́ле, в стака́не, в саду́, на столе́, на коро́бке, в маши́не, на таре́лке, в кварти́ре, на стене́, в столе́, в су́мке, в таре́лке, на окне́, на реке́, в до́ме, на фе́рме, в коро́бке, на ка́рте, в паке́те, на кни́ге, в ча́шке

Check that you remember that «на столе́» can be translated in two ways; that you translated «в таре́лке» as "in a/the dish".

b) Let's try it in Russian. Say in Russian which city is on which river, e.g., Го́род Ту́ла - **на реке́ Упе́**. If you work with someone else, take turns asking questions to get positive and negative answers, as well as using «где?». E.g., Го́род Ту́ла – на реке́ Оке́? – Нет. Го́род Ту́ла – на реке́ Упе́.

го́род Москва́ - река́ Москва́
го́род Яку́тск - река́ Ле́на
город Сара́тов - река Во́лга
город Ряза́нь - река Ока́
город Пермь - река Ка́ма

Братск - Ангара́
Санкт-Петербу́рг - Нева́
Ки́ев - Днепр
Ло́ндон - Те́мза
Пари́ж - Се́на

"New Word" magazine

NEW WORDS: ДИВА́Н - *a sofa, a settee*

ГАЗЕ́ТА - *a newspaper*

ЖУРНА́Л - *a magazine*

Check that you realise that «газе́та» is feminine.

c) Let's get this right. Fill in «В» or «НА» so that the sentences make sense. You might want to work out in English what the sentence is saying first. Make sure you read all the endings correctly – we will have some plurals with «Ы» at the end too.

Де́ньги . . . су́мке, а су́мка. . . . . маши́не.

Ка́рта . . . стене́ . . . ка́рте Росси́я.

Жена́ . . . до́ме, а сын и до́чка. . . . саду́.

Докуме́нты. . . . . столе́? – Нет, . . . коро́бке.

У тебя́ есть тетра́дь? – Да, там, . . . сту́ле.

У Вас есть газе́та «Таймс»? Что . . . газе́те сего́дня?

Извини́. А где мой сыр? – Там, . . . таре́лке, . . . столе́.

Журна́лы. . . . . паке́те? – Нет. Журна́лы. . . . дива́не.

Вот моя́ фотогра́фия. Это я и муж . . . реке́ Во́лге.

Конфе́ты, фру́кты и торт . . . столе́, а вино́ . . . окне́.

Check that you spotted five plural forms with «Ы» at the end.

d) Let's try it in Russian. Find a few things which you know Russian words for. Put, let's say, a pen inside or on top of other things. Say in Russian where the pen is, e.g., Ру́чка на коро́бк**е**. Ру́чка в стака́н**е**. Use furniture (стол, стул, дива́н), crockery (ча́шка, таре́лка), a bag, a book etc. You can do this with someone else, where one puts a pen somewhere and the other says where it is. Remember to swap after a few goes. When you get comfortable, start putting different things (rather than the same old pen) in different places. Keep an eye on «В» and «НА» and do not lose «Е» at the end!

When you are learning it is better to speak slowly to start with, making sure you say things correctly – this way your brain will remember the correct versions. The more you speak, the quicker you will get. If you work on your own, remember to say everything aloud.

To make it clear: This might be a good time to remind you that Russians do not use «мой/ моя́» as much as you use *my* in English – they only need it when they specify that the item is not somebody else's (Do you remember "I put my coat on"?). Don't try using «мой/ моя́» after «В» or «НА» – apart from not sounding Russian, this also might mess things up grammatically, as «мой/моя́» would need to agree with «Е»-forms. If you need to specify, make a separate sentence with «Это», e.g., Ру́чка в су́мке. Это моя́ су́мка.

NEW WORDS: ФЕ́РМА - *a farm*

ФИ́РМА - *a firm, a company*

Check that you palatalised /ф/ in both words.

***RUSSIASCOPE*: ФÉРМА ИЛИ ФИ́РМА**

During the Soviet years, food in Russia was grown in a колхо́з *(collective farm) or* совхо́з *(soviet farm), which were very similar, as they were run centrally, heavily subsidised and generally were not the most efficient enterprises. Most of them did not put any reasonable effort into social developments, which made them extremely unpopular. At that time, «фéрма» meant a large kolkhoz building for keeping cattle, where a lot of women from a* дерéвня *worked (and many still do). After Perestroika, Russia tried to go from state-controlled* колхо́з-*s to privately-owned* фéрма-*s. Despite some occasional good examples, it has been quite hard going, and now the process seems to be reverting back to centralisation.*

The word «фúрма» came into use only during Perestroika, when private enterprises started appearing, and became instantaneously popular. Sometimes I wonder whether the film «Фúрма» (1993) with Том Круз, *which was popular at the time, has in some way contributed to it.*

Note that to use «фéрма» as a location, we need «на» - to get «на фéрме», similar to English *on a/the farm*. This helps to differentiate it from «фúрма» that would need «В» – «в фúрме» (in a firm, in a company).

WORTH REMEMBERING: *There is **NO particular word for "at"** in Russian! Russians use «В» or «НА» instead. E.g., **at** the post-office -* **на** *почте, **at** the theatre -* **в** *теáтре. Unfortunately, there is no easy rule which tells us whether to use «В» or «НА». There are some tendencies, but often we need to remember which words use which. We can easily do this as we go, but instead of remembering two lists, we will focus on «НА»-words (I think there might be fewer of them and they seem to be easier to group into logical clusters). For now, you can assume, if a word is not in our «НА»-list, it would need «В».*

NEW PHRASES:

на заво́де	**на** рабо́те	**на** стадио́не
на вокзáле	**на** по́чте	**на** дáче

Some of my students try to remember these «НА»-words in pairs: two with «З», two to do with work and two to do with leisure. See whether this works for you. Note that these are not the only «НА»-words – there will be others. We will be adding them to the list as we go. You can put «на фёрме» in here if you wish, though strictly speaking, «на фёрме» does not use *at* in English, though it does use «на» in Russian. This box is one which is worth memorising.

Ex.2 a) Big sort out. In the list below, underline all «НА»-words. Try doing this without looking at the box above. Then go through the list adding «В» or «НА» in front and «Е» to the end (find one word where you need a different ending). Make sure you say all the phrases aloud. If learning to write, you can sort out the words into two groups: «В»-words and «НА»-words.

школа, завод, библиотéка, ресторáн, стадиóн, дерéвня, теáтр, почта, фéрма, магазин, вокзал, банк, гóрод, кино, рабóта, сад, дача, университéт

Check that you remember the three meanings of «стадиóн» *(Unit 2).*

b) Reading for meaning. Read three mini-conversations below. See how «НА»-places are used. If you work with someone else, read them in parts, or you can even act them out. More importantly, find the phrases which you think you might find useful and try to add them to your vocabulary.

– У меня́ есть брат. А у вас?
– У меня́ тоже оди́н брат есть.
– А он в кóлледже или в шкóле?
– Он инженéр на завóде!

– Как твоя́ жена́?
– Спаси́бо. Ничегó.
– Онá на дáче сегóдня?
– Нет. На рабóте.

– У тебя́ есть друг в Москвé, да?
– Нет - подрýга, но она на рабóте.
Я сегóдня оди́н*.
– Я тоже. В кафé? У меня есть врéмя.

* оди́н *(here) – alone, on my own*

c) Find a person who works in a factory, has a dacha, is at a leisure centre afterwards, has time today; is at work tomorrow, has a brother who is at college. Keep an eye on your «НА»-words and «Е» at the end of places. This is great to do in a group.

NEW WORD: СОСÉД/КА - *neighbour*

d) It's your turn. Think of where people whom you know are. Make two sentences about each person. For example, I can say «У меня́ есть брат. Он – на дáче в Казахстáне». If you are learning with someone else, you can make a few mini-conversations similar to the above. You can try formal and informal ways. Ask questions in blocks of two: У вас есть сосéд или сосéдка? Он/а на рабóте сегóдня?

Now it is probably time to have a look at our last two vowel letters. First, let's see how they fit in with the other eight Russian vowel letters that we are already familiar with. Remember to name them the Russian way: «Аа», «Оо», «Ии», «Ээ», «Уу», «Ыы», «Яя» and «Ее». In this order they do not seem to make a lot of sense. Let me list them in a different way – I hope it might help you see some logic behind the Russian vowel system.

A (like *a* in *father*) /a/   **Э** (like *e* in *end*) /э/   **O** (like *o* in *for*) /o/   **У** (like *oo* in *moon*) /y/   **Ы** (like back /i/) /ы/

Я (like *ya* in *yak*) /й a/   **E** (like *ye* in *yes*) /й э/   **Ё** (like *your*) /й o/   **Ю** (like *you*) /й y/   **И** (like *ee* in *see*) /и/

Have you noticed that the first four of the bottom row are all two-in-one letters, starting with a /й/ sound, similar to «Я»? Thus, they can be paired up with those above them: A – Я, Э – E, O – Ё, У – Ю. Do they make a bit more sense now? Only «Ы» and «И» make a different kind of pair. *All* letters from the bottom row, if following a consonant, would indicate its palatalization. Try reading all the letters in pairs and then in rows. Now we will have a look at the two new vowels, one at a time.

GROUP III (Funny Shapes) «Ё ё»

«Ё ё» is read more or less **like the English word *your***, perhaps not as back and not as long, in fact very much like the Russian /o/ with a /й/ sound in front. This is a very "stressed" letter because it is **always under stress** (hope this pun works for you). That is why it does not make sense to put a stress mark over it. So, wherever you see the two dots over the letter, you need to put all the power of your voice there. Have a go: ёлка (meaning *a Christmas tree*). There are no other Russian letters with dots like these.

> **How does it sound?** «Ё» is one of the **two-in-one letters**, like «Я» and «E». That is why, when reading it at the start of words and after vowels, the first sound should be /й/, e.g., «ёлка» - /й ó л к a/ and «моё» - /м a й ó/.

Ex.3 a) Try not to trip up! Remember to put your stress on «Ё».

пай - паёк	куй - куёт	край - краёв	пóйма - поём	май - маёвка
буй - буёк	жуй - жуёт	бугáй - бугаёв	прóйма - проём	чай - чаёвник

Check that you remembered to devoice your «B»-s at the end of words.

b) Decoding Cyrillic:

Tip! *You might remember that when you have vowels next to each other in a Russian word, you need to read them both, one after another, e.g.:* EË /й э й ó/.

ЁЛКА	МОЁ	ЧАЁК - ЗУЁК - КУЁМ - ЖУЁМ
ЁМКО	ТВОЁ	ПРИЁМ - ПРИЁМНИК - ПРИЁМЫШ
ЁЖИК	СВОЁ	ЗАЁМ - ВДВОЁМ - ВТРОЁМ - ВОДОЁМ
ЁРЗАЛ	ЕЁ	ЁЖ - ЁЖИК - ЁЖИКИ - ТАЁЖНИКИ

Check that you spotted one «Ж» at the end, which Russians would read as /ш/.

> **NEW WORD: ЁЛКА** - *a Christmas tree*

Check that you put your stress on «Ё».

c) Let's try it in Russian. Think of different phrases where you can use «ёлка». For example, use *my* or *your* (polite and familiar) with it; say that you have one or ask your friend whether they do; or ask in a shop whether they have it and how much it is; imagine what a shop-assistant would say when giving it to you; say the tree is in the garden/in the house/in the garage/in the room etc. Say your phrases and sentences aloud if you can. How long is it till Christmas?

RUSSIASCOPE: Russians used to celebrate **CHRISTMAS** *in a similar way to other Christians, but the Bolsheviks, who came to power in 1917, were against religion and destroyed a lot of churches and cathedrals. Thus, for 70 years most Russians did not celebrate Christmas, and the focus of winter festivities was shifted to the New Year. When I was at school, I did not even realise that there was such a day as Christmas. Since Perestroika, it has been reinstated as a national holiday. For most Russians though, New Year is still a more important celebration, when we have our ёлка, our presents, our visitors and our holidays. Note that Russian Orthodox Christmas is on the 7th of January.*

How does it sound? This is just to remind you that «Ё» (similar to *your*), being a two-in-one vowel letter, joins the club of «Я» and «Е» (together with «И») in **indicating palatalisation**. So, when we have a consonant *before* «Ё» we need to try reading it closer to the palate. «Ё» in this case would give us an /o/ sound, with no separate /й/. E.g., тётя (meaning "aunt") sounds like /т'о т'а/, with both consonants palatalised.

Ex.4 a) Attention: palatalisation! Make sure you palatalise your consonants both before the soft sign («Ь») and before «Ё».

конь - конёк	мать - матёр	путь - путём	король - королёк
огонь - огонёк	кость - костёр	куль - кулём	мотыль - мотылёк

Check that you noticed your unstressed «О»-s.

b) Attention: palatalisation! Try making a small difference between plain and palatalised consonants within each pair.

МОЛ - МЁЛ	иду́ - идёт	крадёт - краду́
ВОЛ - ВЁЛ	ору́ - орёт	грызёт - грызу́
НОС - НЁС	плыву́ - плывёт	ревёт - реву́
СОК - СЁК	расту́ - растёт	бредёт - бреду́

> **NEW WORDS: ВСЁ** - *everything, all (not people); That's all.*
>
> **МАТРЁШКА** - *a Russian nesting doll*   **ТЁТЯ** - *an aunt*
>
> **РЕБЁНОК** - *a chil*   **ДЯ́ДЯ** - *an uncle*

Check that you noticed that there are two palatalised consonants in some words; that you realise that «В» in «всё» would not sound voiced before «С», like in «вход».

To make it clear: «Дя́дя» is one of those not very common words, like «па́па», «Ники́та» and «де́душка», that are masculine despite having «А» (or in case of «дя́дя» - «Я») at the end. So, we would need to use «дя́дя» with other words as a masculine, e.g., мой дя́дя, твой дя́дя, ваш дя́дя.

---

c) What would you say in Russia if you needed to:

say that everything is good;	say that your aunt is in America;
ask how much a Russian doll is;	introduce your uncle;
ask somebody if they have a child;	say that you have everything in the bag;
say that you have one child, a son;	ask somebody whether they have a Christmas tree;
say that your child is at school;	ask somebody whether their uncle is at work.

Check that you realise that «ребёнок» is masculine; that you used «рабо́та» with «на».

says that it represents different generations; some talk about celebrating motherhood; others insist that матрёшка *was an original commercial idea inspired by Japanese nesting boxes. One thing is for sure: the idea of* матрёшка *is not as old as many tend to think – it only appeared at the very end of the 19th century and became instantaneously popular after winning a bronze medal at the Exposition Universelle in Paris in 1900. These days the designs are extremely elaborate and vary immensely, and so does the number of dolls inside.* The Guinness Book of World Records *states that the largest number of dolls is 51, though on the Internet you can find mentions of 72. What I cannot explain is why* матрёшка *is often called "babushka" in the West.*

How does it sound? This is just a small reminder that **after hushers** («Ж», «Ч» and «Ш» so far) «Ё», similarly to «Е» (e.g., in «тóже»), **loses its /й/ sound**; thus it would read just as /o/, without affecting hushers in any way. E.g., «чёрное» in «Чёрное мóре» (which means *the Black Sea*) will sound more or less like /ч ó р н а й e/.

d) Try not to trip up! Put a tick next to the strings with hushers (e.g.: «Ж», «Ш», «Ч»). Then read all the strings in order, making sure that «Ё» does not have its /й/ sound after consonants, while palatalization occurs only in strings with no ticks.

пасёт - несёт - трясёт	зажёг - пожёг - поджёг	слёзы - грёзы - берёзы
ушёл - пошёл - нашёл	очёс - начёс - зачёс	шёлк - чёлка - жёлтая
чёт - почёт - зачёт	тёрка - костёр - вахтёр	жёлоб - жёлудь - жёрнов
завёл - навёл - провёл	гашёная - сушёная - тушёная	дёрнул - дёргал - дёготь

GROUP III (Funny shapes) «Ю ю»

«Ю ю» is pronounced basically **like the English word** *you*, with a slightly **stronger /й/ sound**. «Ю» is the fourth of the Russian two-in-one letters and the last of the ten Russian vowel letters. It's shaped like a number 10 linked with a dash, which is why some of my students call it a "dashing" letter.

How does it sound? We need to make sure that we differentiate between «Ю» (like *you*) and «Ё» (like *your*). When you read «Ю», your **lips need to come much more forward** than when you say «Ё» – similar to how we do it for «У» to make it different from «О».

Unlike our "stressed" «Ё», «Ю» can be stressed or unstressed, though this does not affect the way it sounds much.

Ex.6 a) Watch your stress! (It is different in different columns.) Make sure that you keep the /й/ in «Ю», as here it is after another vowel.

дай - даю́	мой - мо́ю	знай - зна́ю
пой - пою́	вой - во́ю	чита́й - чита́ю
стой - стою́	край - кра́ю	гада́й - гада́ю
куй - кую́	дуй - ду́ю	пыла́й - пыла́ю

RUSSIASCOPE: **СОЮ́З**

«Сою́з» *is a word often associated with Russian spacecraft and their launch systems. In Russian the word «сою́з» means "union" and was also part of the Russian name of the country, the "Soviet Union"* (Сове́тский Сою́з). *The abbreviation of its full name "USSR" runs as «СССР» (Did you read «Р» as* **r** *in error?) in Russian; where the first «С» (for* сою́з) *represents the "U" (for "Union"), while the last letter «Р» stands for* «респу́блика». *Also, people do not always realise that Russia was one of the 15 republics that made up the Soviet Union. After the break-up of the Soviet Union during Perestroika, all of the republics became independent countries.*

---

b) Decoding Cyrillic. Make sure that your /й/ sound is strong at the start of «Ю», particularly at the start of a word.

Ю́РА - Ю́РТА - Ю́МОР	КАЮ́К - КАЮ́Р - КАЮ́ТА	Ю́БКА - Ю́БОЧКА - БАЮ́КАЛ
ЮГ - Ю́НГА - Ю́НАЯ	ЮЛА́ - ЮРИ́СТ - ПРИЮ́Т	Ю́НКЕР - Ю́НОША - ЮНИО́Р

Check that you spotted a word-final devoiced «Г» and a devoiced «Б» before «К» (like in «коро́бка»).

How does it sound? Similarly to the other two-in-one letters («Я», «Е» and «Ё»), «Ю» **indicates** that the **consonant** *before* it **is palatalised**, with no /й/ sound after the consonant, e.g., a girl's name «Лю́да» is read as /л' у́ д а/, with /л/ like *l* in *lit*, with your tongue up and closer to the front of the palate.

---

c) Attention: Palatalisation! Watch your stress too. Keep an eye on palatalised /л'/.

тюк - тю́бик - этю́д	люфт - флюс - флю́геры	сюда́ - сюже́т - сюрту́к
трюк - трюм - трюмо́	плюх - плю́хал - плю́хнули	индю́к - гадю́ка - жадю́га
тюль - тю́лька - тюле́нь	ключ - клю́чик - клю́чники	каню́к - каню́ля - кастрю́ля
лю́ди - блю́до - верблю́д	рю́шка - рю́мка - рю́мочка	слюна́ - слюда́ - Людми́ла

d) Just read and recognise. Underline the words with «Ю» (like *you*), then read all the words, one after the other, making sure that you put your lips forward much more for «Ю» than for «Ё».

дю́на, актёр, маникю́р, меню́, боксёр, бюджéт, сёрфинг, стюардéсса, ликёр, костю́м, репортёр, глюкóза, рюкзáк, жонглёр, сюрпри́з, брошю́ра, манёвр, шофёр, мю́зикл, пюрé, трю́фель, кёрлинг, импортёр, нюáнс, блюз

NEW WORDS: ЧЕЛОВÉК - *a person*

ЛЮ́ДИ - *people*

ДÉТИ - *children*

WORTH REMEMBERING: *Having found out that Russians use «Ы» to make **plurals**, we now have these two plurals in the box above that do not follow the rules. They are **irregular** or sort of "funny" (compare them to their English equivalents). The only way to deal with them is to memorise them. It might help to remember them in pairs:* человéк - лю́ди; ребёнок - дéти.

Ex.7 a) Say it in Russian. Say the plurals below in Russian. Remember to drop a vowel (if you have one) before adding «Ы». If you are learning to write, you can write these down too. Watch your stress.

bananas, cars, schools, fruit, plastic bags, people, shops, cameras, pictures (not photos), rooms, sofas, newspapers, chocolates, farms, children, flats, factories, maps, exits, telephones, magazines, glasses

WORTH REMEMBERING: *Not all words in Russian form a regular plural with the help of «Ы» – it depends on the last letter before the plural ending. If a word ends with «Г», «К» or «Х», for example, we need to add «И», e.g.,* пар**к** - пáр**ки**. *The same happens with feminine words which have «Г», «К» or «Х» just before «А». E.g.,* кни́**г**а - кни́**ги**. *All three, /г/, /к/ and /х/, are pronounced at the back of your mouth and in Russian are not normally followed by /ы/, but they have no problem combining with /и/.*

Tip! *This is just to remind you that «И» indicates that the consonants **before** it are read soft, palatalized.*

b) Let's get this right. Make the following words plural. You might want to underline the letter which would face the ending, to help you decide whether to use «Ы» or «И». Remember to keep your stress in place and watch out for "funny" plurals.

пакéт -..................   фи́рма -..................   класс -..................

банк -..................   ма́льчик -..................   матрёшка -..................

человéк -..................   кварти́ра -..................   ребёнок -..................

ру́чка -..................   су́мка -..................   газéта -..................

c) Reading for meaning. Make sure you read ALL your endings correctly. Once you have read a sentence, find a plural (or plurals) in it and if you have «И» as an ending, underline the letter before it («Г»/«К»/«Х») to see why «И» is used. Translate what you have.

Рóзы в вáзе, на столé. – Спаси́бо.   Бáнки и ресторáны в гóроде, а не в дерéвне.

У вас есть ру́чки? – Да. – Мóжно четы́ре?   Мой сын не ест салáты и фру́кты. – Это плóхо.

Кáрты и кни́ги в корóбке. Это ничегó?   Лю́ди в автóбусе – тури́сты. Там дéти тóже.

Лёша, ты ешь банáны или я́блоки? – Я́блоки.   Собáки в дóме или в саду́? – Сегóдня в дóме.

d) Find a person who has books in their room, has pens in their bag, has more than one female neighbour, does not eat apples, has children, has boxes in the house, has more than one set of Russian dolls.

> **NEW WORD: ПРОДУ́КТЫ** – *food in a shop, cupboard or fridge,*
> *not prepared for eating yet; groceries;*
> *often the sign on a food shop/kiosk.*

You have started discovering that endings of words in Russian are very important. Perhaps it is time to have a look at Russian verbs. Most Russian verbs in a dictionary have «ТЬ» at the end. To give you an example, we can take the word we know «рабóта» which means *a piece of work, a place of work* or *a job*. For it to mean *to work* ("to do some work") we will need «ТЬ» at the end. So we end up with «рабóтать» (keep the stress in place!)

It is in line with what we were talking about before: while English uses separate words, Russian tends to add bits to the same word. Compare: English "need to work" comes out as «нáдо рабо́тать» in Russian ("to" in front of the English verb is represented by «ть» at the end of the Russian verb).

> **РАБО́ТАТЬ** - _to_ work (to do work)

> **WORTH REMEMBERING:** «Рабо́тать» _is the **dictionary form of the verb** (or its infinitive). When you use verbs in English to say that somebody does something, you normally take the "to" off, e.g., "I work", "you work" etc. Something similar happens in Russian: when we need to say "I work" you start with the dictionary form (infinitive) «рабо́тать» and **take «ТЬ» off**. In Russian though, we go one step further: we need to indicate that a person speaking is doing it, not someone else. Russians do this by **adding «Ю»** which links the verb to «Я» (for "I")._
>
> _E.g.: РАБО́ТА**ТЬ** (to work) > Я РАБО́ТА**Ю** (I work / I am working)._

Tip! _Make sure that you read «Ю» as /й у/ as it is after a vowel here. Keep the «А» here too._

Ex.8 a) Reading for meaning. Note the use of «В» or «НА» for _at_. Make sure there is only one stress in your words and keep it on the «О» in рабо́таю. Compare the verb forms below to the verb «я ем». Can you find one difference and two similarities?

Tip! _Keep in mind that the word order is flexible in Russian, and words do not always follow English structures. To make translation easier, **find a verb** first and work out who is doing what. Then attach other words to it, phrasing it correctly in English._

Я рабо́таю в шко́ле.	На фе́рме я рабо́таю. А вы?	Где рабо́таю? В шко́ле в Ту́ле.
Я на заво́де рабо́таю.	Завтра рабо́таю в о́фисе? Да?	Сего́дня я до́ма рабо́таю. А ты?
Сего́дня я не рабо́таю.	Не рабо́таю я на по́чте.	Извини́те, я там не рабо́таю.

> **To make it clear:** I have no doubt that you spotted the difference between «я рабо́таю» and «я ем» - they use different endings. «Я ем» is a bit peculiar and does NOT follow the regular pattern, while «Ю» is used by other verbs. What about similarities? Have you worked out that neither differentiate between different English present forms – thus «я рабо́таю» can mean **"I work" or "I am working"**? Most Russian verbs have only one present tense. Also, neither of the verbs need "do" to make negative sentences – we just put **«НЕ» in front of the verb**, e.g., Я не рабо́таю.

> **NEW WORDS:** ПЕНСИОНЕ́Р/КА - *retired*
>
> СТУДЕ́НТ/КА - *a student*

To make it clear: A lot of Russian words referring to people can have female versions. «Пенсионе́р» and «студе́нт» are only used to speak about men, while «пенсионе́рка» and «студе́нтка» refer only to women. Note that many Russian words for jobs have only one form for both men and women, e.g., Он инжене́р. Она́ инжене́р.

b) What would you say in Russia if you need to tell somebody that:

you do not work, you are a student;

your sister is also a student at college;

your uncle is retired;

you are working in a café today;

you work in the garden;

your aunt is not retired, she is an engineer;

you are not in the office tomorrow;

your neighbour is retired.

c) Now it's your turn. Say in Russian whether you work and, if yes, try to say where. If you do not know the Russian word for where you work, you can try looking it up in the dictionary or on the Internet or ask a teacher to help you. You are most likely to need «В» (or «НА») before the place and «Е» at the end of it. For example, I can say: Я рабо́таю в университе́те в го́роде Ли́дсе. You can also add whether you are working today or tomorrow, if it applies. If you are not working, see if you can explain why not.

> **NEW WORDS:** ЗНАТЬ - *to know*
>
> ЧИТА́ТЬ - *to read*
>
> ПОНИМА́ТЬ - *to understand*

Ex.9 a) Let's get this right. Read the verb forms below aloud. Make sure that two words in each pair have different endings but the same stress. Translate each form. E.g., рабо́тать (*to work*) - рабо́таю (*I work./I am working.*).

To make it clear: Even though «Я» (for *I*) is not written here, the form of the verb with «Ю» at the end can only be translated as a «Я»-form. That is why Russians can often omit «Я» in a conversation if using a verb.

знать - зна́ю   чита́ть - чита́ю   понима́ть - понима́ю

b) Reading for meaning. Watch your stress!

Я понима́ю.   Я чита́ю кни́ги. А вы?   Я хорошо́ зна́ю Ло́ндон. А ты? – Не о́чень.

Не понима́ю.   Газе́ты то́же чита́ю.   Извини́те. Я не зна́ю ру́сский алфави́т.

Я всё понима́ю.   А журна́лы я не чита́ю.   Англи́йский язы́к я зна́ю. – Это хорошо́.

Tip! When you make your phrases in Russian it is best to follow English word order, though you do not have to. To start with, it might also be good to keep «Я» in. You will see when you can skip it.

c) Say it in Russian. Note that you need to say your «A» before «Ю», whether it is stressed or unstressed, e.g., рабо́т**а**ю. Make sure you say the sentences without looking at the verbs in the New Word box or the sentences above.

I work.	I do not work.	I work at a factory in a city.	I am Russian. I work in Moscow.
I know.	I do not know.	I don't know London.	I know London well. And you?
I read.	I do not read.	I read books.	I do not read newspapers.
I understand.	I do not understand.	I am not understanding everything	I don't work at school. I am retired.
I am working.	I am not working.	I am working in a café today.	I am not working tomorrow either.
I am reading.	I am not reading.	I am reading a magazine.	I am not reading it all. I am tired.

Check that you used «НА» with «заво́д»; that you needed «то́же» for "either".

Hopefully, this exercise has given you the idea of how you can combine verbs with other words and what a variety of sentences you can make. Now you can have a go at using these in your conversation.

d) Now it's your turn. Think of what you can say about your work and reading, or perhaps you know another language or a city somewhere. If you work with someone else, take turns making statements about yourself. Make good use of *And you?*. E.g., Я не чита́ю газе́ты. Я чита́ю но́вости *(news)* в Интерне́те. А ты?

NEW WORD: ИГРА́ТЬ - *to play*

---

*Tip! If we talk about playing sport games (or any other games) we need to put «В» in front of the game. E.g., Я игра́ю **в** те́ннис_. (Remember: Russians do not palatalise «т» in «те́ннис».) You do NOT need to add anything to the end!*

Ex.10 a) Reading for meaning. Remember to start with the verb when you try to work out the meanings.

Я игра́ю **в** футбо́л.   Я не игра́ю **в** баскетбо́л. А ты?   **В** гольф я хорошо́ игра́ю.

А я игра́ю **в** хокке́й.   Извини́те. **В** волейбо́л я не игра́ю.   Я **в** кри́кет игра́ю то́же.

Check that you understand that «В гольф я хорошо́ игра́ю.»
is talking about being good at golf.

167

It is interesting that when Russians say «хоккей» they presume ice hockey. For ordinary hockey you would need to add "on grass", so it would be «хоккей на траве́».

> **NEW WORD: ША́ХМАТЫ** - *chess*

Most of the Russian names for sports sound very much like those in English (see Ex.10 b below). There are a couple of exceptions though, with chess being one of them. To help yourself remember it, you might think of checkmate + «Ы» for plural as there are lots of pieces. «Ша́хматы» does not have a singular form.

b) Now it's your turn. Say in Russian whether you play (or not play) the following games: футбо́л, те́ннис, гольф, баскетбо́л, пинг-по́нг, сну́кер, волейбо́л, сквош, рэ́гби, карты, кри́кет, ша́хматы, пул, бейсбо́л, бо́улинг. It is better to make full sentences every time. Remember «В» before the game and NO «Е» at the end. E.g., Я игра́ю в сну́кер. If you are learning in a group, you can work together, where one student says which game he or she plays and then anybody in the group who plays the same one can join in, using «то́же».

> **To make it clear:** When Russians speak about playing an instrument they use «НА» instead of «В». We will have a look at this in the next unit.

> **НО́ВАЯ ФРА́ЗА: Я ЛЮБЛЮ́** - *I like*

> *Check that the stress is at the end and that both «Л»-s are very close to the palate.*

Some of my students remember this as "yellow-blue" (make sure the colours are right though!). Also, note that «я люблю́» is NOT the dictionary form of the verb. We will save that for later (not to complicate things at this stage).

c) Reading for meaning. Remember to find the verb first, to handle the Russian flexible word order.

Я люблю́ кино́. А вы?

Чита́ть очень люблю́. А ты?

Я люблю́ игра́ть в ша́хматы.

Извини́, я не люблю́ ма́сло. – Ничего́.

В шко́ле я ем сандвичи, но я это не люблю́.

Я люблю́ спорт. Игра́ю в баскетбо́л.

О́чень люблю́ мой дом.

Конфе́ты я не люблю́.

Люблю́ рабо́тать в саду́.

> *Check that you realise that «о́чень люблю́» means "I like . . . very much",*
> *though «о́чень» normally translates only as "very".*

To make it clear: You might have already worked this out, but I will mention it just in case: «я люблю» can be linked to a noun (something) or a verb, e.g., «Я люблю кни́ги.» or «Я люблю́ чита́ть.» **The verb following «люблю́» stays in its dictionary form** (with «ТЬ» at the end).

d) Now it's your turn. See what you can say about your likes and dislikes. If you do not know some words you can look them up in the dictionary, on the Internet or ask your teacher. Let's stick to things, though, and not involve people just yet. For example, I can say: Я люблю́ ру́сский язы́к. Я о́чень люблю́ игра́ть в снукер. Я то́же о́чень люблю́ шокола́д.

To make it clear: «Я люблю́» does NOT stand for "*I would like*. . .". It is solely about liking (or not liking). It can mean *I love* too, but words for people would have different endings. If you want to say that you would like (that is, want) something, you need good old «мо́жно».

Ex.11 a) Reading for meaning. Here is something that I can say about myself. Have a look and see whether you can do something similar.

Я Ната́лия Влади́мировна Па́ркер, но мо́жно Ната́ша. Я рабо́таю в университе́те в го́роде Ли́дсе. Я пло́хо зна́ю Ли́дс, но хорошо́ зна́ю Гла́стонбери. У меня́ есть муж Фил и до́чка Са́ша. До́чка - в шко́ле. В го́роде Ту́ле у меня́ есть ма́ма и ба́бушка. Я зна́ю ру́сский и англи́йский языки́. О́чень люблю́ чита́ть кни́ги. Я в сну́кер то́же игра́ю. О́чень люблю́ шокола́д и конфе́ты, но фру́кты то́же ем.

b) Step-by-step guide on how to speak about yourself. Let's pull together a few things that we have learnt. We have done a fair bit – we handle «У меня́ есть», can say where things and people are, and now we are starting to use verbs.

1. Say your *name* starting with «я».

2. Say whether you *work*. If not, see whether you can explain why not. If yes, say where.

3. Say whether you *have* any brothers or sisters, any children or grandparents etc. You can add friends too.

4. Think about *what else* you can say: whether you play any games, know any other languages, have any pets, or like something or doing something.

What a way to finish the unit! What you have done is an achievement, because you have not just memorised the phrases – you have constructed them yourself! You know what you are saying and why. To practice this, you can imagine that you are helping somebody else (who doesn't know anything about Russian) to say a few things about themselves. For example, try speaking on behalf of your friends, family, colleagues, neighbours etc. You can also use a *Hello* or *OK* magazine and speak as a celebrity would (if they knew any Russian!)

ВСЕГÓ ХОРÓШЕГО (*with a funny sounding «Г»*). That's the phrase that I used at the end of the last unit. Or is it already late and you need to be in bed? Then СПОКÓЙНОЙ НÓЧИ is better. (Keep in mind that «Спокóйной нóчи» is not going to do if you are in a class and going home, even if it's very late.) Choose a farewell which is appropriate tonight or just the one you like and try repeating it a few times while you are doing other things. If you happen to think Russian tomorrow night, say the same phrase again. If you feel that you would like a new phrase, we can try «**До встрéчи.**» («В» does not need to be distinctive as it is before voiceless «С», like in «всё» – just catch your lip). «Встрéча» is when you meet somebody, a meeting or an encounter; thus «до встрéчи» means "up to meeting", something like "See you again". If you are tired though, you might decide to stick to «всегó хорóшего» or just to familiar «Спокóйной нóчи», leaving «До встрéчи» for some other time.

Something old, something new (*revision of unit 7*)

Привет. Как у тебя дела? Pick your answer for today (we have a few to choose from) and then try to return this question to me. If you need a reminder, you can look back to the start of the last two revision sections.

> *Check that your return question is informal (А у тебя?)*
> *and that you noticed two cues in my opening greeting.*

My reply today can be «**Ничего.**» *(with a funny sounding «Г»)*, which is not new but is one of the most popular answers in Russia, as well as the one closest to the English *Fine* or *OK*, so I thought it would be good to bring it up. But to be honest, I didn't have the best week, I am afraid – I had a cold. So, a more appropriate answer would be: **Болела.** *((I) was ill/unwell)*. This word is similar to «Устал/а» – we can use it as a question and as an answer; with the right ending it can refer to males *(don't forget to take «А» off)* and females. It might happen to be a useful one in winter. To practice using it, you can think of people around who had a cold recently and make phrases about them (make sure you choose the right form). For example, I can say: Моя дочка тоже болела.

> *Check that you realise that you do NOT need anything for "was" with*
> *«болел/а» – it is already in the past tense.*

Now it is time to look at how we have got on with our Cyrillic letters. Make sure that you name them all aloud and the Russian way.

GROUP I (The Easy): Мм, Тт, Кк, Аа, Оо

GROUP II (The Tricky): Сс, Нн, Вв, Рр, Ее, Уу, Хх *(like . . . but . . .)*

GROUP III (Funny Shapes): Ээ, Яя, Лл, Дд, Ии, Йй, Бб, Зз, Пп, Гг, Чч, Шш, Жж, Фф, Ёё, Юю

GROUP IV (The Strangers): Ьь, Ыы

Find the two new vowel letters in the alphabet below and see which part of the alphabet they belong to:

А Б В Г Д Е Ё Ж З И Й К Л М Н О П Р С Т У Ф Х ... Ч Ш ... ... Ы Ь Э Ю Я. We have three left!

We are going to start our revision with a quick go at our hushing sounds, as we have two more to add to the list. So we need to be fairly comfortable with those that we know at the moment. In addition, we will include a tricky «X» in here. Though it does not belong to the "hushers", it can be a bit challenging.

1. Is Russian /x/ closer to the English /k/ or English /h/?

2. Can you name the three hushing sounds that we have come across so far?

3. What happens to «Е» or «Ё» after hushers, for example, in «тóже» or in «Чёрное море»?

Ex. 1 a) Try not to trip up! And, as always, watch your stress.

пахáл - пожáл - познáл	свáха - свечá - свежá	пожýх - кóжух - хýже
зажáрь - пошáрь - сухáрь	прочь - паршá - порхáл	хочý - хóчет - мáчеха
зачéм - чехóл - черепáха	глóжет - оглóх - галóш	женúх - вы́шел - вы́ехал
урожáй - малахáй - орошáй	шельф - халúф - фурáж	шелухá - шúхта - шáхматы

Now let's focus on vowels. To start with, we need to differentiate between «Ё» (like *your*) with lips slightly rounded, and «Е» (like *ye* in *yes*) when lips are quite narrow. This is an important difference as, apart from giving us different words, e.g., «нёбо» (which means *palate*) and «нéбо» (which means *sky*), they appear to be responsible for certain stress patterns, so we need to watch out for these two.

4. What do «Е» and «Ё» have in common? Why did we call them two-in-one vowels?

5. Can «Ё» be weak?

b) Try not to trip up!

ёлка - Óлька	моё - мáе	éли - ёлка - ёлочка	ежú - ёжик - ежевúка
ёжик - óжиг	своё - свáе	ёрш - ершú - ерóшить	ёкал - ёкнул - ермóлка

Check that in the second column your stress was on different syllables within a pair; that you read two vowels as two separate sounds.

6. What do both «Е» and «Ё» indicate if there are consonants before them?

7. Which Russian consonants are always read the same, whether before two-in-one vowels or not?

8. What sounds do «Е» or «Ё» make if they follow one of the hushers?

c) Watch your stress! Note that «E» is unstressed here, thus weak and would sound more like /и/.

весна́ - вёсны	зёрна - зерно́	шерсть - шёрстка	платёж - платежи́
десна́ - дёсны	рёбра - ребро́	свекла́ - свёкла	кутёж - кутежи́
жена́ - жёны	гнёзда - гнездо́	седло́ - сёдла	грабёж - грабежи́

Check that you have spotted devoiced «Ж»-s.

d) Jog your memory and big sort out. Mark the stresses where needed. First, read out all the words with «Ё», then those with stressed «E»-s and finally those with unstressed weak «E»-s. Remember to highlight the words which you find challenging.

сестра, тётя, где, извините, всё, матрёшка, тарелка, стена, кафе́, ребёнок, тоже, привет, ферма, ёлка, река

e) Watch your stress! The stress patterns here are different in different strings. There are a lot of palatalised consonants too. This might feel like a bit of challenge – take it steady.

пёс - перс - пе́рсик - пёсик	сестра́ - сёстры - се́стрин - сестрёнка
темно́ - тёмное - темнота́ - потёмки	черёд - черёмуха - черемша́ - чёрное
село́ - новосёл - населён - посёлок	плеть - плётка - плете́нь - плетёнка
жесть - жёстко - жесто́ко - жестя́нка	шерсть - шёрстка - решётка - решето́
слеза́ - слёзы - слези́нка - слёзно	галёрка - гале́ра - галере́я - гример́
берёг - бе́рег - бережёт - берегла́	ве́село - весёлка - вёсла - весели́ть

Ex.2 a) Let's get this right. Read through the list of words below – check that you know all the words. It might help to mark the stresses first. Fill in the blanks in sentences underneath using the words from the list. You can use each word only once.

фрукты, хлеб, кофе, матрёшка, ферма, конфеты, офис, сахар, хорошо, кафе, тётя, всё, фотоаппарат, выход, фирма, телефон, ребёнок, дядя, фамилия, плохо

Извини́те, сколько ва́ша ....? – 10 рубле́й.

Алло́. Я ем в .... А ты где сего́дня?

Ма́льчик, твоя́ .... Ерёмин? – Да.

Мой .... фе́рмер. Он на .... сего́дня.

У меня́ есть оди́н ...., сын.

Что это? – Это мой .... «Зени́т».

Мо́жно ....? – Да. Молоко́ и ....?

Как у тебя́ дела́? – .... Спаси́бо.

Ты ешь ....? – Да, и шоколад тоже.

Кто это? – Это моя .... Она́ пенсионе́рка.

Мой муж не ест .... – Это ....

У вас есть ....? – Извини́те, нет. – Ничего́.

Как твоя́ рабо́та? – Я в Москве́, в ....

У тебя́ есть ....? – Да. Там на столе́.

Извини́те, пожа́луйста. А где ....?

Жена́ до́ма? – Нет, она сего́дня в ....?

Check that you put «E» at the end of words after «B» and «HA».

9. Why is it important to look at the end of words in Russian?

10. How would we translate the phrases with «В» or «НА» if there is no «Е» at the end of the places?

11. Spot *two* differences between «на стýле» and «на столé».

b) Let's try it in Russian. Similar to what we did with a pen in the last unit, putting it inside or on top of things, today we are going to work with different things in different places around the room. This time though, you need to place them so you could say TWO sentences each time. For example: Газéта в сýмке. Сýмка на дивáне. Use chairs, walls, desks/tables, sofas, windowsills, boxes, bags, plates, dishes, food items, books etc. If you work with someone else, you can ask questions too, e.g., Где газéта? – Газéта в сýмке. – А сýмка где? – А сумка на дивáне. Watch out for feminines.

Tip! You need to be extremely careful that you put «Е» at the end ONLY (!) if words have «В» or «НА» in front, e.g., Тетрáдь - на столé. Стол_ в óфисе.

To make it clear: Картúна in Russian is a «НА»-word. This means that when you want to say "in the picture", you need «**на** картúне» in Russian. E.g., На картúне - мост.

---

12. Which of these – «фéрма» or «фúрма» – needs «НА»?

13. Is there a particular word for *at* in Russian? What do Russians use instead?

14. How do we know whether to use «В» or «НА» for *at*?

15. Try to remember the six «НА»-words which we identified in the last unit.

c) Let's get this right. Fill in the gaps with «В» or «НА», translate the phrase into English and then give the dictionary form of the place (watch out for feminines).

...... магазúне, ... пóчте, ... шкóле, ... кинó, ... вокзáле, ... дáче, ...
кóлледже, ... теáтре, ... стадиóне, ... университéте, ... бáнке, ... завóде, ... библиотéке, ... кафé, ... рабóте, ... ресторáне

d) What would you say in Russia if you wanted to:

say that you are at the station and you are tired;
say that you are glad that you are at home today;
ask whether the child is at school tomorrow;
say that you are at the sports centre afterwards;

ask whether everything is good at the dacha;
say that your aunt in not in the office, she is at the factory;
say that you are eating in a café in town;
ask somebody whether their husband was ill and if he is at work.

16. What do we need to do to make «Ё» and «Ю» sound different?

? 17. When do we need to read the /й/ sound in *two-in-one letters*?

Ex.3 a) Decoding Cyrillic. Make sure your «Ю» reads as two sounds here but your «У» as one. Remember to put your lips forward for both. Watch your stress.

у́рка - Ю́рка	ю́мор - умо́ра	ую́т - ую́тно - ую́тная
у́зы - ю́зом	баю́кал - бау́л	ду́ю - ду́ют - поду́ю
У́ля - Ю́ля	каю́р - кау́ра	но́вую - ма́лую - ста́рую

18. Can you name all *four* two-in-one letters?

? 19. Can you make four pairs out of these eight vowel letters: А, Ё, О, У, Я, Э, Ю, Е?

b) Try not to trip up! Make sure that all your two-in-one letters start with a /й/ sound, as they are after a vowel here. Watch your stress!

куёт - куют	БОЙ - БО́Ю - БОЯ́М - БОЁВ	ПОЙ - ПОЁТ - ПОЮ́Т - ПО́ЯТ - ПОЁЛ
суёт - сую́т	СЛОЙ - СЛО́Ю - СЛОЯ́М - СЛОЁВ	ДАЙ - ДАЮ́Т - ДАЁТ - ДОЁЛ - ДО́ЯТ
жуёт - жую́т	ЖУЙ - ЖУЮ́ - ЖУЯ́ - ЖУЁМ	КРАЙ - КРА́ЕМ - КРО́ЮТ - КРАЁВ - КРОЯ́Т

20. Do all two-in-one letters indicate that the consonants *before* them are palatalised?

? 21. Which other letter is specially designed to indicate palatalisation?

c) Attention: palatalisation! Remember to palatalise consonants before each of two-in-one vowels.

плёс - плюс - пляс - плен	горя́ч - горю́ч - горе́ - грёб	хлеб - хля́бь - хлюп - водохлёб
кряк - крюк - крест - крёстная	минёр - меня́л - меню́ - мне	салю́т - соля́нка - солён - соле́ние
шлюп - шля́па - шлёпал - лёшем	уте́ря - утю́г - утёк - утя́та	зе́лень - козёл - козю́ля - козя́вочка
сеть - сёмга - ся́ду - сюда́	флёр - флюс - фля́га - филе́	малю́т - маля́вка - малёк - мале́нько

Check that you spotted three devoiced «Б»-s and one devoiced «Г».

d) What's in a name? Match up the full (formal) versions of the Russian names in the top two lines with their diminutive (informal) versions in the bottom line.

Степа́н, Артём, Ю́рий, Пётр, Любо́вь, Семён, Алексе́й, Леони́д, Ю́лия, Серге́й, Людми́ла, Фёдор, Анна, Лев

Check that you noticed two devoiced «В»-s, one of which is palatalised as well.

Алёша, Ю́ля, Серёжа, Лёва, Фе́дя, Лю́да, Аню́та, Стёпа, Ю́ра, Сёма, Пе́тя, Лёня, Тёма, Лю́ба

To make it clear: Similarly to how «Никита» is an exception among male names, «Любовь» is a sort of exception among female names («любовь» also means *love* (as a noun) in Russian).

Reading Challenge: Найдёныш

22. Can you remember a pair of vowels which does not follow the pattern:

    А - Я, Э - Е, О - Ё, У - Ю?

23. What do «Ы» or «И» at the end of Russian words indicate?

24. Which of the two («Ы» or «И») follows «Г», «К» or «Х»?

25. Where do we look in feminine words to decide whether to use «Ы» or «И»?

26. Do you remember "funny" plurals: человек -........................, ребёнок -....................?

Ex. 4 a) Let's get this right. Look at the list below and say that there are more than one of those. You need to choose between «Ы» or «И» and to watch out for "funny" plurals. Keep your stress in the right place.

банан, книга, мальчик, комната, ребёнок, яблоко, пакет, ёлка, тарелка, фрукт, человек, матрёшка, выход, конфета, ручка, фотоаппарат, машина, сумка, коробка

b) Question time. Think of how you would ask a Russian person:

whether they have bananas *(polite)*;

where the pens are;

whether they eat apples;

how the children are;

whether the shops are there;

where the books are;

whether these are restaurants;

how much the sets of Russian dolls are;

whether you can have *(some)* fruit;

whether they have dogs *(informal)*.

27. Does the Russian verb *to eat* follow the general pattern?

28. What is the difference in translation of «работа» and «работать»?

29. Which form of the verb has «ТЬ» at the end?

Ex.5 a) Jog your memory. Read and translate the verbs below.

работать, знать, читать, понимать, играть

Check your stresses.

30. What do we do with «ТЬ» when we speak about ourselves?

? 31. Why do Russians add «Ю» to the end of the verb in «я рабо́таю»?

b) Decoding Cyrillic. Make sure that you read *two* vowels as two sounds, one after the other, e.g., АЮ /а й у/ Watch your stress – it is not always on the «А».

чита́ть - чита́ю	рабо́тать - рабо́таю	понима́ть - понима́ю
гада́ть - гада́ю	зака́пать - зака́паю	помога́ть - помога́ю
лома́ть - лома́ю	похло́пать - похло́паю	выруба́ть - выруба́ю

c) Say it in Russian. If you work with someone else, one of you can pick a verb from Section a) for the other one to make a «Я»-form. Then think of one word (or phrase) to add to your verb to make a sentence, e.g., Я зна́ю – Я зна́ю англи́йский язы́к.

I work	I know	I read	I understand	I play

32. Do Russians use anything for *do* in the word *don't*?

? 33. What do they do to make a negative sentence?

d) Let's try it in Russian. Turn the Russian phrases in Ex.5 c) into negative. Remember that «НЕ» should always be before the verb. Then, as above, add one more word or phrase to make a sentence. See whether you can make it relevant to you.

34. When do «пенсионе́р» and «студе́нт» need «-КА» at the end?

? 35. Do all jobs/occupations have a female version?

e) Let's try it in Russian. Imagine that you are in a Russian city called Но́вгород. You are a student. You are not working – you are a tourist. You don't understand Russian well. You don't know Но́вгород. You have a friend Же́ня. She is a student too. She is waiting for you at the station, you need to find out where the station is, and your telephone has just run out of charge. What a situation! Think of how you phrase it all in Russian.

Note that you do NOT need to translate everything word by word – you might not know all the words. What you need to do is make use of the Russian words that you *do* know. When you speak to Russians, do not try to translate what you think in English – you would quickly run into something you do not know yet. Think of the Russian words you have in stock and build your phrases with them. It might not come out exactly as in English, but when you say it, they are most likely to understand it. And that is what important in communicating. Remember to speak slowly and think about the ends of the words. Good luck.

36. What do we need to use after the verb «игра́ть» if we speak about playing a game?

? 37. Do we need «Е» at the end of a game?

38. Is «люблю́» a dictionary form? How would we translate it?

39. What do you say for *I would like*? (It is nothing to do with «я люблю» – think shopping.)

40. Why is it better to find the verb first to work out the meaning of a Russian sentence?

Ex.7 a) Let's get this right. Match the people on the left with what they say on the right. It might be good to check who the people are first. In the sentences, remember to look for a verb first, in order to handle the free word order.

футболи́ст	Я не рабо́таю. Я в колле́дже.
пенсионе́рка	Чита́ю газе́ты. Очень люблю́ кни́ги.
секрета́рь	Я рабо́таю на заво́де «Штамп».
профе́ссор	Сего́дня я в о́фисе рабо́таю.
ру́сский	Я игра́ю в футбо́л на стадио́не.
студе́нтка	Англи́йский язы́к я зна́ю непло́хо, всё понима́ю.
инжене́р	О́чень люблю́ рабо́тать в саду́.

To make it clear: We have already discovered that, after «люблю» Russians use either a noun (e.g.: Я любл^ те́ннис.) or a dictionary form of verbs with «ТЬ» (e.g.: Я любл^ игр@ть в т&ннис.). It might be helpful to know that there is no separate ing-form in Russian, for example, for "I like playing". It would translate as "I like to play" – Я любл^ игр@ть.

NEW WORD: ПЛА́ВАТЬ – *to swim*

b) Let's try it in Russian. Think of how you can use this new verb. Try to say whether you swim or not, whether you like it, where you swim (if you do), whether you are swimming today etc. If working with someone else, have a competition to see who can make more sentences about swimming. Take turns, with the last sentence being the winner.

c) Now it's your turn! Respond to my statements below – you and I will have an off-line conversation. Keep in mind that these are *not* questions. You need to comment on the same topic about yourself. Remember to watch «Я» or «У меня есть».

E.g.: Я люблю́ конфе́ты. – Я то́же.

Я не люблю́ ма́сло. – Я тоже не люблю́.

Я игра́ю **в** футбо́л. – А я игра́ю **в** те́ннис.

У меня́ есть ма́рки. – А у меня́ нет. Я люблю́ карти́ны.

Tip! *Russians often use «А» at the start when the comment is opposite or different from the original statement.*

Я игра́ю в снукер.

У меня есть брат.

Мясо я не ем.

Я люблю́ я́блоки.

В Ту́ле у меня есть подруга.

Ло́ндон хорошо́ я не зна́ю.

Я кни́ги чита́ю.

О́чень люблю́ пла́вать.

Я боле́ла.

You can do a similar activity with someone else: one says something about what they do or what they have, and the other one comments about themself. Take turns making initial statements.

8

Where do you live?

WHAT'S THE PLAN?

► to recognise and use one more Russian letter (we will save the last two for the next unit);
► to learn more words and to read longer words;
► to say where you live in Russian;
► to understand what is what in a Russian address;
► to ask questions using verbs;
► to try a conversation with a stranger in Russian, with verbs on board;
► to learn how to make some enquiries in a Russian hotel;
► to find out who the first president of Russia was.

We will start with a new letter. I was not sure whether to put it into Group III or Group IV. You will see why in a minute. Though the combination of sounds for it exists in English, it does not have a dedicated letter in the English alphabet and does not come naturally to English speakers. Let's have a look, and you decide where you want it.

GROUP III (Funny Shapes) (or Group IV?)

«Ц ц» stands for *ts* in *its*. I have a feeling you might be a bit unsure about this one. On one hand, there are a lot of words with *ts* in English, for example, plurals (e.g.: bits, cats, flights*)* and verbs (e.g.: eats, fits, concentrates). On the other hand, *ts* is mainly found at the end of words in English, and producing «Ц» at the start or in the middle sometimes proves to be challenging. Finally, Russian «Ц» is a tighter knit than English *ts* – «Ц» is one sound, rather than two separate ones put together. In a way, «Ц» is similar to English /dʒ/ in *Jim*, which is one sound rather than a combination of /д/ and /ж/. Anyway, we might be better starting to see how it goes.

Ex.1 a) Decoding Cyrillic. Watch your stress! When you get to longer words, make sure that you put only *one* stress per word as before.

пал - па́лец	сам - саме́ц	стан - стани́ца	чита́ть - чита́тель - чита́тельница
нем - не́мец	глуп - глупе́ц	тигр - тигри́ца	писа́ть - писа́тель - писа́тельница
хлоп - хло́пец	ларь - ларе́ц	боль - больни́ца	учи́ть - учи́тель - учи́тельница

NEW WORD: У́ЛИЦА

(Watch your stress) - a street

«Проспект Ле́нина в Ту́ле»

RUSSIASCOPE: *In Russia you are probably not going to find a huge variety of words in street names like "road", "drive", "close", "crescent" or "alley". The only other word (in addition to «у́лица») that you are likely to come across is «проспект», which is often translated as "avenue". Проспе́кт is normally a wide and long street, often one of the main streets in a city. Most foreign visitors are amazed at the size of Russian streets. Try to Google "Images of Kutuzovsky Prospekt" (or Куту́зовский проспе́кт) in Moscow, for example, to get the idea. The streets are often named after famous Russians (e.g., у́лица Пу́шкина), important events in Russian history (e.g.,у́лица Револю́ции) or local land-marks (у́лица Университе́тская).*

---

b) What's in a name? Read the names of у́лицы в Ту́ле.

у́лица Сове́тская, у́лица Металлу́ргов, проспе́кт Ле́нина, у́лица Вокза́льная, у́лица Пу́шкинская, у́лица Профсою́зов, у́лица Первома́йская, у́лица Па́рковая, Красноарме́йский проспе́кт, у́лица Октя́брьская

> *Check that you noticed that the actual street names normally (not always, though) follow the words «у́лица» or «проспе́кт».*

c) Try not to trip up! Try pronouncing /ц/ as one sound.

цап - ца́пал - ца́пнул

бо́цман - ло́цман - ла́цкан

пе́рец - гля́нец - фла́нец

у́лица - у́мница - у́стрица

бац - абза́ц - ба́цала

царь - цари́ца - ры́цари

та́нец - танцо́р - та́нцами

цвет - цветы́- цве́тику

гуцу́л - цу́гом - цука́т

царёк - клёцки - зацвёл

юне́ц - ку́цую - юсти́ция

грани́ца - гра́ция - гости́ница

NEW WORDS:

УЧИ́ТЕЛЬ/НИЦА - *a teacher*   **БОЛЬНИ́ЦА** - *a hospital*

ЦВЕТЫ́ - *flowers*   **МЕДСЕСТРА́** - *a nurse*

To make it clear: A male nurse in Russian is «медбра́т».

Check that you put only one stress in each word; that you understand that «цветы́» is a plural form; that «учи́тель» is a male teacher.

d) What would you say in Russia if you wanted to:

say that I (Ната́ша) am your Russian teacher;

say that you like flowers;

ask your сосе́д whether he is a teacher;

ask where a hospital is;

ask my Mum whether she has flowers in the garden;

say that your aunt is a nurse and is at the hospital today;

say that you are not a teacher – you are a student;

find out whether this is Sovetskaya Street;

Check that you chose «ру́сская» for me and «учи́тель» for сосе́д; that you put «у́лица» in front of «Сове́тская».

How does it sound? Technically, /ц/ does not belong to the hushing sounds (like /ж/, /ч/, /ш/), but it does do a lot of things exactly like them. For example, **«Ц» cannot be palatalised**, wherever it is, before two-in-one letters or not. Also, **there will be no /й/** sound in «Е» after «Ц», e.g., в больни́це /б а л' н' й ц э/.

Ex.2 a) Decoding Cyrillic:

цел - цела́

цеп - цепа́

цен - цена́

цех - це́дрой - процеди́л

цепь - це́пкая - зацепи́л

це́ль - це́лая - уцеле́л

прице́л - наце́лил - самоце́ль

целу́й - целу́ю - поцелу́йчик

цени́ть - цени́ла - самооце́нка

b) Let's try it in Russian. Say where the following buildings are in Tula (*they are matched* up to the correct streets). You can find them on the Internet if you are interested (add Ту́ла to your search to get the right places).

Tip! Both «у́лица» *and* «проспе́кт» *in Russian are* «**НА**»-*words. E.g.,* **на** у́лице. *When you put* «**НА**» *in front of street names, the words* «у́лица» *and* «проспе́кт» *need to have* «Е» *at the end, while the actual name can stay as it is, e.g.,* на у́ли**це** Сове́тская, на проспе́к**те** Ле́нина.

заво́д ТОЗ	у́лица Металли́стов
Пу́шкинский лице́й (шко́ла)	у́лица Пу́шкинская
Центра́льная по́чта	проспе́кт Ле́нина
магази́н «Ру́сский сувени́р»	у́лица Сове́тская
Моско́вский вокза́л	у́лица Вокза́льная
больни́ца № (но́мер) 5	у́лица Тимиря́зева
стадио́н «Арсена́л»	проспе́кт Ле́нина
Сберба́нк	у́лица Плеха́нова
Теа́тр дра́мы	у́лица Фри́дриха Э́нгельса

> **To make it clear:** You might have noticed that in Russian names, generic words (like у́лица, вокза́л, шко́ла, заво́д etc.) do not start with a capital, unless they start a sentence.

> **NEW WORD:** ЦЕНТР - *a centre*

b) Reading for meaning. Keep an eye on the endings of the new words.

Это не у́лица Куту́зова - у́лица Куту́зова в це́нтре.

Я хорошо́ зна́ю у́лицы Жу́кова и Шевче́нко.

В го́роде три больни́цы, но э́то не в це́нтре.

Магази́н «Ру́сский сувени́р» - на у́лице Сове́тская.

Я медсестра́, но в больни́це не рабо́таю.

У меня́ есть о́фис в Ту́ле, в це́нтре.

Еле́на и Жа́нна - учи́тельницы в шко́ле.

Цветы́ - в о́фисе, в ва́зе на столе́.

Check that you remember that there is no /й/ sound after «Ц».

> **To make it clear:** Sometimes you can see a dash in Russian sentences. It is a punctuation mark which is sometimes used between two nouns when there is no verb in the sentence.

c) Say it in Russian. Let's see how we can use our new words.

in the street	streets	Are you *(polite)* a nurse?	Is the school in Pushkinskaya Street?
in a hospital	hospitals	Is your *(polite)* hospital there?	I don't work in a hospital. And you?
in the centre	teachers (*f*)	I know streets in London.	Lenin Avenue is in the centre.

Check that "in the street" has «НА» *but "in hospital" has* «В».

d) Let's try it in Russian. Think of a phrase that the following people would say about where they work. Use «Я»-forms. Keep an eye on «В» and «НА».

учи́тель/ница, инжене́р, журнали́ст, медсестра́, профессор, пенсионе́р/ка, секрета́рь, студе́нт/ка

e) Find a person who is a teacher; has an office in the city centre; has a nurse in the family; has a house/flat in the city centre; is an engineer, has a hospital in their city/town; has flowers in the garden or in the office.

RUSSIASCOPE: **РУССКИЙ А́ДРЕС**

If you write to somebody in Russia, you must be familiar with those unusual Russian envelopes with both addresses on the front. If you are only expecting to see one of those, here are some tips for you.

Your address would appear in the bottom right corner, in order to leave some space for the sender's details in the top left corner. To understand what is what in a Russian address, you need to keep in mind that for a long time Russians wrote addresses in reverse order:

1) *country (Росси́я);*

2) *postcode (which is called «и́ндекс» and is made of six numbers and no letters);*

3) *name of the city/town (e.g., «г.Ту́ла» for «го́род Ту́ла»);*

4) *name of the street (e.g., «ул.Приу́пская» for «у́лица Приу́пская»);*

5) *number of the house or a block of flats (e.g., «д.9А» for «дом 9А»).*

6) *apartment number (e.g., «кв.41» for «кварти́ра 41»).*

In the 1990s, Russia officially changed the order in which addresses are written, with the name of the addressee first. As both orders are still in use, it is quite important to "decode" the abbreviations for «г.», «ул.», «д.» and «кв.». Note that in countryside addresses you can have the name of the region (о́бласть) followed by the name of the district (райо́н); and if «д.» is followed by a name rather than a number, it is likely to stand for «дере́вня».

Ex.3 a) Reading for meaning. Have a look at some of the envelopes that I received from my Mum and my Russian friends. Try to "decode" the abbreviations on them and read the addresses aloud in Russian.

How does it sound? We have discovered that the hushing sounds in Russian are in some kind of a different league. (Can you remember what is special about them?). There is one last thing to know: when Russians read «И» **after** «Ж» or «Ш», as the tongue is at the back of the mouth (for /ж/ or /ш/), **«И» sounds like /ы/** (I wonder whether the tongue does not have time to come back to the front . . .). For example, «машина» sounds like /м а ш ын а/. If your «ШИ» sounds like *she*, any Russian would understand you. The question is then – how important reducing your accent is for you. The same happens **after** «Ц» (did I mention that «Ц» is similar to hushers?), e.g., «цирк» (which means *circus*) sounds like /ц ы р к/.

Note that «Ч» is NOT affected by this, as, unlike /ж/, /ш/ and /ц/ which are hard (pronounced more towards the back), /ч/ is pronounced closer to the palate, so the tongue is close to the position needed for /и/. For example, Russian word «чип» would sound more or less like English *chip*.

b) **Try not to trip up!** Try to move your tongue slightly back when reading «Ж», «Ш» and «Ц» and . . . don't forget to smile to get /ы/ after them. Remember not to do this for «Ч».

шип - чип	ужи́ - учи́	цирк - чирк	ши́на - маши́на - машини́ст
ши́на - чи́на	межи́ - мечи́	ци́ник - чи́нит	живо́й - живо́т - живо́тик
ту́ши - ту́чи	пожи́л - почи́л	цита́т - чита́ть	ци́фра - цика́да - у́нция

NEW WORD: ЖИТЬ - *to live*

Check that you tried to move your tongue back to get /ы/ after /ж/.

> **WORTH REMEMBERING:** *Verbs that have only one vowel in them (monosyllabics) do odd things in Russian. (Does the verb "to eat" come to mind?) The verb «ЖИТЬ» is a good example too. To help you produce its «Я»-form, I am listing its three "tricks":*
>
> *1) extra «В» after «ЖИ»;*   Я ЖИВУ́ - *I live (I am living)*
> *2) «У» instead of standard «Ю»;*   *(sounds like /ж ы в у́/)*
> *3) **stress** on the ending («У́»).*

Ex.4 a) Reading for meaning:

– Я живу́ в го́роде.   – Я живу́ в Москве́. А вы?   – Живу́ я в до́ме на у́лице Сове́тская.

– А я в дере́вне живу́.   – В Ту́ле, живу́ и рабо́таю.   – А я на проспе́кте Ле́нина.

     Check *that you have remembered about reading «ЖИ» at the back of the mouth.*

b) Say it in Russian. Let's think of where people can live.

in a city (town)	in London	in a house	in the High Street
in the countryside	in Moscow	in a flat	in Regent Avenue
on a farm	in Somerset	in a room (e.g., in a hostel)	in Oxford Road

     Check *that you remember that actual street names in Russian follow the word «у́лица» and mostly remain unchanged, e.g.,* на у́лице Хай Стрит.

c) It's your turn. Think how you would explain to a Russian where you live. Remember that

some non-Russian names (which do not look like masculine or feminine) do not take «Е» and stay as they are. For example, I can say: Я не живу́ в Ло́ндон**е**. Я живу́ в го́роде Гла́стонбери в Сомерсе́т**е**. У меня́ есть дом на у́лиц**е** А́ндервуд Ро́уд. If you work with someone else, you can take turns making statements and responding to them, using «то́же» or making a different statement starting with «А», e.g., Я живу́ в кварти́ре в це́нре. – А я живу́ в до́ме. (or Я то́же живу́ в кварти́ре, но не в це́нтре.)

«Гости́ница «Москва» в Туле»

> **NEW WORDS:**   ГОСТИ́НИЦА - *hotel*
>
>   НО́МЕР - *room (in a hotel), a number*
>
>   ТУТ - *here*

Ex.5 a) Reading for meaning. See whether you can follow three small conversations at a hotel reception.

- Алло. Это гости́ница «Москва»? Мо́жно но́мер на за́втра, пожа́луйста? – Да, коне́чно. Оди́н? – Да, оди́н челове́к. – Хорошо́. Ва́ша фами́лия? – Стру́гова. Всё, да? – Да. Всё. До за́втра.
- Ваш па́спорт, пожа́луйста. – Вот. Пожа́луйста. Я не ру́сский. Я англича́нин. В Москве́ я тури́ст. Я живу́ в гости́нице «Росси́я». Мой ру́сский друг сего́дня тут, в но́мере 10. – Мину́тку.
- – Здра́вствуйте. Моя́ фами́лия Цибу́льский. У меня́ тут есть но́мер на сего́дня.
  – Извини́те, у меня́ ничего́ нет. А у вас есть а́дрес? Где у вас но́мер?
  – В гости́нице «Интури́ст», но а́дрес я не зна́ю. У меня́ есть телефо́н.
  – А-а-а. Это гости́ница «Тури́ст». А «Интури́ст» в це́нтре на у́лице Тверска́я.
  – Я всё понима́ю. Извини́те, пожа́луйста.
  – Ничего́. Вот ка́рта. Это тут.
  – Спаси́бо.

> **To make it clear:** Russians use the verb «жить» when they speak about a stay of more than one night in a hotel. E.g.: В Москве́ я живу́ в гости́нице «Ко́смос». – *In Moscow I am staying at the Cosmos hotel.*

---

b) Jog your memory or find in the conversations above:

your surname	Can I have a room?	I am English.	I haven't got anything.
a room for today	Your passport, please.	one person	I understand everything.
a room for tomorrow	I am staying in a hotel.	My friend is here today.	I am sorry. – It's OK.

c) Let's try it in Russian. Think of how you would ask for a room in a Russian hotel, what can you say about yourself and what questions you would ask. If you work with someone else, try a short conversation about reserving a room, giving your details and your passport and asking, for example, about tea in the room or water, how much it is, whether there is a restaurant in the hotel or a souvenir shop etc. Enjoy speaking Russian.

«Цирк в Туле»

> **NEW WORD: ЦИРК** - *a circus*
>
> **СТА́НЦИЯ (метро́)** - *underground station or a small station without a terminal building (which would be «вокза́л»)*

Check that you tried to move your tongue back to get /ы/ after /ц/.

d) What would you say in Russia if you:

don't know where your hotel is;

are looking for the underground station;

are asking whether this is a circus or a theatre;

would like to reserve a room for today;

are staying in a hotel in the centre;

don't know hotels in Moscow;

need to say that you do not understand;

need to know whether this is a r/w terminal or an underground station.

> **WORTH REMEMBERING:** *You might remember that, when we were talking about eating, we mentioned that «-ШЬ» in «Ты ешь?» links verbs to «ТЫ». Though «я ем» did not follow the regular pattern for «Я»-forms, «-ШЬ» does work for other verbs. Thus, to ask somebody whether they do something, we need to start with a dictionary form of the verb as always (e.g., работать), get rid of «-ТЬ» as before (as with the «Я»-form) and add «-ЕШЬ». E.g.: РАБО́ТА**ТЬ** - ТЫ РАБО́ТА**ЕШЬ**. Note that «Ты работаешь?» can be translated in two ways – Do you work? / Are you working?*

Check that you keep «А» in front of «-ЕШЬ»,
pronounce «Ш» at the back and stick to one stress only.

Ex.6 a) Reading for meaning. Remember to raise the tone of your voice at the end of questions.

– Ты рабо́таешь на по́чте?

– Нет. Я рабо́таю в магази́не.

– Журна́лы чита́ешь?

– Нет, не чита́ю. У меня́ вре́мя нет.

– Ты Ло́ндон зна́ешь?

– Зна́ю, но не о́чень хорошо́.

– Понима́ешь, как игра́ть в ша́хматы?

– Да, понима́ю. А ты?

– А в те́ннис хорошо́ игра́ешь?

– Игра́ю непло́хо. А ты игра́ешь?

– Ты пла́ваешь?

– Да. Я люблю́ пла́вать.

Check that you noticed that the verb endings in the answers are different from the questions;
that you remember that «У меня́ нет вре́мени» is more grammatically correct.

b) Question time. Use my suggestions below to make questions. If you work with someone else, take turns asking and answering. Note that it is easier to stick to the English word order when speaking.

рабо́тать - заво́д

чита́ть - газе́ты

игра́ть - гольф

знать - англи́йский алфави́т

рабо́тать - за́втра

понима́ть - испа́нский язы́к

игра́ть - ша́хматы

чита́ть - кни́ги

пла́вать - хорошо́

> **To make it clear:** We have not yet made a question with «Я люблю́». The reason is that the verb "to like" (люби́ть) is a different type of verb. So, we will start handling it once we are comfortable with the first type verbs. For now you can do the familiar trick with *And you?*. E.g., Я люблю́ спорт. А вы? or Я не люблю́ абрико́сы. А ты?

c) Let's get this right. Try to think which questions could have been asked to get the answers below. Note that not all answers have «Да» or «Нет», thus questions might require «или» or one of the question words.

E.g., – ....
– Я рабо́таю на по́чте.

– Где ты рабо́та**ешь**?
– Я рабо́та**ю** на по́чте.

– ....?
– Да. Я рабо́таю сего́дня.

– ....?
– А я не люблю́.

– ....?
– Нет. Я не понима́ю.

– ....?
– Да. Я зна́ю испа́нский хорошо́.

– ....?
– Сего́дня «Дэ́йли Те́леграф».

– ....?
– Я игра́ю на стадио́не «Дина́мо».

– ....?
– Нет. Я - медсестра́ в шко́ле.

– ....?
– Да. Сомерсе́т я зна́ю отли́чно.

– ....?
– Да, пла́ваю непло́хо.

– ....?
– Я ем всё - мя́со, сыр, хлеб, фру́кты.

d) Now it's your turn. Now you need to ask your own questions! The easiest way to ask a question is to think of a Russian verb, put «ТЫ» in front, change the verb ending and you have a question! Anything else is a bonus. If you are learning with someone else, you can play a Yes and No Game (игра́ в «Да» и «Нет»). One of you starts by asking questions using the same verb till you get a «ДА» answer. (E.g., Ты рабо́таешь в магази́не? – Нет. – Ты рабо́таешь на заво́де? – Да.) Then you swap, and the one asking questions can keep the same verb or change it. You might want to agree that if you do not get a «ДА» after, say, three goes, you can ask a direct question, e.g., Где ты рабо́таешь? Enjoy it!

> **NEW WORDS:** ИНОГДА́ - *sometimes*
>
> МНО́ГО - *a lot, much*
>
> НЕМНО́ГО - *not much, a little bit*

Ex.7 a) Reading for meaning. Remember to find the verb first. You can underline the new words to remember them better. Try reading with the New Words box covered.

Я очень люблю́ кни́ги, но иногда́ чита́ю газе́ты.

А ты хорошо́ игра́ешь в те́ннис? – Нет, немно́го.

О́чень хорошо́ ты Петербу́рг зна́ешь. – Я там живу́.

Мо́жно хлеб? – Да. Ско́лько? – Немно́го, пожа́луйста.

За́втра игра́ешь на стадио́не? – Не зна́ю.

Я немно́го понима́ю ру́сский язы́к, но не всё.

Ты сего́дня мно́го рабо́таешь. Уста́ла?

А в ша́хматы ты игра́ешь? – Да, иногда́.

We noted before that not all phrases translate directly word for word. Sometimes they sound awkward in English, but when you know what the Russian phrase means, you can adjust it a bit for it to sound right in English. When Russians use «хорошо́» with verbs, for example, in English such phrases might appear as "you . . . . . . well" but also "You are good at . . . . . .", e.g., Ты игра́ешь в те́ннис хорошо́. – *You are good at tennis.* BUT: Ты сего́дня хорошо́ игра́ешь. – *You are playing well today.* The context is very important in understanding the meanings. Keep an eye on it.

Tip! You might remember that I advised you not to use numbers in front of nouns yet, as we need to know how to make them agree correctly. The words «мно́го»/«немно́го» have a similar issue before nouns: the noun endings would have to change to agree with them. For now, use «мно́го»/«немно́го» with verbs or in a separate phrase. E.g., Я мно́го чита́ю. or У меня́ есть цветы́ в саду́. Мно́го. This way you will stay grammatically correct.

b) Now it's your turn. Make a few sentences of your own using the three new words: иногда́, мно́го, немно́го. You can also add our old familiar «хорошо́» here too. The easiest way is to add them to the sentences you already can say. E.g., Я игра́ю в сну́кер иногда́. Or Я мно́го чита́ю в библиоте́ке.

> *WORTH REMEMBERING: One verb that we have not yet used with «ТЫ» is «ЖИТЬ» (to live). You might remember that it was a bit tricky when used with «Я» (try to list its three "tricks" to get «я живу́»). «ЖИТЬ» needs attention when used with «ТЫ» too – this time it has only one "trick" (as long as you know the first three) – the standard «-ЕШЬ»-ending uses «Ё» instead of «Е»: Ты живёшь в Москве́? Note that you still need to add «В» to its dictionary form (ЖИТЬ) and to put the stress at the end.*

Check that you remembered to move your tongue back in «живёшь» and to palatalise «В» before «Ё». From my experience, this is one of the trickiest verb forms to pronounce.

c) Reading for meaning:

– Ты живёшь в го́роде?
– Нет. В дере́вне.

– Где ты живёшь?
– В Ки́еве я живу́.

– Ты на проспе́кте Ле́нина живёшь?
– Нет. Я живу́ на у́лице Ле́нина.

Check that you started translating each phrase by finding the verb.

d) Find the person who . . . lives on a farm; stays in a hotel sometimes; likes the city; has a house in the country; lives in the city centre; works in London a lot; likes staying in a hotel. This is great to do as a group – you can go round asking everybody the same questions. Remember to change the verb ending when you answer!

How does it sound? If you happen to come across **the soft sign («Ь»)** after a consonant but **before a two-in-one vowel**, apart from indicating that the consonant before is palatalised, the soft sign has one more job: it stops the vowel losing its /й/ sound. Remember that /й/ is a strong sound in Russian. E.g., «компью́тер» sounds like /комп'**йу** тэр/.

Check that you understand that «Т» in «компью́тер» is not palatalised (the same as in «те́ннис»).

Ex.7 a) What's in a name? Read the names aloud – remember to say a tense /й/ sound after the soft sign (which is before a vowel here). You also need to palatalise the /н/ in «Нью».

Нью-Йо́рк, Нью-Ка́стл, Нью-Ме́ксико, Нью-фа́ундленд, Нью-Ка́стл-на-Тайне;

Татья́на, Таи́сья, Да́рья, Емелья́н, Ма́рья, Демья́н, Ната́лья, Марья́на

NEW WORD: КОМПЬЮ́ТЕР - *computer*

Check that your /й/ is tense after the Soft Sign.

WORTH REMEMBERING: *Any musical instruments in Russian are «НА»-words. This means that when we talk about playing them, we need «НА» in front of them (rather than «В», which we used with games), e.g., Я игра́ю* **на** *пиани́но. – I play piano.*

Unlike games, musical instruments get «Е» at the end, e.g., Я игра́ю **на** *гита́ре. «Пиани́но» is an exception – it never takes any endings (similar to «кино́» or «кафе́»). Russians use «НА» with computers too – I guess a keyboard looks a bit like an instrument, e.g., Я рабо́таю* **на** *компью́тере.*

Check that you remember that you say «Я игра́ю **в** *теннис_» with NO «Е» at the end.*

b) Let's try it in Russian. Think how you would ask somebody in Russian whether they play the following. If you are learning with someone else, you can answer the questions too. Make sure you have «Е» at the end (except «пиани́но»). E.g.: Ты игра́ешь **на** компью́тер**е**? You can make use of «иногда́» and «не/мно́го» too.

гита́ра, кларне́т, балала́йка, аккордео́н, мандоли́на, фле́йта, пиани́но, тромбо́н, орга́н, саксофо́н

Check that your «пиани́но» did not have «Е» at the end.

> **NEW WORDS:**
>
> ДРУЗЬЯ́ - *friends*   БРА́ТЬЯ - *brothers*

Check that you had a tense /й/ sound in «я» after the soft sign, and that you watched your stress.

To make it clear: «Друзья́» and «бра́тья» are "funny" (irregular) plurals – they need to be memorised, the same as «лю́ди» and «де́ти». If friends are only female, you can use straightforward «подру́ги». «Друзья́» applies to either male friends or a mix of boys and girls.

c) Question time. Think how you would ask somebody in Russian:

whether they have *(familiar)* brothers/ children/friends;

whether people in the hotel are tourists;

whether *(their)* brothers are in New York;

whether the children are at school;

whether Victor and Boris are friends or brothers;

whether they *(polite)* have friends in Moscow.

> **NEW WORD: ОНИ́** - *they*

Tip! As «И» at the end is linked to making plurals, think of «ОНИ́» as «он» with «И» at the end (for plural). Make sure that your stress is at the end – thus the «О» at the front is weak and unrounded, as in «она́».

d) Let's try it in Russian. Make sentences using «ОНИ́» and the words below in their plural form. Translate what you get. E.g., Они́ студе́нт**ы**. – *They are student*s. Keep an eye on which way you make plural – «Ы» or «И» or a "funny" (irregular) form. If you work with someone else, you can take turns asking questions (e.g., Они́ студе́нты?) and giving negative answers, picking a random alternative from the list (Нет, они - инжене́ры.)

студе́нт, инжене́р, студе́нтка, брат, учи́тельница, журнали́ст, челове́к, пенсионе́рка, англича́нка, друг, спортсме́н, акроба́т, ребёнок, подру́га, футболи́ст, спортсме́нка, пенсионе́р, тури́ст

To make it clear: Similar to «друзья́» and «подру́ги», plural forms of other words referring to females (e.g.: студе́нтки) would mean lots of females, while plural forms of male versions (e.g.: студе́нты) can mean either lots of boys or a mix of boys and girls.

*WORTH REMEMBERING: Similar to how words linked to feminines have «А» at the end, a lot of words which are **linked to plurals have «И» at the end**. For example, «мой» if referring to a few things has the form «мои́» (with a long «И»), «твой» turns into «твои́» and «ваш» will become «ва́ши» (Watch your stress). E.g., мой студе́нт - мои́ студе́нты, твоя́ су́мка - твои́ су́мки, ваш друг - ва́ши друзья́. As you see, the plural form of «мой», «твой» and «ваш» does NOT depend on gender or the way of making plural («Ы», «И» or "funny" plural).*

Tip! Make sure that «ва́ши» keeps its stress at the front while «мои́» and «твои́» have all the emphases on the «И». Try shifting your tongue back in «ва́ши», so «ШИ» sounds more like /ш ы/.

To make it clear: «Де́ньги» and «ша́хматы» are plural forms (by default) – they do NOT have a singular. It's good to remember to agree them correctly with other words, e.g., ва́ши де́ньги, мои́ ша́хматы.

Ex.8 a) Let's get this right. Respond to the following questions with «Нет» and say that here is one of those which is yours. E.g., Это ва́ши маши́ны? – Нет. Вот моя́ маши́на. Make sure that «де́ньги» and «ша́хматы» stay in plural.

Это ва́ши пакеты?	Ва́ши картины там?	Книги - твои́ или мои́?	Они́ твои́ бра́тья?
Это твои́ газеты тут?	Это твои́ де́ньги?	Это ва́ши дети?	Ва́ши ша́хматы там?
Они́ твои́ друзья́?	У меня - ваши ручки, да?	Фотоаппараты - твои́?	Матрёшки тут - ва́ши?

b) Now it's your turn. Think of what you have more than one of. Perhaps books, brothers, pens, dogs, friends, desks, bags, a chess set etc. Make a block of two sentences about each of those, e.g., У меня есть ко́шки. Они́ в саду́. If you work with someone else, you can ask blocks of two questions, e.g., У вас есть ко́шки? – Да, есть. – Где ваши кошки? – Они́ в саду́. Remember to take turns after each block of questions.

WORTH REMEMBERING: *You might have already been wondering whether the verb form for «ВЫ» would be different from «ТЫ»-forms with «-ЕШЬ». It is, but it is not completely unfamiliar to you. Do you remember that «здравствуйте» and «извините» had «-ТЕ» as a polite bit, which could come off to make less formal «здравствуй» or «извини»? This «-ТЕ» is in fact the polite bit for the Russian verbs too. The full **ending** for «ВЫ» forms is «-ЕТЕ»*, е.g., Валентина Николаевна, **вы** работа**ете** завтра? *BUT* Валя, ты работаешь завтра? *(Make sure that you keep your «А» before the ending and have only one stress, which might prove to be trickier with an extra syllable).*

Tip! «ВЫ» *can also be used to address more than one person.* Дети, сегодня вы плаваете.

b) Question time. Imagine a three-way conversation in which a friend asks you a question (using «ТЫ»-form) and you need to turn this question to somebody you have just met (using «ВЫ»-form). I will be your friend – see my questions to you below. You need to answer them about yourself (be truthful – you will remember it better) and then rephrase them in a formal way. You can even get an answer, if you work in a group of three. You need to change your endings every time you ask or answer. No double-stressing! E.g.: **Ты** работа**ешь**? – Да, я работаю в офисе. А **Вы** работа**ете**? You do not need to follow the word order in my questions - just make sure you do not lose any words.

Ты работаешь на заводе?

А газеты читаешь иногда?

Ты хорошо знаешь город?

А в футбол ты играешь?

Ты немного понимаешь русский?

Ты живёшь в квартире или в доме?

Что ты читаешь?

Ты где живёшь?

Завтра работаешь?

NEW WORDS: америка**нец** - *an American (m)*

америка**нка** - *an American (f)*

As this book is aimed at English speakers, I decided to introduce the words for somebody who is English (do you remember them?) and now for Americans, as, if Russians hear somebody speaking English, they are most likely to ask «Вы англичанин/англичанка?» or «Вы американец/американка?» If you are not English or American, you might want to learn a Russian word for your nationality. If you don't see it in the table below, you can look it up in the dictionary or on the Internet and fill it in in the blank row. Make sure you choose the correct version for yourself – a lot of male forms have «-ЕЦ» at the end, while most of female nationalities have «-КА». The table is NOT for you to learn but just to give you an idea.

Country	Nationality (male)	Nationality (female)	Language
Испа́ния	испа́нец	испа́нка	испа́нский
Ита́лия	италья́нец	италья́нка	италья́нский
Герма́ния	не́мец	не́мка	неме́цкий
Фра́нция	францу́з	францу́женка	францу́зский
По́льша	поля́к	по́лька	по́льский
Ирла́ндия	ирла́ндец	ирла́ндка	ирла́ндский (гэ́льский)
Уэ́льс (Wales)	валли́ец	валли́йка	валли́йский
Шотла́ндия	шотла́ндец	шотла́ндка	шотла́ндский (гэ́льский)
Кита́й (China)	кита́ец	китая́нка	кита́йский
Ту́рция	ту́рок	турча́нка	туре́цкий

Check that you noticed that neither languages nor nationalities start with the capital.

c) Now it's your turn! Try to make phrases about nationalities of the people whom you know. For example, I can say: Я ру́сская, а мой муж – англича́нин. У меня́ есть друг, он украи́нец. Моя́ подруга Ольга – ру́сская. В Гластонбери у меня́ тоже́ есть подру́ги. Они́ англича́нки. If you would like more practice, speak about celebrities, famous sportsmen etc.

d) Step-by-step guide to a conversation in Russian. A few units back we had a go at starting a conversation with a stranger at a party in Russia. Having learnt a few things since, like formal *your*, plurals and verbs, we can expand what we can say. Think which *questions* you could ask a Russian whom you have just met (to find out about work, where they live, family, hobbies and interests, etc.) This is great to do with someone else – just remember to take turns. Unless you are a teenager, you are better sticking to formal Russian (вы, у вас, ва́ш/а/и) – though you can imagine talking to ма́льчик Са́ша to practice your informal versions.

1. Introduce yourself and think how you can find out the other person's *name* (А вы?).

2. Say your *nationality*. You can mention languages and say you understand Russian a little bit. Don't forget to ask the other one whether he/she is Russian (choosing the right form, male or female).

3. Discuss *work*. Remember to swap questions.

4. Speak about where you *live*. Ask whether your new friend lives in a town or a village or has a flat or a house (you can find out about a garden too).

5. Talk about your *family* and turn the question to your partner (А у вас?).

6. Talk about *hobbies* (ask whether they play sports or musical instruments; you can talk about pets, about what you like/don't like and turn the question the other way.)

Keep talking – this is the only way to learn to speak. Keep thinking Russian – the more often you come back to what you are learning, the better you remember. Finally, make it relevant. Don't make it up – our brains do not want to hold information which is not important. Talk about what you do; think about real people: your friends and family, your neighbours, people at work – what would they say if they spoke Russian.

For now, it is «Всего́ хоро́шего» from me. Quite often, if Russians agree to call each other, they can say «Позвоню́.» at the end of the conversation. As you can tell, this is a «Я»-form of a verb (with «Ю» at the end) – it means *I'll call*. «Позвоню́.» is only used when you are intending to call, rather than a standard farewell. Note there is no «А» before «Ю». I cannot say it to you, as we communicate via the book, not over the phone. So I will settle on «**До встре́чи.**» until the last unit.

Something old, something new (*revision of unit 8*)

Привет. Как дела́ у тебя́ сего́дня? Ничего́? At the start of the last unit, I was ill, if you remember (Боле́ла). Fortunately, today I can say «Всё хорошо.», as I am better, and the Russian word for *better* is going to be our new reply to «Как дела́?» – «**Лу́чше**» (meaning *Better*). It can be used to say *It is better.* or *I am/He is/etc better*; do not use «я», «ты» or «он/а́» or other similar words with it, though. It works best as a one-worder, a bit like «Мо́жно». We can use it as an answer and as a question. E.g.: Лу́чше? – Да. Сего́дня лу́чше. Спаси́бо. Russians only use «Лу́чше» as an answer to «Как дела́?» if something was not quite right the last time the person saw you (like being ill). Let's give it a go.

Я: Здра́вствуй.

Ты: ....

Я: Как дела́?

Ты: .... А.................. ? Я зна́ю - ты боле́ла.

Я: Сего́дня лу́чше. Спаси́бо.

Today we are planning to finish the last two letters of the Russian alphabet, which means you will be able to recognise all 33 Cyrillic letters. I am feeling excited. Are you?

GROUP I (The Easy): **Мм, Тт, Кк, Аа, Оо**

GROUP II (The Tricky): **Сс, Нн, Вв, Рр, Ее, Уу, Хх** (*like . . . but . . .*)

GROUP III (Funny Shapes): **Ээ, Яя, Лл, Дд, Ии, Йй, Бб, Зз, Пп, Гг, Чч, Шш, Жж, Фф, Ёё, Юю, Цц**

GROUP IV (The Strangers): **Ьь, Ыы**

Here they are, 31 of them, how they would appear in the Russian alphabet. Find our new «Ц» here.

А Б В Г Д Е Ё Ж З И Й К Л М Н О П Р С Т У Ф Х Ц Ч Ш . . . . . . Ы Ь Э Ю Я.

As we have finished all Russian vowel letters, shall we start our revision with vowels today?

1. How many Russian letters produce vowel sounds? Can you pick them from the alphabet?

2. You might remember that eight of them make *four* pairs following the same pattern. Can you name them?

3. Which of the vowels indicate palatalisation of the consonants before?

4. What do we call «Е», «Ё», «Ю» and «Я»? Why?

5. How do we read two-in-one letters before the soft sign?

Ex.1 a) Decoding Cyrillic. Watch how you read two-in-one letters: at the start of a word, after a vowel, after a hushing sound and «Ц», and after an ordinary consonant. Watch your stresses – there are no particular patterns within strings.

шёл - сёл - пьём - наём
пять - пьян - паял - ялая
юшка - клюшка - парашют - шуруют
где - угодье - гадает - ежегодное

бьют - дебют - юбок - обоюдно
ёрзал - озёрное - жёрнов - жнивьё
язва - вяжет - веял - деревья
орех - ехал - похмелье - хромое

b) Just read and recognise. Keep an eye on the /й/ sound when reading two-in-one letters!

интервью, юбилей, барьер, миниатюра, медальон, антрепренёр, бильярд, парфюмерия, юмор, партнёр, карьера, биография, иллюзия, павильон, Брюссель

6. What are the *THREE* ways Russian nouns can make plurals?

7. Name the three sounds at the back of your mouth which are followed by «И» in plural.

8. What does «И» indicate if it follows a consonant?

9. Try to remember the *TWO* words which are plural by default and have no singular form.

c) Let's get this right. Here is the list of some Russian plurals. You have three challenges for each of them: 1) mark the stress (it is the same as in singular, unless it's an exception) and read aloud; II) look which way the plural was made («Ы», «И» or "funny"); III) work out its singular (if it has one).

квартиры, ёлки, люди, студенты, фрукты, друзья, матрёшки, студентки, пенсионеры, дети, яблоки, выходы, компьютеры, деньги, конфеты, подруги, шахматы, туристы, братья, книги, фотоаппараты

Check that you realised that «деньги» and «шахматы» haven't got a singular form.

10. What makes Russian hushers different from the other consonants?

11. Is /ц/ classed as a husher?

12. In which way is /ц/ similar to the hushing sounds?

Ex.2 a) Watch your stress! Note that «E» does not produce the /й/ sound after «Ц».

стар - ста́рец - ста́рица   коса́ - косе́ц - коси́ца   конь - коне́ц - ко́нница

гор - го́рец - го́рница   кора́ - коре́ц - кори́ца   ку́зня - кузне́ц - ку́зница

хлеб - хле́бец - хле́бница   гребу́ - гребе́ц - грибни́ца   двор - дворе́ц - дво́рницкая

пти́ца - пя́тница - пу́говица   хитре́ц - сыре́ц - чабре́ц

здра́вица - здра́вница - зарни́ца   ра́нец - ира́нец - иностра́нец

я́дрица - яи́чница - ягоди́ца   лице́й - лицеме́р - лицеде́й

люби́мец - люби́мица - любо́вница   цветы́ - самоцве́т - соцве́тие

b) Jog your memory. Make sure that you read aloud.

у́лица, медсестра́, цветы́, больни́ца, центр, они́, гости́ница, проспе́кт, но́мер, учи́тельница

> **Check** *that you know where the stresses are and would remember them*
> *when they are not marked.*

13. Out of the list above choose the *two* «НА»-words. Do you remember the others that we had?

14. What usually comes first in Russian: words like «у́лица» and «проспе́кт» or the actual street names?

15. Does the actual street name have to take «E» at the end when the word «у́лица» does?

16. What do the following abbreviations in the Russian address stand for: «г.», «ул.», «д.», «кв.»?

17. What if «д.» is followed by a name, instead of a number?

c) Let's try it in Russian. Say that the following people/things are in the following places. Watch «В» and «НА», as well as plurals.

a nurse - in hospital   avenue - in the centre   friends - at work

computers - in the office   a teacher - at school   tourists - in the hotel

brothers - at the stadium   children - in the garden   people - in the street

apples - on the plate   they - in the room *(in a hotel)*   money - in the bag

> **Check** *that "at work" came out as* «на рабо́те» *and "in the garden" as* в «саду́».

d) Let's try it in Russian. Similar to what we did with a pen and other objects in the last unit putting it inside or on top of things, you can work with plurals this time. DO NOT use plurals as locations yet – they would require a different ending. For now, stock up on pens, pencils, apples, books etc., or you can use images on the Internet. E.g., Ру́чки в коро́бке. or Докуме́нты на столе́. You can make sentences about people too. Once you are comfortable, move on to the blocks of two sentences, e.g.: Докуме́нты - на столе́. Стол – в ко́мнате. OR На карти́не – де́ти. Карти́на – на стене́.

Ex. 3 a) Try not to trip up! Watch your hushing sounds + /ц/. Give yourself time to get them right.

жа́рил - ша́рил - цари́л

чини́л - цени́л - жени́л

шприц - шни́цель - шлёпанцы

лы́жница - но́жницы - худо́жница

чепе́ц - черепи́ца - чаровни́ца

каши́ца - божни́ца - горчи́ца

са́женец - царе́вич - швейца́р

цвето́чка - цепо́чка - цы́почки

мы́шца - моло́чница - роже́ница

ключи́ца - кружевни́ца - шелко́вица

18. Is Russian /ш/ shorter or longer than English *sh*?

19. How do Russians read «ЖИ» and «ШИ»? Where do you need to move your tongue?

20. How would «И» in «ЧИ» sound?

b) Decoding Cyrillic. In each line spot the word with «ЧИ» (as in *chin*) to know where *not* to think about moving your tongue back. Note that stress pattern in the second column is random.

тужи́ - туши́ - точи́

чиро́к - широ́к - жиро́к

пожи́ть - почи́ть - поши́ть

суши́л - сучи́л - служи́л

пружи́на - круши́на - кручи́на

жи́то - ши́то - Чита́

лучи́ - у́ши - лу́жи

ре́чи - реши́м - режи́м

ко́ржик - ко́рчик - ко́вшик

вороши́ть - ворожи́ть - воро́чить

21. How do we read «И» after «Ц»?

22. What is the difference between «вокза́л» and «ста́нция»?

c) Just read and recognise: If you are happy learning words and work with Russian a lot, you can pick a couple of useful words from this exercise to learn.

Tip! If you see «-ЦИЯ» in Russian words (except people's names) there is a good chance it might appear as "-tion" in English, e.g. традиция - *tradition. Don't take this as a rule, though.*

концéрт, мотоци́кл, дефици́т, экспеди́ция, инфля́ция, дисциплина, конферéнция, рецéпт, информа́ция, глицери́н, иллюстра́ция, револю́ция, инспéкция, организа́ция, марципа́н, регистра́ция, гиаци́нт, демонстра́ция, публика́ция, би́цепс, вентиля́ция, вице-президéнт, аукцио́н, инициа́лы, колле́кция, процéсс, парацетомо́л, федера́ция, энциклопéдия, ци́трус, делега́ция, модифика́ция

23. What do we put at the end of «ваш» when it is linked with words in plural?

24. What happens with «мой» and «твой» before plurals?

25. What if these are linked to a "funny" plural (like «де́ти» or «друзья́»)?

d) Let's get this right. Put the word in brackets in the correct form. Watch your stress.

Вот (ваш) ко́фе. Са́хар и молоко́ тут.

Это (ваш) учи́тельница? – Нет. Это дире́ктор.

Я живу́ в до́ме № 5. Это (мойу́) у́лица.

Это (ваш) кни́ги? – Да, мой. Я мно́го чита́ю.

У тебя́ есть паке́т? – Да, вот. – А су́мка (твой)?

Ты игра́ешь в те́ннис? – Да. Это (мой) раке́тки.

(Твой) де́ти сего́дня в шко́ле? – Нет, они́ в саду́.

А где (твой) друзья́ за́втра? – На стадио́не.

*Check that you try to move your tongue back when saying «ва́ши»,
but keep the stress at the front.*

e) Let's try it in Russian. Let's think of a situation in which you are trying to organise a trip or an activity for a group of Russians, and you need to check that they have all their things with them. Ask whether they have the following items or where their items are, e.g., У вас есть ру́чка? Or Где ва́ша ру́чка? Alternate these two structures and try not to trip up. Watch plurals and singulars, as well as masculines and feminines.

bags, water, pencils, fruit, telephone, notebook, documents, apples, guitar, books, passport, visas, box, plastic bags, map, computer

Reading Challenge: Револю́цио́нная

26. What do all the verbs that we have learnt have at the end of their dictionary form (infinitive)?

27. What are the two ways of translating the verb «жить»?

28. Try to remember the three "tricks" to make its «Я»-form: 1) an extra letter « . . . »; 2) different ending « . . . »; 3) the stress falls on « . . . ». (Have you got «я живу́?») Well done!

Check that you tried to move your tongue back in «жить» to sound more like /ж ы т'/.

Ex.4 a) Let's get this right. Read the following «Я»-forms and then make their dictionary forms. E.g., Я рабо́таю. (*I work/I am working*) – рабо́тать (*to work*). Watch that you put only one stress, and that it is in the same place (unless you have «жить»).

Я чита́ю.

Зна́ю.

Я пла́ваю.

Я игра́ю.

Я не рабо́таю.

Я живу́.

Не понима́ю я.

b) Let's get this right. Match the people on the left to what they say on the right. If you work with someone else, have only one column in front of you, covering the other. The one who is looking at the right column starts by reading a phrase for the other to work out who, from their list of people on the left, could say that. They need to check by asking, for example, «Вы - клóун?» (with «О» longer than «У»). The first person needs to respond with «Да» (or «Нет») and repeat their initial phrase without reading. Take turns.

КТО?	ГДЕ?
Я дóктор.	Я рабóтаю в цирке.
Я клóун.	Я в университéте. Я немнóго рабóтаю в кафé.
Я русский.	Живý я в Манчéстере. У меня есть друзья в Лóндоне.
Я студéнтка.	Я в банке рабóтаю, в óфисе.
Я мéнеджер.	Сегóдня я рабóтаю в больнúце.
Я пенсионéр.	Я мнóго рабóтаю на завóде, но завтра я в óфисе.
Я актёр.	Дóма я. Живý в дерéвне. Люблю рабóтать в саду.
Я англичáнка.	Рабóтаю в теáтре, иногдá в кинó.
Я инженéр.	Я живý в Москвé на улице Тверскáя.

Check *that you tried to read «ЖИ» and «ЦИ» as /ж ы/ and /ц ы/.*

29. Why do Russians need different verb endings for «Я» and «ТЫ»?

30. What "trick" does the verb «жить» play in the «ТЫ»-form?

c) Let's get this right. Mark the stresses in the list of verb forms below. Add one more word which would agree with a form, for example, рабóтаю - я рабóтаю; рабóтать - люблю рабóтать, знáешь - ты знáешь.

читаешь, живу, ест, играть, не знаю, понимаешь, люблю, ем, живёшь, не играю, плавать, работаешь, читать, не люблю

31. Do you need «В» or «НА» after «игрáть» before a sports game? Do we add «Е» to the end?

32. What do we put after «игрáть» before musical instruments? Do we need «Е» at the end here?

33. Which musical instrument does *not* take any endings in Russian? Do you remember other Russian words that do not take any endings?

d) Now it's your turn. Make questions about playing games or musical instruments. Keep an eye on «В» or «НА» and watch the end of the nouns. E.g.: Ты игрáешь **в** футбóл_? or Ты игрáешь **на** гитáре? Use the list below. If you work with someone else, you can give answers too. Make sure that you take turns.

Tip! In «ре́гби» «Р» is not palatalised, similar to «те́ннис». Also, «ре́гби» would not change its ending. Can you explain why?

кларне́т, те́ннис, кри́кет, балала́йка, аккордео́н, баскетбо́л, ка́рты, гольф, гита́ра, тромбо́н, бо́улинг, мандоли́на, сну́кер, ша́хматы, бейсбо́л, пиани́но, сквош, ре́гби, фле́йта, орга́н, билья́рд, пинг-по́нг, саксофо́н, волейбо́л

34. What ending do Russian verbs take when they are linked to «вы»?

(?) 35. What do you need to do to the standard «-ЕТЕ» ending when you ask where people live?

Ex.5 a) Let's get this right. Judging by the context, choose «ТЫ» or «ВЫ» and the appropriate verb ending.

У вас мно́го книг. .... мно́го чита́........?   Ма́льчик, ... зна........, где тут шко́ла?

Приве́т. Сего́дня игра́ .... в баскетбо́л?   Извини́те, ... рабо́та........ в больни́це?

Добро́ пожа́ловать в Ло́ндон .... зна....... го́род?   Фёдор Харито́нович, ... игра́......... на гита́ре?

Это ва́ша сестра́? А .... то́же жив....... в дере́вне?   ...... хорошо́ понима .... ру́сский язы́к. Ты ру́сская?

b) Jog your memory:

иногда́, мно́го, немно́го, пото́м, тут, они́, ру́сский, ру́сская, англича́нин, англича́нка, америка́нец, америка́нка

c) What would you say in Russia if you wanted:

to say that you	*ask somebody (а вы-person) whether they*
are not English – you are American;	know where the Moskva Hotel is;
understand Russian a little bit;	are staying here;
are not Russian but your teacher *(female)* is;	work at the hospital;
don't live in London; you are in a hotel today;	sometimes play chess;
know that your friends are at a café afterwards;	play a guitar a little;
like flowers and have a lot in the garden;	understand everything;
are glad you know a bit of Russian.	read newspapers.

d) It's your turn! Try to think what you would say if somebody says/asks the following in Russian. See whether you can do it fairly quickly. Great to do with someone else without looking in the book when answering.

Понима́ешь всё?	Извини́те.	Ты игра́ешь в те́ннис?
Вы америка́н/ец/ка?	У вас есть де́ньги?	Вот, пожа́луйста.
Я в о́фисе рабо́таю. А вы?	На гита́ре игра́ешь?	У меня́ есть соба́ка. А у тебя́?
У вас есть ру́чка?	Спаси́бо.	Вы зна́ете, где гости́ница «Росси́я»?
Вы живёте в дере́вне?	Ты ешь мя́со?	Вы хорошо́ пла́ваете?

d) Let's try it in Russian. Today you are going to be somebody else – you can be anybody and live anywhere (you can choose a Russian name and a Russian city if you wish). Think of the following: work (if any), where you live, family and hobbies. Write down the key words on a piece of paper. As you need to say it all in Russian, it might be better to write the key words in Russian too, but you can do it in English if writing is not your priority. If you work on your own, you can follow our last step-by-step guide at the end of the last unit and speak about who you are and what you do. Then put together some questions which you could ask when meeting a Russian. If you work with someone else, ask questions and give answers at the same time. Try to remember what the other person says. When you finish, swap the pieces of paper where you wrote the key words, and check how much you managed to find out.

9

Is Red Square big?

WHAT'S THE PLAN?

► to recognise and use the last two letters of the Russian alphabet (Урá!);

► to learn more Russian words;

► to find out why Red Square is called *Red*;

► to use verbs to speak about your friends and family;

► to see what the Russian Duma is supposed to do;

► to find out about Russian words that describe things;

► to get acquainted with the "mysterious" neuter;

► to find out why the Bolshoi Theater was named that.

Let's try filling the last gaps in the Russian alphabet first, to bring it all together.

GROUP IV (The Strangers) «Щ щ»

Our new letter «**Щ щ**» gives us **a long palatalised hushing sound**. The easiest way to pronounce it is to say *Welsh sheep* in English. It is exactly how Russian «Щ» should read: close to the palate and slightly long.

How does it sound? The immediate question is what we need to do to make our new «Щ» and the old familiar «Ш» sound different. We more or less have the answer already in how we have been trying to pronounce /ш/ – **more towards the** *back* **of your mouth and shorter than the English** *sh*. This is the main difference, as our new

> **«Щ» is the exact opposite** – it is **closer to the front** and to your palate and **is longer** than an ordinary English *sh* (the longer you make it the better it sounds). I actually think that the Stranger might be not the long and front «Щ» *(like in "Welsh sheep")*, but the short and back «Ш» which requires more effort – but this is only my opinion. Try these syllables first: ША - ЩА, ШУ - ЩУ.

To put your mind at rest, I need to mention that whichever way you pronounce your /ш/, Russians will understand you. Also, the long «Щ» is much less frequent and, to start with, you are likely to come across it in not more than half a dozen words. To be honest, I had to think hard to find enough words for your exercise to compare the two.

Ex.1 a) Try not to trip up! To make the words in pairs below sound different, you need to keep moving your tongue back (for «Ш») and forth (for «Щ»). The difference in length will help too.

НИШ - НИЩ	ПИЩУ́ - ПИШУ́	мошна́ - мощна́	лещ - лишь
КУШ - КУЩ	МОЩУ́ - МАШУ́	смешал - смещал	щу́рил - шу́рин
ПЛЮШ - ПЛЮЩ	ЛЕЩУ́ - ЛИШУ́	помешал - помещал	укрощать - украшать
ЧА́ША - ЧА́ЩА	РАСПУЩУ́ - РАСПУШУ́	мешанина - мещанина	веща́ть - ве́шать

b) Decoding Cyrillic. Make sure you read «Щ» long and close to the palate. You cannot make it too long – the longer the better. Note that the stress patterns in the right column vary.

ро́ща - гу́ща - то́лща - тёща   пи́ща - пища́ть - пища́л - пища́ла

хрящ - хрущ - хвощ - о́вощ   щу́пала - щу́плая - ощути́м - трущо́ба

щур - я́щур - щу́ка - щу́пал   треща́ть - враща́ть - отоща́ть - извеща́ть

свищ - прыщ - хлыщ - клещ   поща́да - неща́дно - пощади́л - пло́щадь

Check that you remember that «Дь» in the last word would sound like palatalised /т'/, similar to that in «тетра́дь».

«Пло́щадь Ле́нина в Ту́ле»

> **NEW WORDS:**
>
> **ПЛО́ЩАДЬ** - *a square (in a city)́*
>
> **О́ВОЩ** - *a vegetable*

Tip! «Площадь», *similarly to* «у́лица», *normally goes before the actual name (e.g.,* площадь Ле́нина*), though it can happen the other way round, like in* «Кра́сная пло́щадь» *(Red Square).*

RUSSIASCOPE: КРА́СНАЯ ПЛО́ЩАДЬ

In modern Russian the word «кра́сная» means "red". As a hefty inheritance of Soviet times, with red flags and the Red Army, a lot of Russian places carry this word (or part of it) in their names. Try these: го́род Краснода́р, Красноарме́йский проспе́кт, Краснознамённая у́лица, го́род Краснoя́рск, Красногварде́йская пло́щадь, ста́нция Краснопре́сненская, Краснозвёздный проспе́кт.

*Red Square has the word «кра́сная» in its name for a very different reason, and it is in no way connected to the Reds or the Soviets, as the name goes a few centuries back, long before Bolsheviks appeared on the scene. The red brick walls of the Kremlin were not even there to start with – the Kremlin (*Кремль*) was originally made of wood and then of white stone. It was in the middle of the 16th century when Moscow became the capital of Russia, and Ivan the Terrible ordered the famous St. Basil's Cathedral to be built next to the Kremlin wall in a big empty space left from a huge fire. (*Кра́сная пло́щадь *is NOT inside the Kremlin, as many people tend to picture it, but next to it.) At that time, the word «кра́сный», in addition to denoting the colour, also meant "beautiful", so it is most likely that the name of the square originated from that, as it is a very impressive place.*

c) Reading for meaning. Make your «Щ» long. It is better to make it slightly longer than slightly shorter.

Это Кра́сная пло́щадь, а это Кремль.   Извини́те. Вы зна́ете го́род? А где Кра́сная пло́щадь?
Кра́сная пло́щадь – в Москве́ в це́нтре.   Это не пло́щадь Ле́нина. Это у́лица Ле́нина.

Я не знаю, это пло́щадь Револю́ции или пло́щадь Ильча́.

Вот река́ Москва́. Вот мост. Тут Алекса́ндровский сад. А пото́м Кра́сная пло́щадь.

How does it sound? As «Щ» is read close to the palate, pronouncing «ЩИ» is not an issue and sounds a bit like the English word *she* with a stretched consonant. It is «ШИ» /ш ы/ that we need to watch.

Ex.2 a) Let's get this right! Remember the tongue and the length.

шип - щип	пищи́ - пиши́	кле́ши - кле́щи	щита́ - ши́та	ни́ши - ни́щий
ча́ши - ча́щи	лещи́ - лиши́	ве́шки - ве́щи	лущи́ - лу́ши	су́ши - су́щий

мо́йщик - сва́рщик - сы́щик   лещи́на - лощи́на - морщи́на   я́щик - ямщи́к - я́дерщик
ба́рщина - тре́щина - же́нщина   тащи́ть - защи́п - защи́тная   щипо́к - щито́к - щи́колотка

> **WORTH REMEMBERING:** «ЩИ» *and* «ШИ» *are involved in making plurals. We have discovered that* «Г», «К» *and* «Х» *are always followed by* «И», *e.g.,* кни́ги, я́блоки. *Our hushers (*«Ж», «Ш», «Щ» *and* «Ч»*) also favour* «И», *e.g.,* о́вощи, да́чи. *The small complication is that in* «**ЖИ**» *and* «**ШИ**», «**И**» *sounds like* /ы/, *e.g.,* гаражи́, карндаши́ *(watch the stress in these two).*
>
> *This is important if you are learning to write and for your pronunciation but does not affect understanding.*

Tip! Some of my students remember the letters which produce hushing sounds as "three with the three bits" («Ж», «Ш», «Щ»*) and the fourth (*«Ч»*) looks a bit like a Russian handwritten four* ⁴. *Well . . . it worked for them. You might find a better way.*

To make it clear: Note that /ц/ is officially not a hushing sound and is NOT part of this rule. So if you come across the words where a plural ending would follow «Ц», you can comfortably put a standard «Ы» after it to make plural, e.g., гости́ница - гости́ниц**ы**.

b) Reading for meaning.

Ты ешь о́вощи? – Да. Я о́чень люблю́ о́вощи.

У тебя́ есть о́вощи на да́че? – Да, и цветы́ тоже.

Я ем о́вощи. Я вегетариа́нец. Мя́со я не ем.

Это ва́ши карандаши́? – Да, мой. – Мо́жно оди́н?

У вас есть ру́чки? – Нет, но есть карандаши́. Вот.

А где карандаши́? – Там, на столе́, в коро́бке.

Check that the stress in your «карандаши́» *is at the very end!*

c) Let's get this right. Fill in «Ы» or «И».

Вот ва́ши карандаш . . . ?	Я люблю́ о́вощ. . . .	Ва́ши подру́г. . . - учи́тельниц. . . . ?
У вас есть цвет . . . ?	Это гости́ниц. . . в Москве́.	А где тут гараж . . . ? – Там.
Не зна́ю я у́лицы. . . . . тут. А ты?	Ты фрукт. . . . ешь?	Что это? – Это да́ч. . . .

Check that your stress in «гаражи́» *and* «карндаши́» *was at the end, as well as in* «цветы́».

RUSSIASCOPE: **БОРЩ : ЩИ**

Борщ *is a world-famous soup associated with Russia. Not many people realise, though, that it actually originates from Ukraine, though all Russians happily cook it and enjoy it. It is often described as a "beetroot soup," which might not excite everybody, but beetroot is not the main ingredient and is only used to give* борщ *its lovely dark pink colour.* Борщ *is full of flavours and vegetable goodness, quite nourishing too; it is not pureed. Do you think you would try it?*

Russians love soup. Щи, *unlike* борщ, *is a traditional Russian soup, jokingly called "борщ with no beetroot", which is partially right. In Russia you can also come across summer soups which are served cold.* Приятного аппетита.

d) Now it's your turn. Say whether you like soup, fruit, vegetables, whether you eat meat, pasta, chocolate. Think how you would ask somebody in Russian whether they like them too (at the moment we have not learnt «ВЫ»-forms for eating or liking, so you can use «ТЫ»-form «ешь» or *And you?* to return questions). You can make phrases about your friends and family too. If you are learning with someone else, you might have a little conversation about what you eat/ don't eat and like/don't like. Make sure that you take turns.

How does it sound? As «Щ» is classed as a husher, «Е» and «Ё» (after it) do not affect its pronunciation but are read with no /й/, as one sound /э/ and /о/. So, «ещё» sounds as /й э щ' о/ (meaning *more*).

Ex. 3 a) Decoding Cyrillic. Remember to stretch your /щ/. Watch your stress too.

щека́ - щёки	пу́ще - гу́ще - сла́ще	я́щер - пеще́ра - уще́рб
щего́л - щёголь	бле́щет - хле́щет - ры́щет	щётка - щети́на - щеми́ть
щелка́ть - щёлкать	вещь - мощь - по́мощь	ще́бень - щебёнка - щерби́нка

Check that you understand that the soft sign does not change the way «Щ» is read.
It has a grammatical purpose here, similar to the soft sign in «ты ешь»
or «ты рабо́таешь».

NEW WORDS:

ЕЩЁ - *More. Also.*   **ХВА́ТИТ** - *Enough*

Check you stresses and that there is no /й/ after /щ/.

«Ещё» might feel like a funny little word, but it is most useful if you go to Russia or have Russian visitors. «Ещё» and «Хватит» are similar to «Можно» and are often used as one-word phrases, serving as a question and as an answer. The direct English translations in the box might sound a bit harsh (if not rude), but in Russia these words are commonly used, at the table, for example, when food is served, and are considered polite. We might need more words to put these phrases into appropriate English – «Ещё» might be better phrased as *Would you like some more?* (or *I would like some more please*), and «Хватит» might be closer to *That would be enough, thank you*. Of course, it depends on how you say it, but accompanied by a smile, I am sure it will be taken the right way. At a Russian dinner table these two are priceless.

b) Reading for meaning. Think how you would phrase these sentences in English for them to sound polite.

Ещё? – Да, пожáлуйста.   Мóжно ещё кóфе, пожáлуйста?   Хвáтит? – Извинúте. Мóжно ещё?

Хвáтит? – Да. Спасибо.   Ещё кофе? – Нет. Спасибо.   Ещё спагéтти? – Нет. Хвáтит.

To make it clear: To put «Ещё» and «Хáтит» into sentences, you need to change the endings of some words to make them agree correctly and be grammatically perfect. «Кóфе» and «спагéтти» work in the phrases above, as they do not change at all in Russian (like «кинó» and «пианúно»). You are safe with «Ещё» and «Хвáтит» as one-worders, and I would encourage you to actively use them.

---

c) Say it in Russian. Remember to raise the tone of your voice when asking.

Can I have (*some*) more please?   (*Would you like some*) more?   Yes, please.

(*That's*) enough. Thank you.   (*Is this*) enough?   No. Thank you

d) Question time. Think how you would ask in Russian for more, accept an offer or refuse it. You can try to think of what you might need more of: coffee, milk, sugar, pasta, bread, soup, tea, meat, butter (being a linguist, I picked those words that are not going to require changes to agree with «Ещё»). Remember to practice your Russian aloud. If you are learning with someone else, you can take turns offering each other more food and thinking of different responses.

🔵 *GROUP IV (The Strangers)* «Ъ ъ» is the *hard sign*

To put your mind at rest, I probably need to explain that we have left it till the very end, as it is the rarest letter in Russian. Similarly to the soft sign («ь»), it does not stand for any particular sound – it is a sign. If you think logically – if the soft sign indicates palatalisation (or the "softness") of consonants, the hard sign should indicate that a consonant before it is hard (that is plain, not palatalised). Historically, it was not exactly like that; in the past this letter («Ъ») commonly appeared at the end of masculines, that is after consonants. For example, «брат» looked like «братъ» and «хлеб» looked like «хлебъ». Soon after the 1917 Revolution, the Bolsheviks decided to get rid of this letter at the end of words, along with lots of other attributes of "old life". There were some words, though, where the hard sign («Ъ») was stuck in the middle. That is where you still can find it in modern Russian. As there are not many words like this, «Ъ» is the least used letter of the alphabet.

How does it sound? The only purpose of the *hard sign* now is to separate two-in-one vowels from the consonant before them, leaving it not palatalised. This is similar to how the soft sign does it in «компьютер», for example, but the hard sign appears closer to the front of a word (after a prefix, if you need to know). In both cases, «Я», «Е», «Ё» and «Ю» are read as TWO sounds, with a tense and strong /й/. It might help to think that you are making a little pause after the consonant and read the two-in-one vowel like at the start of the word. Have a go: «съел» /с й э л/ (meaning *He has eaten something*), which is different from «сел» /с' э л/ (meaning *He sat down*), where there is no /й/. This difference in pronunciation is subtle, and if you do not say it perfectly, the context will help Russians understand you. So, no worries – just try.

Ex. 4 a) Decoding Cyrillic. This is just for you to have an idea what to do with the hard sign («Ъ») if you happen to come across it. Remember to make the /й/ sound tense and rapid.

съел - съем - съест	подъём - объём - разъём	изъя́н - изъя́ть - изъяви́ть
съём - съёмка - съёмщик	подъе́зд - объе́зд - разъе́зд	въе́хал - въе́лся - въезжа́л
съе́ду - съеди́м - съедо́бно	подъе́хал - объе́хал - разъе́хались	объясни́л - объясня́л - объясне́ние

Check that you realise that «Д» at the end of «подъе́зд» is devoiced, and, as a matter of fact, so is «З» before it.

Finally, we need to differentiate between three shapes: the hard sign (Ъ), the soft sign (Ь) and the letter «Б». We have already established that «Б» is easily spotted by the "bar" at the top ("bar" starts with *b*). In the hard sign, the "bar" goes in the opposite direction – it sort of points at the consonant before it. This leaves the soft sign, which does not have any bars at all.

I am not giving you any words with the hard sign to learn – at this stage you are highly unlikely to use them in your speech. When the need arises, you will know how to pronounce them, as you now have the complete system of Russian letters and sounds.

Let's have a look at the whole of the Russian alphabet. Could you imagine before you picked up this book that you would be able to read all 33 Cyrillic letters without transcription or repeating after a recording? Are there a lot of English speakers who can do this? I think you need to be proud of yourself. We have put a lot of effort into getting to know how the Russian alphabet works, and I hope that it does not feel like a stranger to you now. You can sound out anything written in Russian now – people's names, street signs, names of Russian cities and villages, an underground map or a train timetable are not a mystery to you anymore. Hopefully, when you look at a Russian word now, it makes sense – some of them might even give you their meaning, once you have read them, as they might sound similar to something in English. I hope that you feel that Cyrillic has now stopped being a hindrance and has become a friend for your learning.

I also hope that when you look at a letter, you have lots of things popping up in your head that are connected with that letter – the sound (or sounds in case of two-in-one letters) it produces, the words where you have it, small little peculiarities of it (like being weak for some vowels, or being palatalised or devoiced for some consonants, or being a "husher"), where you can (or can't) find it (like no «Й» at the start), perhaps some special functions of it (like «Ы» making plurals, or «Е» indicating locations), and so on. Have a look at the full list. Go over it slowly, thinking about all these little things which give you a big picture. Take your time and enjoy it. You have done it! There are no more letters to come.

РУ́ССКИЙ АЛФАВИ́Т

А а	like *a* in *father*	К к	like *k* in *kangaroo*	Ф ф	like *f* in *foot*
	(but not as back or as long)	Л л	like *l* in *fall*,	Х х	like *k* in *kangaroo*
Б б	like *b* in *bar*		*(sometimes like l in lit)*		*(but gentler and flowing)*
В в	like *v* in *van*	М м	like *m* in *empty*	Ц ц	like *ts* in *its*
Г г	like *g* in *golf*	Н н	like *n* in *nut*	Ч ч	like *ch* in *child*
Д д	like *d* in *dog*	О о	like *o* in *for*	Ш ш	like *sh* in *shop* (but
Е е	like *ye* in *yes*		*(but not as back or as long)*		*more to the back and shorter)*
Ё ё	like *your*	П п	like *p* in *pot*	Щ щ	like *shsh* in *Welsh sheep*
	(but not as back or as long)	Р р	like *r* in *error* but rolling		*(long and close to the palate)*
Ж ж	like *s* in *pleasure*	С с	like *c* in *cinema*	Ъ ъ	*the hard sign*
З з	like *z* in *zebra*	Т т	like *t* in *tent*	Ы ы	like *i at the back* of your mouth
И и	like *ee* in *see*	У у	like *oo* in *moon*		*with teeth closed and a smile*
	(the longer the better)			Ь ь	*the soft sign*
Й й	like *y* in *employ* (with no o)			Э э	like *e* in *end*
	(but tense and rapid)			Ю ю	like *you*
				Я я	like *ya* in *yak*

As you see, I have split it into three fairly equal sections, as we did before. The middle one looks much smaller, as most of the sounds in it are similar to those in English and do not require extra comments. We will have another little go at it in the next revision section, but the main job is done.

I am also putting here a separate chart for Russian vowels, which we had before, so it is all in one place.

PAIRS OF RUSSIAN VOWEL LETTERS

Normal vowels: (+ «Ы»)	А а	Э э	О о	У у	Ы ы
	(*a* in *father*)	(*e* in *end*)	(*o* in *for*)	(*oo* in *moon*)	(like *i* at the back)

Two-in-one vowels (+ «И») :	Я я	Е е	Ё ё	Ю ю	И и
	(*ya* in *yak*)	(*ye* in *yes*)	(like *your*)	(like *you*)	(like *ee* in *see*)

Shall we move on now, as there are lots of meanings that we are still to discover behind Russian words, phrases and sentences. Our next step might be learning to use verbs to speak about other people, not just ourselves.

*WORTH REMEMBERING: We have already established that Russians use different endings at the end of the verb when they speak about themselves («Я»-form) or when they ask somebody («ТЫ»-form or «ВЫ»-form), e.g., я рабо́таю/ты рабо́таешь/вы рабо́таете. If they want to speak about somebody else, a third party, like a friend or a brother, the verb needs yet another ending. It's all because of Russian's flexible word order that requires "identifiers", bits to link words into sentences. As always, we **start with a dictionary form** (e.g., рабо́тать) and again take the end **«ТЬ» off, in order to add «-ЕТ»** this time. E.g.: РАБО́ТА**ТЬ** - ОН РАБО́ТА**ЕТ** / ОНА́ РАБО́ТА**ЕТ**. For once, it does not matter (in present tense!) whether you're talking about a male or a female.*

Check that you keep your «А» before «-ЕТ» and the same stress in all forms of the verb.

Ex.5 a) Reading for meaning. Remember to find the verb first.

Ми́ша рабо́тает в фи́рме «Бо́рус», в Ту́ле.

Ва́ша учи́тельница мно́го чита́ет?

На балала́йке она́ игра́ет, а не на гита́ре.

У меня́ муж - англича́нин, но ру́сский язы́к понима́ет.

А ваш дя́дя хорошо́ зна́ет францу́зский?

Брат в ша́хматы не игра́ет, он всё вре́мя на да́че рабо́тает.

Check that the tone of your voice went up in questions; that you understood «всё вре́мя» as "all the time".

b) Now it's your turn. My students really like this as a group activity, but if you work on your own, you can think about what you can say about people you know, using different Russian verbs (at least four), as well as «не/мно́го» and «иногда́». Make sure that you attach the right ending and note that we have not done this form for «люби́ть» and «жить» yet.

As a great group activity, pick a Russian verb, e.g., игра́ть, and make a sentence about yourself using it. For example, I can say: Я игра́**ю** в сну́кер немно́го. The next person on your right needs to speak about me, e.g., Наташа игра**ет** в снукер немного. Then they would need to make a phrase about themself, using the same verb. What would you say? Keep going until everybody in the group has said two sentences and the round comes back to me, who started it – then you can pick a different verb.

> **WORTH REMEMBERING:** *Let's have a look at what our monosyllabic «ЖИТЬ» is going to do. Try to remember its three "tricks" and how we say "I live" and "You live" in Russian. Similar to how the regular endings acquired dots in «ты живёшь» and «вы живёте», when we speak about a third party, the «-ЕТ»-ending gets dots too, e.g.,* ОН ЖИВ**ЁТ**/ОНА́ ЖИВ**ЁТ**.

> ***Check*** *that you tried to move your tongue back for «ЖИ» and palatalised your «В» before «Ё». If you forget to read your «В» closer to the palate, «живёт» will sound like «живо́т», which means "stomach".*

c) Question time. Think of the questions which need to be asked to get the answers below. We had a similar exercise in Unit 8, but with other verbs. Watch the endings and the palatalised «В»!

– .... ?
– Да. Мой брат живёт в Москве́.

– ....?
– Нет. Извини́те. Я не живу́ в Ло́ндоне.

– ....?
– Он в Новосиби́рске живёт. А ваш?

– ....?
– Моя́ тётя. Она пенсионе́рка и там живёт.

– ....?
– Тут в Ту́ле я живу́ в гости́нице «Москва».

– ....?
– Да. Живу́ в кварти́ре на у́лице Ле́нина.

> ***Check*** *that you have spotted a phrase where «Я живу́» would translate as "I am staying".*

d) Now it's your turn. Say in Russian where each of your family and friends live. Try to use as many different places as you can, for example: го́род, дере́вня, кварти́ра, у́лица, гости́ница and so on. Names of places will work too. Note that not all non-Russian names would get a «Е» at the end.

E.g.: Мама живёт в Ту́ле, в кварти́ре в до́ме 9 «А» на у́лице Приу́пская. А ле́том* в дере́вне. Ми́ша (или Михаи́л) живёт в доме, а не в кварти́ре, но это не в це́нтре. А работает он в це́нтре. О́льга, моя подруга, живёт в Ту́ле, но иногда́ она работает в Москве и живёт там в гости́нице.

---

* ле́том – *in summer*

NEW WORDS:

ПОМОГА́ТЬ - *to help*   ДУ́МАТЬ - *to think*

Check that you put the stress at the front in «ду́мать».

RUSSIASCOPE: **ДУ́МА** *is a term which you might occasionally hear on the news when some new Russian laws are mentioned. In modern Russia, the* Ду́ма *is the lower house of the Russian parliament (officially called the Federal Assembly of Russia). Following the collapse of the Soviet Union and the Russian constitutional crisis of 1993, the* Ду́ма *replaced the Supreme Soviet (the highest legislative body of the former USSR). The* Ду́ма *appeared as a result of the new constitution introduced by* Бори́с Е́льцин.

*Neither the idea nor the name are new. In ancient Russia, Dumas were assemblies of nobles and worked as advisory councils to Russian tsars and princes, not restricting them in any way, though. The last Tsar of Russia, Nicholas II, tried to establish a first representative Duma, but that was short-lived, and the 1917 Revolution put an end to the attempts to reinstate it. «*Ду́ма», *as you might have already worked out, comes from the verb «*ду́мать». *Let's hope that the democratically elected deputies of the new Russian* Ду́ма *do just that.*

Ex.6 a) Let's get this right. Use the correct ending for each person. Your main job, though, is to watch your stress (I have tried to group the verbs by their stress patterns). Make sure that you understand what you are saying – it might be good to translate each form, on your own or with someone else.

2nd syllable	*1st syllable*	*3rd syllable*	*2nd syllable*
ты игра́......	вы ду́ма.....	я не понима́.....	я жив....´
он чита́......	я зна́.....	он помога́....	я любл....´
рабо́та....	она пла́ва....	вы понима́.....	ты жив....

b) Say it in Russian. Watch your stress and your endings.

What do you *(familiar)* think?	She knows everything.	I am helping tomorrow too.
Does she help a lot?	I like swimming.	Do you *(polite)* think this is good?
I understand a bit.	He plays golf sometimes.	Does he live here?

Tip! *To link «*Я ду́маю» *or «*он/а́ ду́мает» *to the next clause, you can use «*что» *as "that", e.g.,* Я ду́маю, что он мно́го рабо́тает.

c) Let's try it in Russian. Let's try to "gossip" in Russian – we will say what people think about themselves. This is great fun to do as a group where a student on your left, for example, can say what they do a lot or well/badly (e.g., Я хорошо́ зна́ю ру́сский алфави́т.) and you turn to the person on your right and say what the other person thinks (Он ду́мает, (что) он хѳрошо́ зна́ет ру́сский алфави́т). Then you need to say something about yourself for it to be passed on by the person on your right. If you are on your own, you can make similar sentences about people whom you know.

Ex.7 a) Let's try it in Russian. You have four short paragraphs about four of my people from Tula (and its о́бласть). Each paragraph talks about a different person – you need to work with one at a time. Start by reading, sentence by sentence, and following what you are reading (remember to look for verbs). Keep track of the information, rather than memorising sentences. Then you can try to say what you remember about that person – stick to our step-by-step guide: 1) name; 2) lives; 3) works (if they do); 4) hobbies. Don't try to recreate my phrases – make your own, using the information you have. It is best not to do all the paragraphs in one go – we learn better if we keep coming back to what we have learnt.

Мой друг Михаи́л (мо́жно Ми́ша) живёт в Ту́ле. Он инжене́р, но он не рабо́тает на заво́де. Рабо́тает он в фи́рме «Бо́рус». Англи́йский он зна́ет непло́хо, но понима́ет не всё. Иногда́ он игра́ет на гита́ре. Ещё, он игра́ет в те́ннис, но немно́го.

Ле́на - моя́ подру́га. Живёт и рабо́тает она́ в Ту́ле. Она́ учи́тельница в шко́ле. Там она́ Еле́на Константи́новна. Ле́на о́чень хорошо́ зна́ет англи́йский язы́к. Она́ не игра́ет в футбо́л или в те́ннис, но она́ чита́ет кни́ги и отли́чно игра́ет на пиани́но. Ле́том[1] иногда́ пла́вает в реке́.

Ва́ня не живёт в Ту́ле, он студе́нт в Москве́, в университе́те. Ве́чером[2] он рабо́тает в газе́те. Ва́ня о́чень мно́го чита́ет и рабо́тает на компью́тере. Иногда́ игра́ет в бадминто́н на стадио́не. Немно́го зна́ет англи́йский язы́к, но ду́мает, что зна́ет пло́хо.

Валенти́на Никола́евна - моя́ ма́ма. Она́ пенсионе́рка, и живёт в кварти́ре в Ту́ле. Ле́том[1] она́ живёт в дере́вне. Она́ мно́го рабо́тает в саду́. Она́ хорошо́ зна́ет, как вы́растить[3] о́вощи, фру́кты и цветы́. Англи́йский она́ не понима́ет, но зна́ет англи́йский алфави́т.

---

[1] ле́том - *in summer*　　[2] ве́чером - *in the evening*　　[3] вы́растить – *to grow (something)*

b) Let's try it in Russian. You can do this exercise only after you have read all the paragraphs. If you were reading throughout the week or a while ago, it might be worth having another look through the paragraphs before you start. It is good to try answering the questions without reading from the texts. Note that to answer some questions you might need to name more than one person.

Кто не работает?

Лена играет на гита́ре или на пиани́но? А Миша?

Кто живёт в Москве?

Где работает Валенти́на Никола́евна?

Кто знает англи́йский язы́к?

Ваня играет в бадминтони или в те́ннис?

Кто живёт в дере́вне?

Кто пла́вает в реке́?

Ваня играет на компью́тере?

Кто много читает?

c) Now it's your turn! Think about somebody (a friend, one of your family, a neighbour, a celebrity etc.). Think how you would say a few things about them. Remember not to translate from English – use Russian verbs that you know and build your phrases around them. Also, try not to look things up in dictionaries, unless you absolutely have to. It might be easier to stick to the same plan:1) name; 2) lives; 3) works (if they do); 4) hobbies. Remember «-ET»/«-ЁT» at the end of your verbs.

Now we will have a look at some other words like «большо́й». In linguistics, words that describe things and people are called adjectives – for example, "little", "old", "new" and similar.

RUSSIASCOPE: **«БОЛЬШО́Й»** *in Russian means "big", "large" or "great". In size, the* Большо́й теа́тр *is indisputably impressive. With ten floors above ground and four basement levels, the* Большо́й теа́тр *houses more than 400 dressing rooms and has seating for 1,700 spectators, definitely justifying its name. More than that, the Bolshoi Ballet and Bolshoi Opera are amongst the oldest and most renowned ballet and opera companies in the world. Since 1776, when it was founded, it has grown into the world's biggest ballet company by far, having more than 200 dancers.*

«Это Большо́й теа́тр в Москве»

The Russian ballerina whose name is most known outside Russia is most likely А́нна Па́влова *(hopefully, not only because of the dessert named after her). Though* А́нна Па́влова *(Did you do one stress?) did dance on the Bolshoi's stage at the start of her career, she is mainly associated with St. Petersburg and Paris.*

Ticket prices vary and certain seats can be affordable; sometimes you can even buy them on the day. If you are in Moscow, even if you are not a regular theatre goer, it might be worth a visit, to see what it is like.

> **NEW WORDS:**   МОЛОДÓЙ - *young*
>
> БОЛЬШÓЙ - *big, large*   НÓВЫЙ - *new*
> МÁЛЕНЬКИЙ - *little, small*   СТÁРЫЙ - *old*

Check that you noticed that «большóй» and «молодóй» have the stress at the end, while the other three words have it at the very start (with «мáленький» having the same stress pattern as «кóмната»).

WORTH REMEMBERING: *The words in the box above are used to describe things or people. In Russian dictionaries, all **descriptive words (adjectives)** have «Й» at the end, but the ending in these words is made of TWO letters: it can be «-ÓЙ», «-ЫЙ» or «-ИЙ». E.g., большóй, нóвый, мáленький. This is NOT a choice we make – we learn these words with a particular ending.*

Tip! *You might have noticed that «-ÓЙ» has a stress mark over «Ó» – in descriptive words «-ÓЙ» always carries the stress. E.g.,* большóй, молодóй.

From our experience with Russian plurals, you might remember that «Ы» does not "agree" with the three sounds at the back of the mouth (/г/, /к/, /х/) or with the four hushing sounds (/ж/, /ш/, /щ/, /ч/). This rule works for adjectives too – it is called the "seven letter rule". For this reason we have «ИЙ» (rather than «ЫЙ») in «мáленький» and «рýсский». This rule is not that important to know here, as you will learn the ending as you learn an adjective, but as it works for other endings, it might be worth keeping an eye on.

Ex. 8 a) Say it in Russian:

Tula is a big city.	Do you have a small room *(in a hotel)*?
I have a small desk.	My very old friend *(male)* lives in the village.
Is your *(polite)* phone new?	The young engineer works at a factory.
I like the old park.	Can I have a big glass, please?

To make it clear: «Молодóй» *cannot* refer to a young child in Russia – that would be «мáленький ребёнок». It is normally used with young adults, e.g., молодóй человéк, молодóй учи́тель.

WORTH REMEMBERING: *In a dictionary, ALL descriptive words* (**adjectives**) *are found in their* **masculine** *form, that is, they are ready to describe masculine words* (большо́й паке́т, но́вый стол, ма́ленький сын). *Their gender is NOT fixed – it depends on which noun they describe. To describe* ***feminine words,*** *we need to put a feminine "identifier" on them. For that we take the* **LAST TWO** *letters off and add «-АЯ» instead, e.g.,* больш**а́я** су́мка, но́в**ая** кни́га, ма́леньк**ая** ко́мната.

To make it clear: The three masculine descriptive endings (-ÓЙ, -ЫЙ, -ИЙ) mainly behave in the same way and are normally replaced by «-АЯ» when describing feminines.

b) Reading for meaning. Make sure you put only ONE stress in each word and keep it in the same place in masculine and feminine forms.

молодо́й студе́нт - молода́я студе́нтка

но́вый каранда́ш - но́вая ру́чка

большо́й го́род - больша́я дере́вня

ру́сский язы́к - ру́сская матрёшка

ма́ленький сын - ма́ленькая до́чка

ста́рый друг - ста́рая учи́тельница

c) Let's get this right. Fill in the correct endings.

Твой ма́леньк....... брат сего́дня в шко́ле?

Молод...... челове́к, извини́те. А где Больш....теа́тр?

Это твоя́ но́в.... сумка? – Да. – Отли́чно.

Где ва́ша нов..... студе́нтка? – В кла́ссе, я ду́маю.

моя́ учи́тельница - русск...... , но живёт тут.

Твой стар..... дя́дя живёт в го́роде или в дере́вне?

To make it clear: Though Russian descriptive words (adjectives) agree with the gender of the words they are linked to, similarly to «мой», «твой» and «ваш», keep in mind that «мой», «твой» and «ваш» change only ONE letter (мо**я́**/тво**я́**/ва́ш**а**), while adjectives change the last TWO! E.g.: больш**о́й** - больш**а́я**, ма́леньк**ий** - ма́леньк**ая**. Also, note that adjectives prefer to keep their stress in the same place.

d) Now it's your turn. Think of how our new adjectives can apply to you. For example, you might have a big dog, an old car, a new book and so on. Try putting them into a sentence, e.g., У меня́ есть больша́я соба́ка. Or Моя́ ста́рая маши́на – на у́лице. (Avoid using adjectives with locations yet – the agreements would change). If you work with someone else, start with making a statement about something, but leave the adjective out. Then your partner needs to ask a question with an adjective, and you answer. e.g., Моя́ маши́на - на у́лице. – А ва́ша маши́на - ста́рая или но́вая (больша́я или ма́ленькая)? Watch how many letters you take off and add in both your adjectives as well as «мой», «твой», «ваш».

Speaking of young and old, we now will look at some other words for people. Somehow, they have a few hushers in them – so, we will start with those.

Ex. 9 a) Decoding Cyrillic. Watch your hushers and your stress. Be aware of double-stressing – we need one stress only.

бáба - бáбочка - бáбушка   полу́чка - полу́шка - пáлочка

лáпа - лáпочка - лáпушка   галу́шка - галóшка - гáлочка

дéва - дéвочка - дéвушка   лóдочка - ладóшка - лáдушка

> **NEW WORDS:** **ДÉВОЧКА** - *little girl (younger than 14–15 years old)*
>
> **ДÉВУШКА** - *older girl (between the ages of 15 and 30)*

Check that your stresses in both words are at the front and that there is just one stress.

b) Let's get this right. Choose the correct word from the right column for each person on the left; one entry will be used twice. Watch your stress. Note that you do not need to do anything with the ages – they are for your information.

Name	Age (no need to read or match them up – they are just for your information)	What would Russians call them? Choose the right word.
Я́на	25	бáбушка
Дéнис (или Дени́ска)	5	дéвочка
Андрéй Николáевич	27	дéдушка
Анастаси́я Андрéевна	84	молодóй человéк
Ли́дочка	9	дéвушка
Антóн	19	мáльчик
Влади́мир Алексéевич	72	

c) Question time. Use the table above to make ИЛИ-questions. E.g.: Сáша - это дéвочка или мáльчик? If you work with someone else, you can answer these too. Questions like this might come extremely handy if you are trying to work out who is who in a list or in a host family.

If we think about the age slot allocated for, let's say, «дéвочка», 0–15 years old, it is still fairly wide and includes toddlers and early teenagers. So, some of them can easily be «мáленькая дéвочка» or «большáя дéвочка» before they become «дéвушка». You also need to keep in mind that the word «молодóй» can only refer to «дéвушка» or «молодóй человек» (or older), but not to children under 15, and thus cannot be used with «дéвочка» or «мáльчик».

d) Reading for meaning. Work out how you can describe the following people in English; give age spans.

ма́ленький ма́льчик	молода́я де́вушка	ма́ленькая де́вочка	ста́рый инжене́р
молода́я студе́нтка	ста́рый де́душка	молодо́й челове́к	молода́я учи́тельница
ста́рая ба́бушка	большо́й ма́льчик	больша́я де́вочка	ма́ленький сын

e) Now it's your turn. Among the people you know, find people who in Russia would be called «де́вочка», «ма́льчик», «де́вушка», «молодо́й челове́к», «ба́бушка», «де́душка». Try using adjectives. Say their names and what they are. E.g., Дени́с - ма́ленький ма́льчик.

NEW WORDS:

ЖЕ́НЩИНА - *a woman*   **МУЖЧИ́НА** - *a man*

How does it sound? «Ж» and «Ч» in «мужчи́на» are not read separately – they merge into one long husher which sounds more or less like our «Щ». There is nothing wrong with pronouncing it as it is written, but it might be easier to run two hushers one into the other, like in *Welsh sheep*.

To make it clear: «Мужчи́на» is a masculine word (by default). It is similar to «де́душка», «па́па», «дя́дя», «Ники́та» and some others that need to be agreed as masculines, despite having «А» (or «Я») at the end. E.g., мой де́душка, молодо́й мужчи́на, who is older than «молодо́й челове́к» and is normally about 30–35 years old. A similar age span would apply to «молода́я же́нщина».

---

f) Now it's your turn. To practice the new words, make a list of names of some people you know, of different genders and ages. Swap lists with your partner. Your purpose is to find out who is who in your partner's list without using any English. E.g., Сэм – это мужчи́на или же́нщина? – Мужчи́на. – Он молодо́й мужчи́на? – Нет, не очень.

RUSSIASCOPE: ГОСПОДИ́Н, ГРАЖДАНИ́Н, ТОВА́РИЩ **или** МОЛОДО́Й ЧЕЛОВЕ́К?

Knowing the words like «де́вушка», «же́нщина», «мужчи́на» and similar in Russian might be more important than in English, as they often work as a way of addressing strangers. I will explain.

The difficulties with terms of address started in 1917, when the titles which had been traditionally used before then, «господи́н» (for Sir and Mr.) and «госпожа́» (for Madam and Mrs.), were abolished by the Bolsheviks, who introduced their unisex «това́рищ», which stands for "comrade" and was actively used for a few decades. Since the collapse of the Soviet Union and with the popularity of the Communists waning, «това́рищ» has fallen out of use as a title. There have been suggestions to re-introduce the pre-revolutionary titles, but they have not really caught on. Some tried to use «граждани́н», which means "citizen", but that did not catch on either, possibly due to it being used in Soviet times to prisoners (who supposedly were not това́рищи). The bottom line is that nowadays there are no settled equivalents for Sir or Madam. The solution emerged from the use of words like «де́вушка», «молодо́й челове́к», «же́нщина», «мужчи́на» and even «ба́бушка» and «де́душка», which are successfully used to address strangers in Russia. E.g., «Де́вушка, извини́те, пожа́луйста. А где Кремль?». In this situation, «де́вушка» is of course not translated as "girl", but rather as "Miss", "Madam", "Young lady" or even "Excuse me". «Де́вушка» is often used towards shop-assistants, receptionists, waitresses etc., and is not formal, but is not condescending either. «Ба́бушка» and «де́душка» have also been traditionally accepted by elder people as a sign of respect for their age. Mind you, times change, and in Moscow perhaps not all ба́бушка-s might want to be called that.

Ex. 10 a) Reading for meaning. Think how you would translate «де́вушка» and «мужчи́на» here.

– Де́вушка, можно меню́, пожалуйста?

– Да. Коне́чно. Вот, пожалуйста.

– А о́вощи у вас есть? Я вегетариа́нец.

– Да. Это вот тут. Пицца, макаро́ны, сыр.

– Спаси́бо.

– Пожа́луйста.

– Мужчи́на, извини́те. Это почта?

– Нет, молодо́й челове́к. Это не почта. Это вокза́л.

– А почта где, вы знаете?

– Ду́маю, почта на проспе́кте Ле́нина.

– Спаси́бо.

– Пожа́луйста. До свида́ния.

Male	Female
ма́льчик	де́вочка
молодо́й челове́к	де́вушка
мужчи́на	же́нщина
де́душка	ба́бушка

Check that you spotted that all words for females have the stress at the front.

b) Find a person who. . . Think how you would ask different people whether they have something (in a polite or in familiar way) and whether they do something. See below for the list of people and the list of things they might have. This is great to do as a group. The words for people can go into one hat and all the items into another. Don't show each other the slips you pulled out – the others need to find out who you are and what you have. They need to start with something like «Вы ба́бушка?» or «Ты ма́льчик?». Then depending on your answer they would need to choose between «У вас есть . . . ?» and «У тебя́ есть . . . ?». Finally, if you wish, you can think of a verb which can be linked to the item and ask the second question using «вы» or «ты». E.g.: Вы мужчи́на? – Нет. – Вы же́нщина? – Да. Я же́нщина. – У вас есть кни́га? – Нет. – У вас есть саксофо́н? – Да. У меня́ есть саксофо́н. – Вы игра́ете на саксофо́не? – Да. Я немно́го игра́ю на саксофо́не. Then it's the other person's turn to ask questions. After that you need to change partners.

де́вочка, молодо́й челове́к, де́душка, же́нщина, де́вушка, ма́льчик, ба́бушка, мужчи́на

конфе́ты, ша́хматы, кни́га «Англи́йский язы́к», гита́ра, ка́рта Ло́ндона, я́блоки, компью́тер, ру́сский алфави́т

> **To make it clear:** With «молодо́й челове́к» and «де́вушка», either «ты» or «вы» are possible, depending on your age, their age and the situation. You are safer with «вы», but if «молодо́й челове́к» looks younger than your son and is in your friend's family you can confidently use «ты». If you are going through passport control, though, he would definitely need «вы». If you are a teenager, you would only use «ты» to the same age group or younger.

> **WORTH REMEMBERING:** *The time has come to have a look at that mysterious neuter gender which we have been leaving for later. Similarly to how feminines tell you that they are feminines by having «А» or «Я» at the end, Russian **neuters** have «О» or «Е» at the end, e.g., окно́, кафе́.*

Here are some new neuters for you.

> **NEW WORDS:** МО́РЕ - *sea*
>
> СЛО́ВО - *a word*   ПИСЬМО́ - *a letter (from a friend)*

Tip! You need to be aware of "hidden" neuters which do not have the stress on the last «О». This means you cannot hear clearly what is at the end and need to note for yourself that it is a neuter word, e.g., я́блоко, мя́со.

Ex. 11 a) Jog your memory. These are some other neuter words we have come across. Watch your stresses and find five hidden neuters.

мясо, окно, кафе́, метро, сло́во, я́блоко, вино, масло, мо́ре, ра́дио, молоко, письмо́, кино

> **WORTH REMEMBERING:** To link adjectives (descriptive words) with neuter nouns, we need to start with a dictionary form (which ends with either «-ÓЙ», «-ЫЙ» or «-ИЙ») (e.g., но́в**ый**), take TWO letters off the end and put TWO new letters for neuter «-OE», e.g., но́в**ое** окно́.

b) Reading for meaning. Make sure you read all your endings correctly. In each phrase, underline the adjective and say which gender it is describing.

Он чита́ет большо́е письмо́.

У меня́ есть ма́ленький пакет.

Вы зна́ете ру́сское сло́во «спу́тник»?

Моя́ тётя немолода́я же́нщина.

Она́ не ру́сская, а англича́нка, но немно́го зна́ет русский.

Я живу́ в до́ме №8 на проспе́кте. Это но́вый дом.

Вот ва́ша англи́йская кни́га. Спаси́бо большо́е.

Улица Оборо́нная – это о́чень ста́рая улица в Ту́ле.

> **To make it clear:** Russians actively add «НЕ» to the front of adjectives (written together), for example, «немолода́я же́нщина», rather than «ста́рая». (Remember that «НЕ» is always separate from verbs).

RUSSIASCOPE: **МОСКО́ВСКОЕ МЕТРО́**

A first visit to the Moscow underground leaves most foreign visitors speechless, as its central stations look more like museums: marble walls, sculptures, pictures, mosaics etc. (Stalin liked to impress). So if you happen to be in Moscow, it is definitely worth popping in (or rather down) to the underground stations within the "ring". The map is simple to understand (it helps if you read Russian, of course). Also, Moscow trains are cheap (for less than £1 you can go anywhere within the city) and exceptionally reliable – they come every two minutes in any direction. If you are not going to Moscow just yet, the Internet has a good selection of pictures that give you an idea of what it is like.

NEW WORD: КРА́СНЫЙ - *red*

c) Say it in Russian. Each string has three genders in it. Work out which word is which gender before translating.

red pencil - red pen - the Red sea

new book - new word - new desk

big movie - big library - big city

small plate - small glass - small apple

old hotel - small room *(in a hotel)* - big window

small letter - young woman - old man

old hospital - new university - English underground

red juice - old wine - Russian vodka

WORTH REMEBERING: *You might question the ending in «Кра́сная пло́щадь» (for Red Square), as «пло́щадь» does not seem to have «А» at the end. «Пло́щадь» in Russian belongs to a tiny cluster of **soft sign feminines**. So does the female name «Любо́вь» (Лю́ба for short) that we came across earlier. Dictionaries will always tell you if you stumble across one of these, and we will learn them as we go. Within the first year of learning, though, you are unlikely to come across more than half a dozen of these. The only other soft sign feminine you know at the moment is «тетра́дь», e.g., моя́ ма́ленькая тетра́дь.*

НО́ВАЯ ФО́РМА: МОЁ - *my (for neuter)*

Check that you realise that the stress is at the end and «О» is weak; that here we pronounce a strong /й/ sound but do not write «Й» before «Ё».

To make it clear: Make sure you realise that when we agree «мой»/«твой»/«ваш» with feminines or neuters we change ONE letter, while to agree adjectives (descriptive words) we need to change TWO. E.g.: мой но́вый каранда́ш - моя́ но́вая ру́чка - моё но́вое сло́во

d) Let's try it in Russian. Choose one or two Russian adjectives that you know to describe the following things and people. E.g., мо..... .... каранда́ш – мо**й** кра́сн**ый** каранда́ш

мо.... .... стол

мо.... .... сумка

мо.... .... окно́

мо.... .... учи́тельница

мо.... .... сло́во

мо.... .... фотоаппарат

мо.... .... я́блоко

мо.... .... друг

мо.... .... ручка

WORTH REMEMBERING: **ТВОЁ** - *your/s (informal) for neuter*

ВА́ШЕ - *your/s (formal) for neuter*

Check that you noticed that the stresses are different in the two words.

e) Let's try it in Russian. Look at what different people have to say and think of a question to ask them using an *adjective* and a correct form of *your/s*. E.g.: Жéнщина: Я живý в квартѝре. – *You:* Вáша квартѝра стáрая или нóвая?

Дéвушка: Я работаю в офисе.

Мáльчик: У меня есть сестра.

Студéнт: Я знаю слово «плóщадь».

Бáбушка: Я люблю мой сад.

Ребёнок: А у меня есть собака.

Молодой человек: У меня есть машина.

Русская туристка: Вот мой паспорт.

Дéвочка: Это моё яблоко.

Англичáнин: Мой друг живёт в Москве.

Мужчина: Я читаю журнал.

Check that you remembered to raise the tone of your voice at the end of your questions.

d) Find a person who has a new bag, a red apple in the bag or a small exercise book, owns a Russian doll, a large garden or a small dog, has a Russian friend. Enjoy going round asking questions in Russian.

Think Russian. Look for adjectives around you, noting the genders that they would need in Russian. Try to remember which words are neuter. Every time you look out of the window or pick up an apple, think that they have «О» at the end. Find an adjective to link to them. Not agreeing adjectives is NOT a dangerous mistake – any Russian would understand you, but it sounds better if we try speaking correctly.

Tip! Avoid using adjectives after «В» or «НА» at the moment. When a noun gets a new ending (e.g., «Е» in «в гóроде») the adjective will have to agree with a new form. As you might have noticed, the set of endings for an adjective is different from that for a noun. To be grammatically perfect, try putting your adjectives in a separate sentence, e.g., Я живý в дóме №8 на проспекте Лéнина. Это большóй дом.

Today our good-bye is going to be with a /щ/ sound (long and close to the palate). The word looks like this «СЧАСТЛИ́ВО!» and sounds something like this /щ а с л и́ в а/. Make sure your stress is in the right place. It comes from the word "happy" and means sort of "Stay happy". In this form it is used only when you leave. It is quite informal, so might not be the best to say to your teacher, but I would be happy for you to say it to me.

Something old, something new (*revision of unit 9*)

Здра́вствуй. Do you remember that you can use this greeting with no «-те» as a halfway version between «Приве́т» and «Здра́вствуйте»? **У меня́ всё хорошо́ сего́дня. А у тебя́?** Can you give a quick answer and then think of a different one? Today I can also say **«Мно́го дел.»** which means *lots to do* ("lots of doings" technically, as «дел» from «дела́» is not a verb). «Мно́го дел» is an equivalent to *Busy* in English. You can often hear «О́чень мно́го дел.» or «Ужа́сно мно́го дел.» (*Very busy* or *An awful lot to do*). «Ужа́сно.» actually can be used on its own if the things go terribly wrong, which I hope they won't, but this gives you one more option of answers to «Как дела́?».

Anyway, as in the last unit we proudly went through the last two letters of the Russian alphabet, today we have no new letters to come, which might actually feel a bit like an end of something you enjoyed doing (well, hopefully). But there are plenty of other things to learn, as well as practicing what we have learnt in the last couple of units. We will have a look at the alphabet again, because when you look up a Russian word in a Russian-English dictionary, you will need to know in which part of the alphabet to look. This will be the last time when the four groups of letters appear in this book, as we only had them to help you remember them better. Make sure you read all the letters the Russian way.

GROUP I (The Easy): **Мм, Тт, Кк, Аа, Оо**

GROUP II (The Tricky): **Сс, Нн, Вв, Рр, Ее, Уу, Хх**

GROUP III (Funny Shapes): **Ээ, Яя, Лл, Дд, Ии, Йй, Бб, Зз, Пп, Гг, Чч, Шш, Жж, Фф, Ёё, Юю, Цц**

GROUP IV (The Strangers): **Ьь, Ыы, Ъъ, Щщ**

РУ́ССКИЙ АЛФАВИ́Т:

Аа Бб Вв Гг Дд Ее Ёё Жж Зз Ии Йй

Кк Лл Мм Нн Оо Пп Рр Сс Тт Уу

Фф Хх Цц Чч Шш Щщ Ъъ Ыы Ьь Ээ Юю Яя

1. What letter does the Russian alphabet start with? (*Did you read it in Russian?*)

2. In which part of the alphabet can we find the other four letters of Group I?

3. What is the last letter of the Russian alphabet?

4. In which section are you going to look for «В» and «З»?

5. Can you find all seven of the Tricky Letters (Group II)? In which part are most of them situated?

6. Try finding four two-in-one vowels. You might notice that they are paired up. Where are the two pairs?

7. Identify the two signs (which do not stand for any sounds). Can you remember their place in the alphabet?

8. Can you find the other two Strangers in the alphabet («Ы» and «Щ»)?

9. Find the letters which make hushing sounds. Note which one of them is in the first part.

Ex.1 a) Decoding Cyrillic. Read aloud the names of the Moscow underground stations. Make sure that there is only ONE stress per word. There is either a hushing sound or a «Ц» in each name – keep an eye on them. Note that some names are made up of two words. You do not need to understand what the words mean (names would sound the same in English); you might recognise some of the words within them, though – they will talk to you.

Ту́шинская, Печа́тники, Кузне́цкий мост, Ю́жная, пло́щадь Револю́ции, Молодёжная, Че́ховская, у́лица Милашéнкова, Цари́цыно, Ма́рьина ро́ща, Пу́шкинская, Черки́зовская, Кожухо́вская

One of the letters we had a look at in the last unit was a husher and a Stranger. Do you think it might be good to have another look at it?

10. Which of the two letters is pronounced at the back of your mouth: the old and familiar «Ш» or the new Stranger «Щ»?

11. How do we need to pronounce «Щ»?

12. Do you remember how we read «ЖИ» and «ШИ»? How is «ЩИ» read?

13. What are the main two differences between «борщ» and «щи»?

14. Is «Щ» and «ЩЬ» read the same or differently?

15. What happens to «Е» after «Щ» (or after any other of the hushers)?

b) Decoding Cyrillic. Make your «Щ» as long as possible and watch your «Ц» in the last column (their shapes are somewhat close).

му́сор - му́сорщик	жена́ - же́нщина	жил - жили́ще	сме́нщик - сме́нщица
бето́н - бето́нщик	куста́рь - куста́рщина	уди́л - уди́лище	убо́рщик - убо́рщица
фона́рь - фона́рщик	война́ - вое́нщина	святи́л - святи́лище	упако́вщик - упако́вщица

c) Try not to trip up! Take your time working out which hushing sounds you need in each word. Mind your «Ц» too.

ку́ща - ку́ча - ку́шка	ро́жа - ро́ща	плащ - плац
плащ - плач - пло́шка	мо́жно - мо́щно	щель - цель
мощь - мочь - мо́шка	вы́ражен - вы́ращен	пи́ща - пицца

плечу́ - плещу́ - пляшу́	ращу́ - рожу́	це́дра - ще́дро
туши́ть - тащи́ть - точи́ть	лещи́ - лежи́	це́пко - ще́пка
замеща́л - замеча́л - замеша́л	полощи́ - положи́	цеди́л - щади́л

c) Jog your memory. And a big sort out too. In the list below, underline the words with «Щ» in them and then read the list as it is, making sure that your «Щ» is at the front of your mouth and as long as possible. If you are learning to write, sort out the words into two groups: those with «Щ» and those with «Ц». Keep an eye on what your words mean.

у́лица, пло́щадь, центр, больни́ца, това́рищ, учи́тельница, ещё, ста́нция, о́вощ, же́нщина, цирк, гости́ница

> ***Check*** *that you read* «ЦИ» *as* /ц ы/ *in* «цирк» *and* «ста́нция».

d) What's in a name? Read the names of some places in Russia. Keep an eye on «Щ» and «Ц».

Луцк, Городе́ц, Щёкино, Шацк, Мценск, Черепове́ц, Городи́ще, Ща́пово, Ли́пецк, Сла́нцы, Тро́ицк, Щёлково, Целиногра́д, Горохове́ц, Ще́рбинка, Новокузне́цк, Ли́повцы, Ку́нцево, Щу́чье, Черновцы́, Еле́ц

> ***Check*** *that you read* «Е» *in* «Щу́чье» *with a strong* /й/ *sound like in* «компью́тер» *or* «друзья́».

16. If a word has «Ж», «Ч», «Ш» or «Щ» at the end, which ending would it take to make plural: «Ы» or «И»?

17. Why are «ЖИ» and «ШИ» the trickiest in this rule?

18. Why are «гаражи́» and «карандаши́» worth remembering?

19. Can you name the other three letters which are never followed by «Ы» in Russian words?

20. What do we write in plural after «Ц»?

e) Let's get this right. Put the following words into plural, choosing «Ы» or «И».

Tip! Do you remember the seven letters which need «И» *in plural: three pronounced at the back of your mouth and four hushers (three with the three "bits", and the fourth looks a bit like a Russian handwritten four).*

ба́бушка, же́нщина, де́вочка, о́вощ, больни́ца, гара́ж, цирк, мужчи́на, у́лица, де́вушка, ёлка, центр, каранда́ш, това́рищ, гости́ница, матрёшка

> ***Check*** *that you tried to read «ЖИ» and «ШИ» in at the back of your mouth; that «гаражи́» and «карандаши́» had the stress at the end; that «Ж» and «Ч» in «мужчи́на» sound more like a long front /щ/.*

f) What would you say in Russia if you needed to ask somebody:

whether this is Red Square;

whether they know where the hospital is;

whether they would like some more;

whether they have any vegetables;

whether their teacher is Russian;

whether they had enough;

where the Lenin(a) Library (*underground*) station is;

whether the hotel is in the centre.

21. Why do Russians have no words like *Sir/Mr.* or *Madam/Mrs.*? What do they use instead if they do not know people?

22. Why is it OK to use «де́вушка» to address a girl you don't know? How would you translate it then?

23. What is the difference between «де́вочка» and «де́вушка»?

24. Which words can we use in Russian in place of English *Sir*?

Ex.2 a) Big sort out. From the list below read out all the words with «Ч», then with «Ш» and finally with the letter «Ж». You might want to mark the stresses first. Then sort out the words into males and females. Finally, put them in order, starting with the youngest.

молодой человек, бабушка, девушка, мальчик, мужчина, дедушка, женщина, девочка

> ***Check*** *that you read «мужчи́на» in the last group (words with the letter «Ж»), but that it sounded like «Щ».*

b) Question time. Watching «ТЫ»- and «ВЫ»-people, ask in Russian:

a gentleman – whether he works here;

a little girl – whether she knows where the school is;

a very elderly lady – if she is OK;

a young man – whether he can swim (swims);

a lady of about 40 – if she is a nurse;

a very elderly gentleman – where the Kremlin is;

a young girl of 20 – whether the head is in the office;

a little boy of 10 – whether he has a pen.

c) If you are learning to write, you can try doing the exercise above in writing. If you want to challenge yourself, try writing the lists of males and females without looking at the list above.

d) Say it in Russian:

men and women	friends and brothers	fruit and veg
boys and girls (*little*)	women and children	chocolate and sweets
teachers (*fem*) and students	people and dogs	pens and pencils

Check that «шоколáд» *stayed in singular as it does not have a plural form; that your stress in* «карандашú» *is at the very end.*

Reading Challenge: Шифровáльщик

Ex.3 a) Reading for meaning:

Турúст в Москве

— Мужчина, извините. Я турúст. Мой телефон не работает. У меня есть карта, но я не знаю, где Крáсная плóщадь?

— Дýмаю, это станция метро «Библиотéка Лéнина».

— А где это на карте?

— Вот ýлица Моховáя. Это Алексáндровский сад. А это Кремль и Красная площадь.

— Я понимáю. Спасибо. До свидáния.

— Однý минýту, молодóй человéк. Можно ещё на «Плóщадь Револю́ции». Это лучше. Там ýлица Никóльская и Крáсная плóщадь недалекó*.

— Большóе спасибо.

— Пожалуйста.

---

* далекó - *far*

Подруги в ресторáне

— Привет, Гáлочка.

— Привет, Óленька. Как делá?

— Сегóдня лýчше. Спасибо. Вот твой сок.

— Спасибо.. . . . Ты болéла?

— Да. Немнóго. Сегóдня много лучше. А у тебя как?

— Ничегó. Спасибо. Дел ужáсно много! А где меню́?

— Вот. Тут неплохóе мясо.

— Да? А óвощи?

— Не знаю. Это ты óвощи ешь, а я в мясе понимаю лучше.

— Я очень люблю óвощи, а мясо я не ем.

— Правда*? А твой муж?

— Нет, он óвощи не ест, он ест мясо. А твой?

— Он иногдá ест, но он, как ты - óвощи-фрýкты.

— Я дýмаю, иногдá ничегó.

— Ещё сок?

— Нет, хвáтит. Спасибо.

---

* Правда. – *Is that true? = Really?*

b) Jog your memory or find in the text:

I don't know.	You were ill.	Thank you very much.	A little bit.
I think.	It's much better.	It's also possible. . .	Awfully busy.
I understand.	It's OK sometimes.	More juice?	It's enough.

233

c) Let's try it in Russian. Pick a conversation and make a 5–7 point plan (sort of your own step-by-step guide for it). If you work with someone else, have a go at a similar conversation (you might want a plan each). You do not need to remember everything – just the gist, and try to keep it going. If you are working on your own, it might be easier to talk through what happened in the second conversation – say who was ill, who works a lot, who eats vegetables, who prefers meat (you would need «ОН/А»-endings).

In the last unit, among other things, we had a look at the adjectives, the words that describe things. Let's see what we know about them.

25. Name a few descriptive words (adjectives) in English.

26. Try to remember the three combinations of the last TWO letters that Russian descriptive words can have at the end of their dictionary form.

? 27. Do we choose between «-ÓЙ», «-ЫЙ» and «-ИЙ», or do we learn an adjective with a particular ending?

28. What do we need to note about adjectives with «-ÓЙ»?

29. Can we use the seven-letter rule for choosing between «Ы» and «И» (that we use in plural) to determine whether we need «-ЫЙ» or «-ИЙ» in an adjective?

Ex.4 a) Jog your memory. See whether you remember the following adjectives. Watch your stresses – read out the adjectives with the stress on the first syllable, then on the last and finally find one with the stress in the middle. Then read out all the adjectives with the «ИЙ» ending, all with the «ЫЙ» ending and finally with «ÓЙ» at the end.

большо́й, ма́ленький, но́вый, ста́рый, молодо́й, кра́сный, ру́сский, англи́йский

b) Let's get this right. Fill in the last two letters in the following adjectives, without looking at the line above. Mark the stresses.

больш. . . .   маленьк. . . .   стар. . . . .   англи́йск. . . . .

русск. . . . .   нов. . . . .   молод. . . .   красн. . . . .

30. Which words can we describe using the dictionary form of an adjective?

31. What do Russian adjectives need to have at the end to describe feminines?

? 32. Can «-АЯ» replace any of the original endings in the descriptive words that we had («-ÓЙ», «-ЫЙ» or «-ИЙ»)?

33. Do we need to move the stress when we change the ending?

34. How would you read the two vowels: «АЯ», «ОЕ», «ИЯ», «АЮ», «УЮ», «ОЁ», «ОЮ».

Check that you put the stress on the «Ё» in «ОЁ».

c) **Decoding Cyrillic.** Make sure you read the last two letters correctly. Watch your stress – no double-stressing!

мой - молодо́й - голубо́й   бе́лый - сме́лый - бе́ленький   ту́ю - пусту́ю - голосу́ю

ста́я - проста́я - подраста́я   ко́лкий - ме́лкий - ма́ленький   бо́ю - тобо́ю - китобо́ю

ма́ю - лома́ю - долома́ю   ма́лое - ста́рое - но́вое   дво́е - друго́е - дорого́е

> **Check** *that you read «E» at the end and that you spotted weak «O» in some endings.*

Ex.5 a) Reading for meaning. Keep an eye on the last two letters of the descriptive words. Say which gender they describe.

русский язык	молода́я студентка	ва́ша больша́я дере́вня	моя русская подруга
но́вая школа	Кра́сная пло́щадь	мой красный карандаш	ваш новый офис
старый де́душка	ма́ленький самовар	твоя новая ручка	твой молодой учи́тель

b) **Let's get this right.** Match the descriptive words in the top line with the right nouns from the bottom line to make sensible phrases. You would need to match the endings as well as the meanings.

но́вая, молодо́й, ста́рая, большо́й, англи́йская, ру́сский, ма́ленький, кра́сная

бабушка, человек, ребёнок, город, гости́ница, язы́к, ручка, газета

> **Check** *that you remember that you cannot use «молодо́й» for young children; that you understand that «ребёнок» needs a masculine adjective, as the word is masculine.*

c) **Say it in Russian.** Remember to change the endings when you describe feminine nouns.

a big house - a big flat	an old friend (*m*) - an old teacher *(fem.)*	a young man - a young nurse
a little boy - a little girl	a Russian man - a Russian woman	a red chair - a red car
a new pencil - a new pen	the English language - an English newspaper	a small glass - a small cup

> **Check** *that you described "a man" as masculine and said «ру́сский мужчина»; that the word «ма́ленький» has only one stress, on the very first syllable.*

35. How many letters did we change to agree adjectives with the words they describe?

36. How many letters do we change in «мой»/«твой»/«ваш»?

? 37. Is the word «пло́щадь» masculine or feminine in Russian? Say *Red Square* in Russian.

38. What other Russian word that you know does not have «A» at the end but is classed as a feminine?

d) What would you say in Russia if you would like to

introduce your old friend;	offer somebody your English newspaper to have a look at;
ask for a red pen;	find a big glass;
find a small plate;	show a picture of your little sister;
show your new phone;	find your Russian exercise book.

Check that you realise that both «кни́га» *and* «тетра́дь» *are feminine.*

39. Does the hard sign (Ъ) stand for any sound?

40. Where can you find it within a word in modern Russian: in the middle or at the end?

41. How do we read two-in-one vowels after «Ъ»?

42. How do we differentiate between the shapes of the two signs: the hard sign (Ъ) and the soft sign (Ь)?

43. Why haven't we learnt any words with the hard sign?

Ex.6 a) Big sort out. Mark the stresses where needed. Underline the words with the soft sign (Ь). Then read out the words with the hard sign (which you have not underlined). Finally, read and translate the underlined words with the soft sign. If you are learning to write, you can write the words into two columns.

ма́льчик, съем, пло́щадь, во́семь, объе́хал, изъя́н, большо́й, тетра́дь, подъе́зд, ско́лько, разъём, ма́ленький, де́ньги, въе́лся, знать

b) Jog your memory. See whether you remember the following verbs. Mark the stresses. Find *one* monosyllabic verb and *two* verbs where the stress is at the beginning.

чита́ть, пла́вать, игра́ть (в/на), знать, помога́ть, рабо́тать, ду́мать, понима́ть

44. What do we call the form of the verbs above? When do we use it?

45. Can we use it after «я», «ты», «он/а́» etc.?

46. Why do we need to change the verb ending in Russian every time the doer changes?

47. What does the soft sign do in «рабо́тать» but does *not* do in «рабо́таешь»?

c) Let's get this right. Match the endings to the doers. Note that one ending is used twice.

	РАБО́ТА/ТЬ	
Я		-ЕТ
ТЫ		-ЕТЕ
ОН		-Ю
ОНА́		-ЕШЬ
ВЫ		

d) Big sort out. Put the forms of the verb «жить» in the same order as above (starting with «Я»). Read them aloud.

живёшь, живёт, живу́, живёте

e) Let's get this right. Imagine that somebody tells you what they do, and you want to know whether their partner does that too. Change each «Я»-form below to the «ОН/А́»- form. Watch your stress and raise the tone of your voice, since youare asking a question. It is fun to do with someone else. E.g., я рабо́та**ю** – А он/а́ то́же рабо́та**ет**?

Я чита́ю.	Я так ду́маю.	Я тут живу́.	Я непло́хо игра́ю.	Пла́ваю.
Зна́ю я.	Я ем всё.	Помога́ю иногда́.	Рабо́таю мно́го.	Я э́то понима́ю.

48. Which verb that we know does NOT follow the general pattern?

Ex.7 a) Now it's your turn. Think of a couple of phrases which you can say in Russian about what you are doing today or tomorrow. After each phrase, say what somebody else is doing, whether it is the same or different. E.g., За́втра я рабо́таю в о́фисе. А моя́ подру́га не рабо́тает. If you work with someone else, take turns commenting on the same topic or changing the topic. E.g., Я то́же рабо́таю сего́дня, но пото́м я игра́ю в ре́гби. А мой брат в ре́гби не игра́ет.

b) Let's get this right. Answer the following questions and then think which form of *And you?* you would choose to return them (А вы? А ты? А у вас? А у тебя́?). This is good to do with somebody else. E.g., Ты игра́ешь на саксофо́не? – Нет, не игра́ю. А ты? Try to make use of the words like иногда́, мно́го, немно́го, не о́чень, сего́дня, всё, тут, пото́м, ве́чером and similar.

Вы игра́ете на гита́ре?	У вас есть о́вощи в саду́?	Ты иногда́ пла́ваешь?	У вас есть де́ньги?
У тебя́ есть пиани́но?	А компью́тер у тебя́ есть?	У тебя́ есть каранда́ши?	Ты помога́ешь до́ма?
Ты зна́ешь Ло́ндон?	Вы понима́ете ру́сский?	А газе́ты вы чита́ете?	Вы рабо́таете за́втра?

c) Let's try it in Russian. Have a look at the list of people below. You need to make at least one sentence in Russian about each of them. You CANNOT use a dictionary! Think of what they are likely to do and find a Russian verb you know. The words under the line might help you. Remember to put the verb in the correct form. You can also try starting with «Я ду́маю, (что) . . . ».

пенсионе́рка, ру́сский, медсестра́, футболи́ст, студе́нт, англича́нка, профе́ссор, испа́нец, капита́н, гитари́ст, инжене́р, бизнесме́н

язы́к, стадио́н, компью́тер, сад, о́фис, Ло́ндон, мо́ре, заво́д, Мадри́д, больни́ца, гита́ра, кни́ги

d) Now it's your turn. We will use verbs, combining the three endings in one exercise. You need to say blocks of TWO sentences + a question: 1) say something about yourself («я»-form), 2) use the same verb to speak about somebody else («он/á»-form) and 3) ask a question using the same verb («ты-» or «вы»-forms). E.g., 1) Я мно́го помога́ю до́ма. 2) Мой брат то́же иногда́ помога́**ет**. 3) А ты помога́**ешь** до́ма? It is good to do this in a group or working in pairs with somebody else. If you work on your own, you can think of interviewing a Russian for, say, a college project – make sure that you use different verb forms.

49. Does Russian have lots of neuter words?

? 50. What do Russian neuter nouns have at the end?

Ex.8 a) Big sort out. Read out all the neuters. Watch your stresses.

ко́мната, молоко́, ша́хматы, стол, мя́со, чай, де́ньги, сло́во, матрёшка, челове́к, ма́сло, кафе́, ребёнок, де́вочка, вино́, тетра́дь, кни́ги, письмо́, таре́лка, го́род, метро́, у́лицы, язы́к, лю́ди, кино́, компью́тер, мо́ре, су́мка, друзья́, карти́на, стул, я́блоко

51. Which TWO letters do adjectives need at the end to describe a neuter?

b) Big sort out. Read out all the phrases with the *same* adjective. Watch your endings. For each phrase say which gender is described and make sure you know the meaning.

ру́сская де́вушка, но́вый го́род, большо́е я́блоко, ста́рый дом, ру́сское сло́во, ма́ленькая де́вочка, большо́й стака́н, Кра́сная пло́щадь, но́вое кафе́, ма́ленькое письмо́, ру́сский журнали́ст, ста́рая гости́ница, ма́ленький каранда́ш, Кра́сное мо́ре, больша́я таре́лка, но́вая больни́ца, ста́рое кино́, кра́сный флаг

> ***Check*** *that you remember that* «кино́» *in conversational Russian often means "film".*

c) Say it in Russian:

red pencil - red wine	English village - English underground	small banana - small apple
old house - old window	big copybook - big letter	red plastic bag - the Red Sea
little shop - little cafe	Russian newspaper - Russian word	new station - new cinema

52. Do you remember the neuter forms of «мой», «твой» and «ваш»?

? 53. What is the difference in the stresses of these three forms?

d) Let's get this right. Put the following plurals into their singular form. E.g., мои́ су́мки - моя́ су́мка. Watch your stress. If you feel comfortable, halfway through you can start adding an adjective to your singular.

мои́ стака́ны	твои́ друзья́	ва́ши у́лицы	мои́ о́вощи	твои́ кни́ги
ва́ши ча́шки	ва́ши шко́лы	мои́ кафе́	твои́ студе́нты	мои́ ра́дио
твои́ я́блоки	мои́ карандаши́	твои́ де́ти	ва́ши бра́тья	ва́ши больни́цы

e) Now it's your turn. You need to ask blocks of TWO questions: the first one to find out whether the other person has a particular item and the second one to ask whether it is big, little, old, Russian etc. E.g., У вас есть ру́чка? – Да. – А ва́ш**а** ру́чк**а** кра́сн**ая**? – Нет, чёрная *(black)*. Note that to ask the second question, you need to work out which gender the item is and to change the end of «твой/ваш» and the two letters of the adjective that you are using. Remember to take turns asking questions. You can start with being formal and then switch over to the informal way. It is good to do this with someone else. Try using neuters. You also can ask about people and pets.

f) What would you say in Russia if:

you don't understand;	somebody is leaving (think of something different);
somebody was not well;	somebody is better;
somebody wants a red pen and you've got one;	you'd like more coffee;
you don't want any more;	you need to know where the underground station is.

10

What is he/she up to?

WHAT'S THE PLAN?

▶   to consolidate your knowledge of Russian;
▶   to learn a few more Russian words;
▶   to read a Russian village boy's letter;
▶   to say that things are *his* or *hers*;
▶   to use another way of introducing yourself and others;
▶   to say that he/she has something;
▶   to know the difference between *well* and *good* in Russian;
▶   to learn when not to say "good evening" in Russia;
▶   to say a few things about the place where you live.

As we have no new Russian letters to do (Ypá!), we will start with new words (there are still a few of these for us to get on with). Today we are going to concentrate on talking about other people. Though our first two new words are short, they need a lot of attention to pronounce them correctly. No rush – read and watch your stress.

Tip! *Make sure you have **a strong /й/ sound** at the start of both of them; that the letter «**Г**» in the first word needs to **sound like /в/** (like in «ничего»); that the **stress** in both words **is at the end**. Ready. Steady. Go.*

NEW WORDS:

ЕГÓ - *his (Did you read the "funny" «Г» as /в/?)*
ЕЁ - *her (Did you pronounce both vowels, with two /й/ sounds?)*

***Check** that you realise that the first vowel in both words is weak.*

Ex.1 a) Reading for meaning. Give the gender of each noun. Make sure you keep track of who the things and people belong to. Before you read my note below, could you summarise how «его» and «её» are different from «мой/моя́», for example?

его́ сын, моя́ до́чка, её рабо́та, ва́ше молоко́, твои́ паке́ты, его́ жена́, ваш друг, её друзья́, мой дя́дя, твоё вино́, её муж, твоя́ кни́га, его́ студе́нты, ва́ша кварти́ра, её окно́, мои́ су́мки

To make it clear: You will love ЕГО́ and ЕЁ because they never change! They look and sound exactly the same whether used with masculines, feminines, neuters or plurals. E.g., его́ друг, его́ подру́га, его́ кафе́, его́ друзья́; её каранда́ш, её ру́чка, её ра́дио, её кни́ги.

---

b) Let's get this right. Read what people say and then say a sentence about each person, changing «мой/моя́/моё/мои́» to «ЕГО́» or «ЕЁ» accordingly, without looking in the book.

Де́вушка: Это моя́ ма́ленькая сестра́.

Де́душка: Мой ста́рый друг – то́же пенсионе́р.

Мужчи́на: На вокза́ле мои́ друзья́.

Же́нщина: За́втра мой ребёнок в шко́ле.

Студе́нт: Сего́дня моё ру́сское сло́во «тетра́дь».

Ба́бушка: Мой сын живёт в Москве́.

Молодо́й челове́к: Моя́ но́вая маши́на – на у́лице.

Ма́льчик: Я игра́ю в футбо́л. Мой друг то́же.

Учи́тельница: Мои́ кни́ги в кла́ссе на столе́.

Де́вочка: Ма́ма моя́ в больни́це рабо́тает.

Check that you have spotted one neuter and two plurals. They do not affect «его́» or «её», but it is still good to note them.

To make it clear: Make sure that having learnt the new words, you have not forgotten the old «он» and «она́». Compare: Это его́ жена́. **Она́** рабо́тает в шко́ле. Это её сын. **Он** в колле́дже сего́дня.

---

c) Say it in Russian. Try not to trip up between «он» and «его́», «она́» and «её».

I have a friend. He is an engineer. His wife is a nurse.

I have a friend. She works at school. Her brother lives in Moscow.

This is her brother. He is good at hockey (ice). *(He plays hockey well.)* His little son plays hockey too.

This is his grandmother. She lives in the village. Her garden is very big.

He is a tourist. He does not know Russian. This is his bag. And here is his passport.

She works in a hotel. Her husband is a taxi driver. His car is new. He knows the city very well.

Ex. 2 a) Reading for meaning. Here is a letter that was written by one of the schoolboys from my Granny's village in an attempt to find a pen-friend in England. His village, called Апу́хтино, is situated in Tula region (Ту́льская о́бласть) in Odoyev district (Одо́евский райо́н), about 120 miles to the south of Moscow. Read it aloud and remember that to translate a phrase we need to find the verb first.

RUSSIASCOPE: Russians treat a personal letter as a conversation – they say "hello" at the start and "good-bye" at the end.

«Это ма́льчик Са́ша»

«А это его мама Антони́на»

Здравствуй, дорого́й¹ друг!

Я Са́ша. Я русский. Живу я в деревне Апу́хтино. Моя деревня большая. В деревне есть школа, почта и магазин. А где ты живёшь, в городе или в деревне?

У меня есть мама, папа, сестра и брат. Моя мама Антони́на работает на ферме. Ле́том² я тоже помогаю на ферме или в саду. Мой папа Никола́й - шофёр в колхо́зе. Мой брат Серге́й - тоже шофёр, но он работает в Москве́. Сестра Ле́на в деревне не живёт, она живёт в городе Одо́еве. Она работает в больнице, но она не медсестра́. А у тебя брат или сестра есть?

Я в школе, но английский язык я не знаю. Я люблю спорт. В школе есть маленький стадион, и я играю там в футбол. Лето́м я плаваю в реке́. У меня есть друг Рома́н. Он тоже в футбол играет и отлично плавает. А ты в футбол играешь? А плаваешь хорошо?

Ещё у меня есть собака Да́мка, кот Му́рзик и коро́ва³ Буре́нка. А у тебя есть кошка, собака или коро́ва?

Пиши́ мне⁴, пожалуйста. Бу́ду очень рад. До свидания.

Твой русский друг Саша.

---

¹ дорого́й - *dear*   ² ле́том - *in summer*   ³ коро́ва - *a cow*   ⁴ Пиши́ мне. – *Write to me.*

Check that you realise that «шофёр» in conversational Russian stands for "a driver", rather than "a chauffeur"; that you remember that «колхо́з» stands for "collective farm", and «фе́рма» for a cattle building.

Have you noticed that apart from personal names and new words there are not many stresses marked in this letter? I am hoping that you feel that you did not have a lot of problems reading it, did you? Well done! Now we will try working with this letter as a text to help you improve your speaking skills.

b) Jog your memory or find in the text. If you look a phrase up in the text, make sure that you repeat it without looking in the text.

I live in the village.	My Mum works on a farm.	dear friend	Where do you live?
I help on a farm.	My Dad is a driver.	small sports ground	Do you have a brother?
I swim in the river.	Sister doesn't live in the village.	My village is big.	Do you play football?
I play football there.	He is an excellent swimmer.	your Russian friend	Are you good at swimming?

> *RUSSIASCOPE:* «ПРА́ВДА» *is a fairly famous word in Russian history because it used to be the name of the most influential Communist Party newspaper in the former Soviet Union. It actually stands for "truth". In conversational Russian, the word* «Пра́вда» *is often used to say "True!", "right", and* «Непра́вда» *often means "wrong" or "false".*

c) Пра́вда или непра́вда? (True or false?) Read the phrases below about Sasha and his family. Not all of them match what Sasha has written in his letter. Check them one after another. If the information is right, say «Да» (or «Пра́вда») and repeat it (*without looking in the book*). If it does not match the letter, say «Нет» or («Непра́вда») and say what is right. Try not to read from the book when speaking. You can check the information, but try speaking yourself. Keep in mind that these are statements, NOT questions, so the tone of your voice does NOT need to go up.

Са́ша ру́сский.	Са́ша пла́вает в мо́ре.
Он живёт в дере́вне.	Его́ ма́ма рабо́тает в фи́рме.
Дере́вня небольша́я.	Па́па Никола́й в колхо́зе рабо́тает.
Са́ша зна́ет англи́йский язы́к.	Па́па и сын - шофёры.
В дере́вне есть ма́ленький стадио́н.	Брат Серге́й рабо́тает в Москве́.
Са́ша игра́ет там в футбо́л.	Его́ сестра́ живёт в дере́вне.
Его́ друг Рома́н в футбо́л не игра́ет.	Она́ рабо́тает в шко́ле.

Check that you spotted the difference between «в фи́рме» *and* «на фе́рме», *and that you know which one means "on a farm".*

d) Let's try it in Russian. Think of what you can say about Sasha. Check all the information you might need *before* you speak. Don't worry about names. Think of our Step-by-step guide and how you would phrase that he is at school, where he lives, what he does after school etc. Then think of 3–5 people from Sasha's family and friends, and say at least one sentence about each of them – make a good use of your new word «ЕГО́». E.g., Его́ друг хорошо́ пла́вает. Note that we have NOT learnt the phrase for *He has* yet, so rely on your verbs. Remember to start by thinking of a Russian word you could use. And no writing at this stage, unless you want to do a small plan – one word per point. You can write the whole story afterwards, if you wish.

Now we will have a look at a different ways of phrasing certain things – how to introduce yourself, to start with.

> **НÓВАЯ ФРÁЗА:**
>
> **Меня́ зову́т . . . . . .** = *My name is . . . .*
> **КАК ВАС/тебя́ ЗОВУ́Т?** = *What is your name?*

*Check that your «зову́т» starts with /з/ like z in **zebra** and that the stress is at the end.*

Though the phrase «**Меня́ зову́т**» translates as *My name is*, there is no word for *my* and no word for *name* in it. Does this remind you of how we started with the Russian "I have" construction that did not have *I* or *have* in it, but we now have no problem using «У меня́ есть». The same will happen with «Меня́ зову́т . . . .» » - we will learn it as a phrase and, as Russians use it quite a lot, you will get used to it fairly quickly.

Let's see what it is made of. We know «меня́», which is a form of *me* (note that it is not *my* but *me*). «Зову́т» translates as "[they] call" – it is a verb in *they*-form. So, all together we get "Me [they] call . . .". We are not going to dissect it like this every time, though. What is important is not to start with «мой» or «моя́». For example, I can say: «Меня́ зову́т Ната́лия, или Ната́ша. А тебя́?» Hope you know how to answer.

If you want to start with a question, then it is crucial not to start with "What", as «Как» in «Как вас/тебя́ зову́т?» means *how*. As you are familiar with «вас/тебя́», you can work out the rest for yourself. As it is always "they" who call everybody, «зову́т» remains unchanged, whosever name you're talking about. Now that you know how the phrase is constructed, we can have a go at using it. Keep an eye on formal and informal versions. E.g., Как тебя́ зову́т? – Меня́ зову́т Ната́ша. BUT Как вас зову́т? – Меня́ зову́т Ната́лия Влади́мировна. Keep in mind that if you forget, you can always fall back on our familiar «Я Ната́ша. – А ты?»

Ex.3 a) It's your turn! Using the new phrase, say in Russian what your name is. Think how you would ask somebody about their name. If you are working in a group, you can do a round in which you ask the person on your right what their name is; they would answer and then ask the person on *their* right and so on. It might be best to use the formal option to start with. You might want to employ «Óчень прия́тно» too.

> **To make it clear:** You might remember that «Óчень прия́тно» literally translates as *Very pleasant*. Quite often it appears as «Мне óчень прия́тно», where «мне» stands for *for me*. Thus, to return this and say "It's nice to meet you too", we would need to do the same as before – use the identical form of *me*, which is in this case «мне». E.g.: Óчень прия́тно. – Мне тóже.

b) Reading for meaning:

В офисе

– Здравствуйте. Как вас зовут?

– Меня зовут Галина Петровна.

– Óчень приятно. Меня зовут Михаил Николаевич.

– Мне тоже очень приятно. У вас есть моё письмо?

– Да-да. А документы у вас есть?

– Да. Вот, пожалуйста.

Лéтом в школе

– Мальчик, тебя как зовут?

– Меня зовут Саша. А вас как?

– А меня зовут Елéна Викторовна.

– Óчень приятно.

– Мне тоже. Я ваша новая учительница.

– *(Calls his friend)* Рóмка, это новая учительница, Елéна Викторовна.

– Здравствуй. Тебя зовут Ромáн?

– Да. Здравствуйте.

Света и Дима

– Дéвушка, вас как зовут?

– Светлана. А вас?

– Меня – Дмитрий. Можно Дима.

– Óчень приятно, Дима

– Мне тоже, Света.

– Лучше Светлана.

– Извините, Светлана.

– Ничего.

c) Find in the text different versions of:

What is your name? My name is ...... And what's yours? Nice to meet you too.

c) Let's try it in Russian. Imagine asking different people their names and having similar conversations. If you are working with someone else, try re-enacting one or two of the conversations above to get confident (remember that you do not need to memorise everything – just the gist). Then you can make a similar one of your own.

WORTH REMEMBERING: Similar to how the English word "her" can be used in two different contexts ("her bag" and "I know her"), Russian «ЕГÓ» and «ЕЁ» are used after verbs, e.g., Я знаю её. (I know her.) Ты понимаешь его? (Do you understand him?). That is why to speak about somebody else's name, we would need to change «меня» /«тебя»/«вас» for «егó»/«её». We will end up saying "Him (they) call . . ." «Егó зовут . . .» or "Her (they) call . . . " «Её зову т. . .». E.g., Это мой брат. Егó зовут Сергéй. А это его женá. Её зовут Люба.

«Мой брат и его женá»

Ex.4 a) Now it's your turn. Think of how you would introduce people you know in Russian. E.g.: У меня есть муж. Егó зовут Фил. If you are working with someone else, you can say what friends or family you have; the other student can ask what their name is, and you answer. Remember to take turns. E.g., У меня есть подруга. – Как её зовут? – Её зовут Óля. The idea is to speak about as many people as possible in order to practice «Егó/её зовут . . .».

> **WORTH REMEMBERING:** «ЕГÓ» *and* «ЕЁ» *will come in handy for us to speak about other people having something. Remember that* «У меня есть . . . » *literally stands for "By me is . . . ". Thinking logically, to say "He has . . . " we need to put together "By him is . . . ". So we will have* «У + его + есть». *The only minor addition here is that* «Н» *is attached to the start of* «его». *For now, think of it as "n" in "an apple". So we end up with* «У негó есть . . . » *which means "He has . . . ". Using the same logic, we would arrive at* «У неё есть . . . » *that translates as "She has . . . ". We always need* «Н» *at the start of* «его» *and* «её» *after* «У».
>
> *E.g.,*   У негó есть сын. – *He has a son.*   У неё есть кнúга. – *She has a book.*

b) Reading for meaning. Have a look at the *two* passages below: the first one is about *him* and the second is about *her*. You need to read them paying attention to the use of «ОН», «ЕГÓ» and «У негó есть» («ОНÁ», «ЕЁ» and «У неё есть»). Make sure that you understand what you are reading.

1) У меня есть друг. Егó зовут Олéг. Он живёт в гóроде Тýле на улице Гáлкина. У негó есть большáя квартира, но это не в центре. Олéг инженéр, но он не работает на заводе. У негó есть новая работа в фирме. У негó есть жена. Её зовут Диáна. У него есть сын Платóн.

2) Вы уже знаете, что у меня есть старая подруга. Её зовут Óльга, можно Óля. Она живёт в гóроде Москве. У неё есть отлúчная квартира в центре на проспéкте Лéнина. Недалекó* у н её есть маленький магазин. Она очень много работает. У неё есть дети: сын Антóн и дочка Яна. Ещё у неё есть большая собака Лóра.

---

* далекó - *far*

c) Let's try it in Russian. Have another look at the passages above. Find the phrases that talk about 1) name; 2) work; 3) where one lives; 4) family. You are going to speak about each of my friends. While you are reading, try *not* to memorise the sentences, but remember the information. Then without looking at the texts, say what you remember first about Олéг and then about Óльга (stick to our Step-by-step guide). If you are working with someone else, one of you can speak about Олéг and the other one about Óльга. Take turns saying sentences, e.g., Олéг живёт в гóроде. – Óльга тóже живёт в гóроде.

> **NEW WORDS:** ДÉВУШКА - *a girlfriend (a partner)*
>
> ПÁРЕНЬ - *a boyboyfriend (a partner)*

«Пáрень» is a conversational word for *a young man* (sort of a "*lad*", but 15–30 years old). For partners who are older than the age of «дéвушка» and «пáрень», Russians use «жéнщина» and «мужчúна». The context always prompts when these words refer to partners. E.g., Это моя дéвушка. *OR* У неё есть нóвый мужчúна.

> **To make it clear:** Just in case you questioned how you would know whether a word with the soft sign at the end is a masculine or a feminine, it might be helpful to assume that the words ending in the soft sign, like «Кремль», «рубль» or «па́рень», are masculine unless specified otherwise (like «пло́щадь» and «тетра́дь», which are feminine). There are far fewer soft sign feminines, and they need to be memorised.

Ex.5 a) Reading for meaning. Some of these phrases might sound a bit like gossip – let's try it in Russian.

Э́то ва́ша де́вушка? – Нет, э́то моя́ жена́.　　А жена́ у него́ есть? – Нет, но ду́маю, есть же́нщина.

У тебя́ есть па́рень? – Да. Его́ зову́т Дени́с.　　Кто э́то? – Зна́ешь, у меня́ тётя есть. Э́то её мужчи́на.

Зна́ете, что у неё есть па́рень? – Да. В Москве́?　　Его́ де́вушка рабо́тает на стадио́не, где он игра́ет.

b) Say it in Russian. Watch out for «ОН»/«ЕГО́»/«У НЕГО́ ЕСТЬ» and for «ОНА́»/«ЕЁ»/«У НЕЁ ЕСТЬ».

I have a friend *(fem.)*. Her name is Galya. She has a son. He has friends in Moscow.

I have a brother. His name is Sergey. He has a daughter. Her name is Olya. She is a teacher.

Do you have a wife? What's her name? Does she have (*any*) brothers? How many?

I know (that) you have a son. Is his name Ivan? I think he has a girlfriend. True? What is her name?

This is my aunt. She lives in the village. She has a house and a big garden. Her children are in the city.

Is this your Russian uncle? What is his name? Does he live in Moscow? Does he have a wife?

He has a daughter. She is not a little girl. I think she has a boyfriend. I don't know what her name is.

c) It's your turn. Let's speak about what other people have. We will make blocks of two sentences each time. Start by saying that you have, let's say, a friend/brother/teacher/etc. Then say what/whom *they* have got. E.g., 1) У меня́ есть ма́ма. 2) У неё есть дом в дере́вне. This is great fun to do in a group, when the person on your left says what/whom they have, and you make a sentence about them. For example, I can say: У меня́ есть друзья́ в Ту́ле. – *You:* Её зову́т Ната́ша. У неё есть друзья́ в Ту́ле. Then it would be your turn to say a phrase about yourself for the person on your right to speak about you. If you want, you can add one more phrase about your people. E.g., У меня́ есть брат. Он живёт в Казахста́не. – *You:* У неё есть брат. Её брат (*or* «он») живёт в Казахста́не.

> **To make it clear:** At the moment, avoid putting names or any other nouns after «У» in «У него́/неё есть», as they would have to have a different ending after «У». Rather than saying "My brother has a dog" split the information between the two phrases: У меня́ есть брат. У него́ есть соба́ка.

You might have realised that one verb which we have not used when speaking about «он» or «она» is the verb *to like*. So far, we only know how to say «Я люблю». Let's see what it does in other forms.

НО́ВОЕ СЛО́ВО: ЛЮБИ́ТЬ – *to like*

Check *that you put your stress at the end and that you did NOT put the second «Л» in.*

WORTH REMEMBERING: *The verb «люби́ть» does not behave quite like the other Russian verbs we have learnt, but it is not an exception. There are two types of verbs in Russian, which have slightly different endings. «Люби́ть» belongs to the second type. To know how to handle it, we will try to remember its three "tricks", like we did with the verb «жить»:*

*1) «И» before «ть» in the dictionary form (люби́ть) is going to stay when you agree «люби́ть» with other people. So, for «ты»-form we will get «-**И**ШЬ» instead of «-ешь» and for «он/а́»-form – «-**И**Т» instead of «-ет»*

2) There is NO second «Л» like in «Я люблю».

*3) The **stress** moves to the front. Make sure you still put only one stress in each form with all the effort on the first vowel, making it longer than «И»*

ТЫ ЛЮ́БИШЬ   **ВЫ ЛЮ́БИТЕ**   **ОН/ОНА́ ЛЮ́БИТ**

Ex. 6 a) Let's get this right. Read the pairs of forms with the correct stress. Translate each form as you read.

люби́ть - лю́бишь	люблю́ - лю́бишь
люби́ть - лю́бите	люблю́ - лю́бите
люби́ть - лю́бит	люблю́ - лю́бит

b) Reading for meaning. Watch your stress, particularly in the forms of «люби́ть».

Ты лю́бишь шокола́д? – Да. И конфеты тоже.
Его де́вушка лю́бит баскетбо́л. Отли́чно играет.
Футбо́л я не очень люблю́. А ты? – Иногда́.
У неё есть большой сад. Она лю́бит цветы́.

Её па́рень хорошо́ плавает. Лю́бит мо́ре.
Вы лю́бите джаз? – Да. Я на саксофо́не игра́ю.
Это ва́ша книга? – Да. Очень люблю́ читать.
Мой дедушка пенсионер и лю́бит жить в деревне.

c) Now it's your turn. Say what other people like. If you work in a group, you can do a round in which the person on your left says in Russian what *they* like (e.g.: Я люблю́ пла́вать.). You need to say in Russian what *they* like (e.g.: Он/а́ лю́бит пла́вать.) and then make a phrase about yourself for the person on your right to speak about you. Watch your stresses and your endings. Speak slower to give yourself time to think.

Tip! If you happen to like something which is feminine in Russian, e.g., мýзыка, it needs to change its «А» to «У». E.g.: Я люблю́ мýзыку. We have not got time to practice it now, but it might be worth keeping in mind if you like music.

> ## НÓВАЯ ФРÁЗА: Я УЧУ́ РУ́ССКИЙ ЯЗЫ́К – *I am learning Russian*

To make it clear: The verb «учи́ть» is similar to «люби́ть» and has some peculiarities of usage, but I thought you might just like to have this phrase up your sleeve. Watch your stress in «УЧУ́», with the second «У» longer than the first.

*WORTH REMEMBERING: There is **NO special word for** "it" in Russian. To refer to masculine or feminine words, Russians use «ОН» or «ОНÁ». (E.g.: У меня есть каранда́ш, но он кра́сный. – I have a pencil, but it is red. OR Я живу́ в кварти́ре. Она́ о́чень ма́ленькая. – I live in a flat. It is very small.). For neuter words, Russian has a special word «ОНÓ». (E.g., Вот письмо́. Оно́ о́чень большо́е. – Here is the letter. It is very big/long).*

So, when Russians speak about things, they can use one of THREE words for "it": «ОН», «ОНÁ» and «ОНÓ». The choice depends on the gender of the item they are talking about. «ОНИ́» can be used to speak about both things and people.

Ex. 7 a) Let's get this right. Read the strings of words below. Translate each word and then replace it with «ОН», «ОНÁ», «ОНÓ» or «ОНИ́» (you should have one of each in each line).

дом, ванна, окно, ко́мнаты

мясо, о́вощи, пи́цца, хлеб

гости́ницы, проспе́кт, пло́щадь, метро

тури́ст, друзья́, письмо́, почта

каранда́ш, тетрадь, книги, слово

гита́ра, аккордео́н, пиани́но, балала́йки

море, мосты́, сад, река́

со́ки, молоко́, вода́, чай

b) Let's get this right. Fill in the gaps with «ОН», «ОНÁ», «ОНÓ» or «ОНИ́».

У меня́ есть маши́на, но .... о́чень ста́рая.

Мо́жно твои́ каранда́ши? – Да ...... там, в столе́.

Я зна́ю прия́тное кафе́ .... на у́лице Бо́лдина.

Это твоя́ коро́бка? – Извини́. .... не моя́.

Алло́. Я на у́лице. У меня́ пакет. ...... большо́й.

О́чень люблю́ кра́сное вино, но в кафе́ ...... дорого́е*.

У вас есть де́ньги? – Да, ... в номере в гости́нице.

Он игра́ет на гита́ре. ...... ненóвая, но играет хорошо́.

* дорого́й – *dear, expensive*

c) Let's try it in Russian. We need to have a go at using «ОН», «ОНА́» and «ОНО́» in the meaning of *it* in our own phrases. Make blocks of TWO sentences with the adjective in the second one, e.g., Я рабо́таю в о́фисе. Он но́вый, но о́чень ма́ленький. If you work with someone else, you can ask each other blocks of TWO questions, e.g.: У тебя́ есть су́мка? – Да, есть. – А она́ но́вая? – Нет, она́ ста́рая.

I think I have convinced you by now that endings in Russian words help you understand people correctly, and they also help Russians understand you better. We have discovered that the same stem (main part of the word) can have different endings attached to it: «рабо́та» *(a place of work, a job)*: «рабо́тать» *(to work, i.e. "to do work")* OR «дом» *(a house, a home)* : «до́ма» *(at home)*, «в до́ме» *(in the house)* Today we will have a look at another familiar stem which might have a different ending, if it starts describing things. Watch your stress!

> **НО́ВОЕ СЛО́ВО: ХОРО́ШИЙ** - *good, nice (as an adjective)*

Check *that you tried to put your tongue back when reading «ШИ».*

> **To make it clear:** The word «хорошо́» that we learnt earlier has NOT been and cannot be linked to a noun. E.g., Он хорошо́ пла́вает. OR Как дела́? - Хорошо́. For it to describe a thing or a person, it needs to turn into an adjective, which means getting an adjectival ending («-ИЙ» here as it would follow «Ш», according to the seven-letter rule). A different stress is not a rule – just a nuisance.

Ex.8 a) Reading for meaning. Try not to trip up too. In each sentence, underline a word with the «хоро́ш-» stem and say whether it is describing a noun (and is therefore an adjective) or a verb. Watch your stresses and your endings.

Э́то хоро́ший магази́н, он в це́нтре.

Я ду́маю, его́ шко́ла о́чень хоро́шая.

Ваш сын чита́ет о́чень хорошо́ сего́дня.

Гости́ница ничего́, а но́мер о́чень хоро́ший.

Она́ мно́го ест то́рты, конфе́ты, джем. Э́то нехорошо́.

Э́то ру́чка нехоро́шая. Вот лу́чше каранда́ш.

Он ду́мает, что вы хорошо́ игра́ете на гита́ре.

Ты зна́ешь, что у неё есть хоро́ший друг в Аме́рике?

Tip! *In a similar way, we can convert «отли́чно» to «отли́чн**ый**» and «прия́тно» to «прия́тн**ый**» to describe things and people. E.g.,* отли́чн**ая** су́мка, прия́тн**ое** письмо́. *See whether you want to remember these, or whether it is getting to be too much for you. They are not essential.*

251

> **To make it clear:** The **neuter form** of «хоро́ший» comes out as «хоро́ш**ее**». I don't think at this stage we need to go into details why it is like this – it is a spelling rule to do with hushing sounds and unstressed endings, and we really do not have time for it in this book. If you like nice wine, it might be worth remembering «хоро́шее вино́». Keep in mind that this is mainly about the spelling and is important if you are learning to write.

b) Let's get this right. Looking at the list of words below decide whether a word is a noun or a verb to help you use «хорошо́» or «хоро́ший/ая» with it. E.g., ко́мната - *noun* - хоро́шая ко́мната; пла́вает - *verb* - хорошо́ пла́вает. Note that if you try translating the verb phrases into English word by word, they might come out clumsy (хорошо́ пла́вает = *swims well*, which is probably better phrased as *is a good swimmer* or *is good at swimming*). Watch that your stress is different in «хоро́ший» and «хорошо́».

кварти́ра, читает, мальчик, собака, играю, помогает, гостиница, чай, тетрадь, плаваете, работа, друг, знаешь, пицца, номер, работает, водка, фотоаппарат

> *Check whether you remember how to say "nice wine", if you need it.*

c) Now it's your turn. Think of things that you have or somebody else has which you think are nice/good and use «хоро́ший/ая» with them. Then think of what you or someone else is good at in order to use «хорошо́». If you feel comfortable, try using «отли́чный» and «прия́тный» to describe things and people. E.g., отли́чный друг, прия́тная же́нщина. If you work with someone else, take turns saying your sentences, but without the words «хорошо́» or «хоро́ш/ий/ая», so that the other person can ask you follow-up questions using those words. E.g., Я игра́ю на пиани́но. - Хорошо́ игра́ешь? OR У меня́ есть сестра́. У неё есть кни́га. - Хоро́ш**ая** кни́га?

> **НО́ВОЕ СЛО́ВО: ДО́БРЫЙ** - *kind, good (not about things)*

In modern Russian, the word «до́брый» refers mainly to people in the meaning of *kind*. It is also used in greetings such as *Good evening* or *Good day*.

> **NEW WORDS:**
>
> | | |
> |---|---|
> | **У́ТРО** - *morning* | До́бр**ое** у́тро. |
> | **ДЕНЬ** - *afternoon, day* | До́брый день. |
> | **ВЕ́ЧЕР** - *evening* | До́брый ве́чер. |
> | **НОЧЬ** - *night* | Споко́йной но́чи. |

> *Check that you noticed that «у́тро» is neuter, and «до́бр**ое**» has the ending to match it.*

You might remember «Спокойной ночи» from our late-night farewells. «Спокойный» means *peaceful* or *calm*. The word «ночь» has a different ending in the box because when Russians wish something, they put words into a special form, hence the words in «Спокойной ночи» do not appear in their dictionary forms (which are the first nouns in the box). At this stage, we will just remember it as a fixed phrase, and make sure that you never use it when you leave a place. In fact, none of the above greetings can be used as a farewell.

Also, I have a suspicion that you might have worked out that «день» is a masculine word, as it agrees with the dictionary form of «добрый». «Ночь», on the contrary, is a soft sign feminine (like «площадь» and «тетрадь»).

d) Let's get this right. Among the words below find *four* which you can use «добрый» with. Use «хороший» with the rest. Make sure you agree them all correctly. Translate what you have got. Keep an eye on the stress in «хороший».

.... книга	.... чай	.... утро.
.... вечер.	.... ручка	.... номер
.... женщина	.... день.	.... сумка

e) What would you say in Russia when:

you are arriving for somebody's dinner party;

you are phoning somebody;

you are leaving an office at the end of the day;

you feel that something is good;

your friend is leaving;

you see somebody you know at breakfast;

you meet somebody for the first time;

you are going to bed in a hotel where you are staying;

you want to compliment the host on their nice flat;

somebody is leaving but you will see them tomorrow;

somebody walks into your office in the afternoon;

you bump into your friend in town.

> НОВОЕ СЛОВО: **КРАСИВЫЙ** - beautiful *(about appearance, view)*

The words «красный» (for *red*) and «красивый» (as *beautiful*) look very close – you might remember that they came from the same word in Old Russian. To keep from confusing them, watch the stress and the letter «В». The stress in «красный» is at the beginning (think that we learnt it first or "to begin with"). You can also think that there was no «В» to start with, as there is no «В» in красный. Have a go: красный - краси**в**ый *(with a long and loud «И»)*.

Ex. 9 a) Try not to trip up! Read aloud and translate correctly. The stress here is crucial.

красный дом - красивый дом

красная сумка - красивая сумка

Красное море - красивое море

Красная площадь - красивая площадь

красная ручка

красивая женщина

красивый мужчина

красное яблоко

красивая деревня

красный диван

красивая машина

красное вино

To make it clear: The word «краси́вый» is used to speak about how things and people look, that is, about their appearance, but NOT about how something feels, tastes or smells. For example, you can say «краси́вый го́род» or «краси́вая де́вушка», but you cannot use it to say "beautiful wine" or "beautiful day". You would need «прекра́сный» (meaning "splendid, wonderful") in this case. E.g., прекра́сное вино́, прекра́сный день. Alternatively, you can use «о́чень хоро́ший» or «отли́чный».

NEW WORD: БЕ́ЛЫЙ - *white*

---

b) Let's try it in Russian. See which adjectives on the left can describe the nouns on the right. Remember that «до́брый» and «краси́вый» have restricted use. Make phrases which would be correct in Russian. Watch your endings. If you work with someone else, make random phrases for each other to translate. Make sure you take turns. You can add «отли́чный» and «прия́тный» to the list if you feel comfortable.

хоро́ший	день
до́брый	машина
кра́сный	вино
бе́лый	девушка
краси́вый	ве́чер
	пло́щадь
	у́тро
	дом
	ручка
	деревня
	челове́к

WORTH REMEMBERING: *In Russian* **things DO NOT have things***. The phrase «У него/неё есть» is only used to speak about people. To say, for example, that "a town has a theatre", Russians would say "There is a theatre in the town".* **"There is" in Russian is «ЕСТЬ».** *So, we will have «В го́роде есть теа́тр». Note that you do not need «там» with it. Also, it is better to start this kind of sentences with the location (e.g.: В го́роде), rather than «есть». Compare:* **В Москве́** *есть Кремль. — There is a Kremlin* <u>in Moscow</u>. *OR Moscow has a Kremlin.*

НО́ВОЕ СЛО́ВО: **ЕСТЬ** *—There is/are*

Ex. 10 a) Reading for meaning. When reading each phrase in Russian, try thinking about two ways of translating «ЕСТЬ» into English. E.g., В го́роде есть теа́тр. – *1) There is a theatre in town. 2) The town has a theatre.* Keep an eye on the correct stress in «краси́вый». Also, note the genders of the adjectives here.

Москва - очень большо́й город. В Москве есть Кремль. Он очень краси́вый.
Тула - большо́й и старый город. В Туле тоже есть Кремль. Он ма́ленький, но интере́сный.

В Москве есть метро́. Оно - очень краси́вое. Ста́нция метро́ «Библиоте́ка Ле́нина» очень краси́вая!

Тула - нема́ленький город, но в Туле нет метро. В Туле есть вокза́лы и ма́ленький аэропо́рт.

В Москве есть Кра́сная площадь. Она очень ста́рая, большая и краси́вая.
В Туле есть площадь Ленина. Она в центре. Это центра́льная площадь в городе.

В Москве есть Большо́й теа́тр. Он в центре. Это очень старый и очень большо́й теа́тр.

В Туле есть драмати́ческий теа́тр. Он на проспе́кте Ле́нина. Он новый, но небольшо́й.

To make it clear: The word «**интере́сный**» does not normally have connotations of being peculiar or odd. It is a very positive description. Russians can say «интере́сная де́вушка» meaning "interesting to talk to" or even "sophisticated". Note that, unlike in its English equivalent, there is NO second «Т» in Russian «интере́сный».

---

b) Find in the text above all forms of "it" and say which words they refer to («он» refers to «Кремль» which is masculine). Then, find all adjectives (descriptive words) and say which gender they describe.

c) Say it in Russian. Remember that it is better to start with the location rather than the word «есть» *(for "There is/are")*. Watch the gender of *it* too.

There is a Kremlin <u>in Moscow</u>. It is very beautiful.

There is a very old square <u>in Moscow, Red Square</u>. It is very big.

There is an old theatre <u>in Moscow, the Bolshoi Theatre</u>. It is very interesting.

There is an underground <u>in Moscow</u>. It is very beautiful.

d) Let's try it in Russian. Now, following the same pattern, think about what you can say about Tula. Remember to start with «В Ту́ле есть. . . . . . .» and watch your genders.

> **NEW WORDS:** ЦЕ́РКОВЬ - *church*
>
> СОБО́Р - *cathedral*

> **To make it clear:** The word «це́рковь» is classed as a feminine word. It belongs to the same small cluster of "funny feminines" with the soft sign as «пло́щадь», «тетра́дь» and «ночь». We definitely need to know that they are feminine, if we want to describe them. E.g., В дере́вне есть це́рковь. Он**а** о́чень стар**ая**.

d) Let's get this right. Go through the list of adjectives below, one by one, using «це́рковь» *(fem)* or «собо́р» *(masculine),* depending on the form they have. Say the phrases in Russian, aloud. Make sure that you understand what you are saying.

большо́й, ма́ленькая, хоро́шая, прекра́сный, бе́лая, краси́вая, интере́сный, ста́рый, но́вая, англи́йский, ру́сская

e) Step-by-step guide of how to describe a place where you live in Russian.

1. Say *where you live*. (Remember «В» in front and «Е» at the end, unless the name of the place cannot be classed as masculine or feminine in Russian, like «в Гла́стонбери».)

2. Specify whether this is *a city/ a town or a village* and whether it is big or little. (Keep in mind that «го́род» is masculine, while «дере́вня» is feminine.)

3. Say whether it has *a central street or a square*. Describe them or say what buildings are there. (You would need to use «ЕСТЬ» for *There is/are* instead of a "having" construction). Remember to start with the location, e.g., В це́нтре есть у́лица Хай-Стрит.

4. Describe what your city/town/village has. Make *blocks of TWO sentences*: the first with «ЕСТЬ» and the second with one of Russian words for *"it" and an adjective*. (E.g., В дере́вне есть це́рковь. Она́ о́чень ста́рая.)

If you live in a big city which has lots of shops, stations, banks etc. you can use it as a chance to practice your plurals. Keep in mind that you do not know yet how to describe plurals, so to use your adjectives choose ONE, the most prominent feature, and make two sentences about it. E.g., В це́нтре есть ста́рый собо́р. Он о́чень краси́вый.

Think how you can pay compliments in Russian. It should definitely help you handle Russian genders. You can use one adjective one day and another the next. When you get confident, try using a different adjective each time. You can add other words that you know to these small phrases, e.g., Сего́дня прекра́сный день. OR У него́ (есть) отли́чная маши́на. OR Ва́ша сестра́ - краси́вая де́вушка.

We have now got to the end of our last unit in this book. You still have the overall revision for your next session. I do hope you enjoyed learning with me. I definitely enjoyed writing this book. I am thinking about doing another one, so look out for it. Whatever you do – УДА́ЧИ! Keep thinking Russian.

Final revision

Дóбрый день. Or is it already «Дóбрый вéчер»? Perhaps it is still morning for you, and I can say «Дóброе ýтро» to you? Choose the one which is right for you today. «Как дела?» How do you return it to me? – **Прекрáсно!** Do you recognise this word? We came across it at the end of Unit 10. It means *wonderful, splendid,* but it had a different ending then. As a reply to «Как делá?» it does not describe anything in particular, so it does not need to agree with feminine or masculine etc. Here it is similar to some other answers we used like «Хорошó», «Отлúчно», «Неплóхо» etc.

One of our main aims in this book was for you to learn to read Russian, and we gave it a good go, didn't we? Today we shall have a look at the Cyrillic alphabet once again. It is not a stranger to you now but a good friend, I hope. Enjoy using it.

А Б В Г Д Е Ё Ж З И Й К Л М Н О П Р С Т У Ф Х Ц Ч Ш Щ Ъ Ы Ь Э Ю Я

Ex. 1 a) Let's get this right. Looking at the alphabet above, name (phonetically) the letter following «Б», «Е», «Ж», «Й», «П», «Т», «Ф», «Ш», «Ъ», «Ю». Have another look at the alphabet above (remember it might help to split it into three parts). Now cover it with your hand or a sheet of paper and name the same letters again. If you had to peep, do it again.

b) Fill in the gaps. Try doing it without looking at the alphabet above.

А ... В Г Д ... Ё ... З И ... К Л М .... О .... Р ... Т ... Ф ... Ц Ч ... Щ Ъ Ы .... Э ... Я

c) Let's get this right. Pick ten letters which stand for vowel sounds. Then, without looking at the alphabet, complete the pairs:

А -....   Э -....   О -....   У -....   Ы -....

1. Can you name four Russian letters which give us hushing sounds?

2. Which two of them are read at the back of your mouth?

3. Name the two which are close to the front and to the palate and do not affect the reading of «И».

4. How do we read «Е» after each of them?

Ex.2 a) Try not to trip up! Watch your «Ц» here too. Read these strings slowly and give yourself time to get the right sound.

нищ - ниц - ни́ша - ни́же - ничко́м

плачу́ - плацу́ - палашу́ - полощу́ - положу́

причáл - прижáл - пришёл - прицéл - прищéпка

щи - шью - чу́ю - жую́ - целу́ю

жени́ть - чини́ть - цени́ть - щени́ть - шамáнить

Шу́рка - чу́рки - щу́рит - жури́т - цари́т

грéчка - Грéция - грешу́ - грущу́ - гружу́

рéжет - ры́щет - ры́царь - рычи́т - реши́т

цóкал - щёлкал - шёлка - чёлка - жёлтый

венéц - вéнчик - вéшний - вéщий - свéжий

b) Decoding Cyrillic. Read Russian anagrams, keeping «ШИ» and «ЖИ» at the back of your mouth.

пиши́ - шипи́   кричи́ - чири́к   цéли - лицé   щéли - лещи́

лы́жи - жи́лы   пищáл - щипáл   лишáл - шали́л   нáши - ши́на

c) Big sort out. In the list below, underline words with the long front «Щ», and then read the list as it is, keeping «Ш» at the back. If you are learning to write, sort out the words into two groups.

школа, карандаши́, óвощи, чашка, дéвушка, машины, женщина, бабушки, шоколад, плóщадь, ешь, борщ, лу́чше, дедушка, щи, шесть, матрёшка, ещё, большой, знаешь, хорошо

d) What's in a name? Here are some more names from the Moscow underground map. Watch out for hushers and «Ц». Make sure that there is only ONE stress per word – no double-stressing.

Щу́кинская, Шáболовская, Чи́стые пруды́, Преображéнская плóщадь, Вы́стовочная, Цветнóй бульвáр, Бáбушкинская, Тексти́льщики, Окружнáя, плóщадь Ильичá, Борови́цкая, Шоссе Энтузиáстов, Полежáевская, Щёлковская, Нóвые Черёмушки, Жулéбино, Речнóй вокзáл

e) Try not to trip up! Now you might have a couple of challenging sounds in one word. Take your time.

щенóк - щелчóк - щёлочь

щёточка - щёлочка - пощёчина

шармáнщик - шипя́щий - пищи́шь

хи́щник - хищéние - похищáл

дружи́ще - жили́ще - убéжище

жéнщина - жестя́нщик - живу́щий

щипцы́ - вещи́ца - щу́пальца

я́щерица - защи́тница - сокрóвищница

5. How many words in Russian can be used to translate the English word *it*?

6. In how many ways can we translate «он» and «онá»?

7. When do we use «онó»?

8. How do we know that a noun is neuter?

9. How many words for *they* does Russian have?

Ex.3 a) Let's get this right. Read the words below. Translate each word, then decide whether it is masculine, feminine, neuter or plural and replace it with «он», «она́», «оно́» or «они́».

цирк, му́зыка, ра́дио, карти́ны, кни́ги, дере́вня, де́ньги, но́мер, больни́цы, я́блоко, компью́тер, матрёшка, ма́сло, фру́кты, са́хар, мо́ре, карандаши́, конфе́ты, у́ лица, пло́щадь, газе́та, сло́во, кафе́, ша́хматы, де́вочки, фотоаппара́т, мужчи́на, ёлка, вино́, о́вощи, мя́со, сыр, вы́ход, учи́тель, соба́ка, тетра́дь, бра́тья, спорт, письмо́, гаражи́, же́нщины, дя́дя, ста́нция, метро́, де́ти, челове́к, шко́ла

Check your stress in «гаражи́» *and* «карандаши́»;
that you remembered that «пло́щадь» *and* «тетра́дь» *are feminine;*
that you replaced «де́ньги» *and* «бра́тья» *with* «они́».

b) Reading for meaning. Keep an eye on the highlighted words – see how you translate them.

– Извини́те, пожа́луйста. Это ваш паке́т?

– Нет, не мой.

– **Он** тут на сту́ле . . . Я не зна́ю, что де́лать.

– На паке́те англи́йское сло́во «Сувени́ры», а челове́к на у́лице - англича́нин. Ду́маю, что паке́т – **его́**.

– Спаси́бо. Ду́маю, что это хоро́шая иде́я.
(to the Englishman) Это ваш паке́т?

– Это твоя́ маши́на?

– Нет. У меня́ есть друг, **она́ его́**.

– Хоро́шая?

– Не зна́ю. **Она́** – не о́чень но́вая, но **он её** лю́бит.

– А у меня́ мотоци́кл есть. **Он** то́же нено́вый. Моя́ де́вушка о́чень лю́бит мотоци́клы.

Reading Challenge: Моро́женщица

10. Name three pairs of letters which adjectives (descriptive words) can have at the end of their masculine form.

 11. Which of them *always* has the stress on it?

c) Let's get this right. Fill in the correct *two* letters at the end of these adjectives (their dictionary forms). Read and translate.

больш́.... .   ма́леньк....   англи́йск.... .   краси́в......

но́в.... .   ста́р....   молод́....   хоро́ш.....

ру́сск....   до́бр.....   кра́сн......   бе́л......

d) Big sort out. Mark the stress without checking the section above. First read out all the adjectives with the stress at the front, then those with the stress at the end and finally those left.

бе́лый, ма́ленький, молодо́й, краси́вый, англи́йский, до́брый, большо́й, ру́сский, ста́рый, кра́сный, хоро́ший, интере́сный, но́вый

12. What do we need to do with the last TWO letters of the dictionary form to agree an adjective with a feminine noun?

(?) 13. What do we put at the end of a descriptive word (an adjective) to link it to a neuter noun?

Ex.4 a) Decoding Cyrillic. Make sure you read the TWO letters at the end correctly. Watch your stress.

тáлый - тáлая - тáлое   золотáя - золотóе - золотóй

сáмая - сáмый - сáмое   дорогóй - дорогóе - дорогáя

крéпкое - крéпкий - крéпкая   голубóе - голубáя - голубóй

b) Let's try it in Russian. Mark the stresses in your adjectives (descriptive words) first. Then, using the table, put the adjectives and nouns together to make meaningful phrases. You can use each word only ONCE! Remember to change the *TWO* letters at the end of the adjectives to agree with feminines or neuters. If you work with someone else, say the phrases for each other to translate.

большой	дéвочка
маленький	мóре
новый	человек
старый	мýзыка
русский	плóщадь
красный	вéчер
молодой	цéрковь
добрый	яблоко
белый	студент

> *Check that you remembered that the word «цéрковь» is feminine; that you did not use «молодóй» with «дéвочка», as «молодóй» can only refer to those over 15 years old.*

14. Think of two distinctive differences in pronunciation of «крáсный» and «красúвый».

(?) 15. Give a couple of examples when you cannot use «красúвый». Name a couple of words which can be used instead.

c) Try not to trip up! крáсный : красúвый : прекрáсный. Translate the phrases and name the gender.

крáсный стул, красúвая кóмната, красúвое метрó, прекрáсная картúна, красúвый дом, крáсная рýчка, прекрáсный сад, крáсное винó, красúвый собóр, прекрáсное ýтро, крáсное яблоко, прекрáсный день,

красúвая жéнщина, крáсная машúна, прекрáсное кафé, красúвое слóво, прекрáсная книга, крáсный пакéт

16. Do you remember that the old familiar «хорошо́» cannot be used to describe nouns (as it is normally linked to a verb to, e.g., хорошо́ пла́вает)?

17. What happens to «хоро́ший» (which IS an adjective) if it describes a feminine word?

18. Can you remember its neuter form?

Ex. 5 a) Let's get this right. Fill in the correct endings and mark the correct stress. Keep in mind that you have «хорошо́» if there is no noun to describe.

У неё есть хорош..... подруга Лю́ба.   Его сын – ма́ленький, но читает хорош...... и лю́бит кни́ги.

Он хорош..... игра́ет на саксофо́не.   Вот меню́. Мясо ешь? – Иногда. – Тут мясо о́чень хорош.....

Ду́маю, это хорош...... журна́л.   У вас хорош..... дом и краси́вый сад. – Спаси́бо.

Как дела́? – Хорош...... А у тебя́?   Ты хорош..... зна́ешь го́род? – Немно́го зна́ю центр.

Check that in the second sentence on the right you spelt «хоро́шее» *with two* «Е»*-s.*

b) Say it in Russian.

Good evening.	nice wine	good woman	Good! *(well)*	Good night.
good hotel	beautiful bag	nice morning	beautiful garden	nice flat
beautiful city	Good day.	beautiful picture	good word	beautiful day

Check that you used «прекра́сный» *or* «о́чень хоро́ший» *in the last phrase.*

c) Reading for meaning. After you read this, find all the adjectives, mark the stress in them and say which gender they describe.

ЧТО ДЕ́ЛАТЬ?

В Ту́ле у меня́ есть прекрасный друг, Оле́г (вы его́ зна́ете). Он о́чень лю́бит мотоци́клы. У него́ есть большо́й красный мотоцикл «Урал». Он не о́чень новый, но, я ду́маю, что хоро́ший. Мой друг мно́го чита́ет Автожурна́л. У него́ есть хоро́шая рабо́та и де́ньги. Немно́го, но есть. Он ду́мает купи́ть[1] но́вый мотоцикл «Хонда». Его́ жена́ Диа́на лю́бит маши́ны. У неё есть ста́рая бе́лая маши́на. Она́ ду́мает, что она́ ужа́сно некраси́вая. Я ду́маю, что е́сли[2] у неё бу́дет[3] ма́ленькая но́вая маши́на, она́ бу́дет[3] о́чень ра́да. Диа́на то́же рабо́тает, но маши́на – это до́рого[4]! Что делать: но́вая маши́на или но́вый мотоци́кл? А мо́жет быть[5], лу́чше Чёрное[6] мо́ре ле́том? А вы как ду́маете?

---

[1] купи́ть – *to buy*   [3] бу́дет – *will (Future)*   [5] до́рого – *expensive*

[2] е́сли – *if*   [4] мо́жет быть – *maybe*   [6] чёрный – *black*

d) Say it in Russian. Having read about Олéг, complete the sentences below. In the last sentence write in what you think is better. Then try to think how you would tell somebody about Олег и Диáна and their dilemma.

Это мой друг. У него есть .... мотоцúкл. Он ...., но....................
У него есть .... работа.

У него тоже есть женá Диáна. У неё есть .... машина. Онá.........................
Диáна думает, что её машина ...., и ....
машúна будет лýчше.

Я думаю, что лýчше ....

e) Now it's your turn. Say in Russian what you or somebody among your family and friends have, which is new or old, nice or not very; perhaps you own something beautiful. Watch that your descriptions match the genders of the things. E.g., У меня есть машúна. Онá óчень стáрая, но я её óчень люблю́. Думаю, она хорóшая.

? 19. How many letters do you need to change to agree the possessive words like «мой», «твой», «ваш» with their nouns?

Ex.6 a) Let's try it in Russian. Imagine yourself as a teacher or a guide who is trying to organise a group of Russian students. Show them that you have got your item and ask where theirs are. E.g., Вот мой карандáш. А где вáши карандашú? Watch your plurals.

Tip! Make sure that the stresses in «моя́»/«моё» and «вáша»/«вáше» are at the opposite ends of the words.

ручка, пакет, книга, тетрадь, билéт, карта, письмó, телефон, виза, сумка, альбóм

20. How do we read «Г» in «егó»?

? 21. What is the first sound in both «егó» and «её»?

22. Where is the stress in both words?

23. Do «егó» and «её» change to agree with masculines, feminines and neurters that they describe?

Ex.7 a) Let's try it in Russian. Fill in «егó» or «её» according to the context.

Это мой брат Валéрий. А это ...... дочка Óля.	Учительница и ...... студенты в школе.
Это твоя тётя? – Да. – А это .... муж?	Это ваш менеджер? Это .... тетрадь?
.... дéвушка хорошо знает русский.	.... муж тоже работает на заводе.
Её друзья – в кафе. .... пáрень тоже там.	Журналúст Иванóв. Вот ..... телефон.

b) Say it in Russian. Choose the correct form of «мой», «твой» and «ваш».

my map, her pencil, your *(formal)* child, his flat, your *(inform.)* Dad, his newspapers, my desk, her room, your *(formal)* café, his children, your *(inform.)* car, her bags, his plastic bag, my plate, your *(inform.)* chair, her uncle, your *(formal)* wall, my wine, his chocolates, my Russian doll, your *(form.)* farm, her apple, my glass, her brothers, his fruit, your *(inform.)* box, my bread, your *(formal)* friends, his money

c) Let's get this right. Change the words in brackets <u>where needed</u> to match the gender of the nouns. Watch the number of letters that you need to change in «мой»/«твой»/«ваш» and in the adjectives, e.g., (мой) (красный) ручка - мо**я́** кра́сн**ая** ру́чка.

(ваш) (англи́йский) учи́тель	(её) (маленький) дочка	(его) (добрый) дядя
(мой) (русский) учи́тельница	(твой) (кра́сный) карандаш	(ваш) (большо́й) письмо́
(твой) (ста́рый) ра́дио	(ваш) (белый) церковь	(твой) (хороший) книга
(его) (краси́вый) де́вушка	(мой) (новый) сло́во	(мой) (отли́чный) па́рень

24. Does «зову́т» in «Меня зову́т» mean *name*? What *does* it mean?

25. Is there a word *my* in «Меня́ зову́т»? What does «меня́» stand for?

26. Though «Как вас зову́т?» is translated as *What is your name?*, what is the direct translation of «как»?

27. Can you remember the familiar version of «Как вас зову́т?»?

28. What is the English equivalent of «Мне о́чень прия́тно.»? What does each word stand for?

Ex.8 a) Let's get this right. Fill in the gaps with the correct words from «Как вас/тебя́ зову́т?» or «Меня́ зову́т. . . .». or «Мне о́чень прия́тно.» Note that some sentences may not have *all* the words in them.

– Здра́вствуйте. Как вас ....?	– Это моя́ дочка.	– Извини́те. .... вас зову́т?
– .... зову́т Ири́на. А вас?	– Как .... зову́т, де́вочка?	– Евге́ний, но можно Же́ня.
– А меня́ Игорь.	– Ка́тенька.	А .... как?
– .... прия́тно.	– О́чень ...., Ка́тенька.	– А .... Валенти́на, или
– Мне	А меня́ .... Ири́на	Ва́ля.
	Серге́евна.	– ....
		– .... тоже.

b) Let's get this right. Read the statements below. Follow them up with the correct form of *And you?* Start formal on the left and go informal on the right. You now have *THREE* forms of each to choose from: 1) А вы? 2) А у вас? 3) А вас? (with informal versions: А ты? А у тебя́? А тебя́)?

Я живу́ в го́роде. А ....?	Сего́дня у меня́ есть маши́на. А ....?
У меня́ есть соба́ка. А .... ?	Влад меня́ зову́т. А .... ?
Меня́ зову́т Ири́на. А ....?	Я понима́ю. А ....?

Виза у меня есть. А .... ?   На гита́ре непло́хо игра́ю. А .... ?

Очень мно́го чита́ю. А ....?   Меня́ зову́т Татья́на. А ....?

Меня́ зовут Ви́ктор. А .... ?   У меня́ есть па́спорт. А ....?

c) Now it's your turn. Try practicing *And you?* questions. Think of what you can say about yourself in Russian, and after each phrase choose the right form of *And you?* If you are working in a group, do a round in which you say a phrase about yourself and then turn to the person next to you with the right form of *And you?* They need to answer it and then make a new phrase about themselves. Try using different constructions: verbs, "I have" and «Меня́ зову́т . . . »

29. What are the *two* translations of «ЕГО́»?

30. How do we literally translate «Как его́ зову́т?» and «Как её зову́т?»

c) Let's try it in Russian. Think of the people you know. Say in Russian that you have, let's say, *a friend*, and what their name is. For example, I can say: У меня́ есть подру́га. Её зову́т Га́ля. If you work in a group, you can do two rounds: first you have a conversation with one person (following our step-by-step guide), and then change partners and tell your new partner about your first partner. Remember to take turns.

31. How do we translate «У него́ есть . . . » ?

32. Do you remember what each of the words in «У него́ есть . . . » means?

33. What does «У неё есть . . . » stand for?

34. When do we need to put «Н» at the start of «его» and «её»?

d) Let's get this right. Have a look at what people say about themselves. Think how you would speak ABOUT them in Russian. Say the sentences aloud and keep an eye on the use of «он» /«его́»/«У него́» («она́»/«её»/ «У неё»). Make sure you always put «Н» at the start of «его́» and «её» after «У». E.g., Де́вочка: У меня́ есть сестра́. – У неё есть сестра́.

Англича́нин: Я англича́нин. У меня́ есть па́спорт и виза.

Пенсионерка: Мои дети в Смоле́нске. Дома у меня́ есть кошка.

Такси́ст: Я рабо́таю на такси. Моя́ машина - новая.

Русская: У меня́ есть кварти́ра в Туле. Я не живу́ в Москве́.

Молода́я де́вушка: Меня́ зову́т На́стя. Я студентка. У меня́ есть очень хорошая учительница.

Её па́рень: У меня́ есть раке́тки. В те́ннис я игра́ю очень мно́го. Я люблю́ спорт.

До́ктор: Меня́ зову́т Алексе́й Петро́вич. Моя́ больница - не в центре, но у меня́ новый офис.

Медсестра: А я не рабо́таю в больни́це. Я рабо́таю в школе. Меня́ зову́т Гали́на Серге́евна.

Женщина: У меня́ всё хорошо. Муж рабо́тает в банке. Я тоже рабо́таю. У меня́ есть ребёнок.

Мужчина: Я очень люблю́ чита́ть. У меня́ есть книги. Ещё я немного зна́ю английский язы́к. Мой сын – в университете.

35. Why are we looking at the verb «любить» separately? How do we translate this form?

36. Try to remember its three tricks. Name the *extra* letter which appears *only* in the Я-form.

37. Which vowel makes its other endings (for example, in its «ты» form), unlike in other verbs which we have come across?

38. Which form has the same stress as the dictionary form? Where is the stress in the other forms? Write in «И» in the endings and read aloud with the correct stress: ты люб. . . . .шь, он/á люб. . . .т, вы люб. . . . .те.

Ex. 9 a) Jog your memory. Without looking at the forms above, mark the stress in the following verb forms. Read aloud and translate each form.

любит, люблю, любишь, любить, любите

b) Say it in Russian. Watch your stress and your endings.

| to like – he likes | I like – she likes | he likes – Do you like? *(familiar)* |
| I like – Do you like? *(familiar)* | to like - Do you like? *(formal)* | I like – to like |

c) Let's try it in Russian. Have a look at the sentences below. Think what those people might like. Make one phrase in Russian about each of them using the verb «любить» in the correct form. You might use the words under the line to give you a clue.

Антон хорошо играет в теннис.

Лидочка ест шоколадный торт.

Валентина Николаевна работает в саду.

Олег живёт в Ялте летом. Он много плавает.

Сегодня Света – в Третьяковской галерее.

Яна знает итальянский, французский и английский.

Николай - шофёр. У него есть мотоцикл и машина.

Ольга ест бананы, абрикосы и яблоки.

Галя много читает в библиотеке.

Лёна играет на пианино. Завтра она на концерте.

машины, цветы, читать, спорт, фрукты, музыку, шоколад, картины, языки, плавать.

d) Now it's your turn. Think how you would ask a Russian about what they like, in both formal and informal ways. Watch your stress! Use the words below to make questions. E.g., Вы любите теннис?/Ты любишь теннис? If you are working with somebody else, you can try a conversation. Remember to take turns rather than doing a cross-examination. If you have time, you can tell somebody else about what the other person likes or dislikes.

шоколад, футбол, музыка (!), радио, читать, фрукты, чай, мясо, шахматы, играть в снуккер, театр, матрёшки, фильмы, плавать, сыр, русский язык, кофе, магазины, играть на гитаре, кино, Лондон

Check that the word «музыка» got its «У» after «любит» (музыку).

b) Find a person who

plays piano	reads a lot	helps at home
knows London well	likes fruit	is tired
has a dog	plays tennis sometimes	does not know French
likes music	has a car	likes swimming

Ex.10 a) Reading for meaning: МОЙ ДРУЗЬЯ́ В БЕЛАРУ́СИ

Tip! The word «Белару́сь» is another soft sign feminine. All soft sign feminines have the ending «И», instead of «Е», after «В» when talking about place.

У меня́ есть о́чень хоро́ший друг. Его́ зову́т И́горь. Живёт он в Бори́сове. Бори́сов - небольшо́й го́род в Белару́си. У него́ там есть но́вая кварти́ра в до́ме на у́лице Вату́тина.

У него́ есть жена́. Её зову́т Ната́ша. У него́ есть де́ти то́же. Его́ сын Па́ша - большо́й ма́льчик, он в шко́ле. Сын Алёша - ма́ленький ребёнок. Ната́ша - медсестра́ в больни́це, но сейча́с[1] она́ не рабо́тает, потому́ что[2] Алёша - о́чень ма́ленький.

И́горь - инжене́р, он рабо́тает на заво́де «Кра́сный октя́брь». Это ма́ленький заво́д о́птики в Бори́сове, но его́ рабо́та - о́чень интере́сная. Ещё у него́ есть ста́рая маши́на, но он её о́чень лю́бит. Иногда́ ве́чером[3] он рабо́тает на такси́. И́горь чита́ет «Автожурна́л». Ещё он о́чень лю́бит спорт. Он мно́го пла́вает и иногда́ игра́ет в хокке́й.

b) Пра́вда или непра́вда? We did a similar exercise about Sasha in Unit 10. Remember that the sentences here are NOT questions – they are statements, but not all of them are correct. Read each sentence. If the sentence is correct say «Да» (or «Пра́вда») and repeat it without looking in the book. If it is wrong, say «Нет» (or «Непра́вда») and give the correct sentence (again, without reading it)

И́горь живёт в Росси́и.	Его́ де́ти - до́ма, а не в шко́ле.
Бори́сов - большо́й го́род.	Его́ жена́ сейча́с не рабо́тает.
И́горь живёт в кварти́ре.	Её зову́т Ната́ша.
У него́ есть но́вая кварти́ра.	И́горь рабо́тает на вокза́ле.
У него́ есть жена́ и до́чка.	У него́ есть мотоци́кл.
Его́ сын Па́ша - молодо́й челове́к.	Иногда́ И́горь рабо́тает на такси́.
Алёша - ма́ленький ма́льчик.	И́горь лю́бит спорт.

Check that «И́горь» has the stress at the front.

---

[1] сейча́с - *now*   [2] потому́ что - *because*   [3] ве́чером - *in the evening*

c) Question time. You can check the text if you need the information, but you need to make sure you DO NOT read when you answer.

Где живёт Игорь?	Алёша - большóй или мáленький?
Борúсов - большóй город?	Кто в школе: Алёша или Пáша?
У него квартира или дом?	«Крáсный октя́брь» - это стадиóн?
Его квартира - нóвая?	Игорь работает на завóде вéчером?
У него есть семья́*?	Где он работает вéчером?
Его женá дóктор в бóльнице?	У него есть машина или мотоцúкл?
Онá рабóтает сейчáс?	Что он лю́бит?

* семья́ - *family*

d) Say it in Russian. Say what you can remember about Игорь. Our Step-by-step guide might keep you on track. Make sure that you make your own sentences using the information in the text, rather than trying to remember the sentences from the text.

Now think of how you would tell me in Russian about somebody you know: a friend, a colleague, a neighbour or a relation. Think of RUSSIAN phrases you know to say a few things about him/her. Try not to use a dictionary if you can help it — see whether you can rephrase things instead.

e) Step-by-step guide on how to speak about somebody in Russian.

1. Start by explaining who they are to you. E.g., У меня́ есть подрýга. OR Я живý в дóме №14, а Дэвид живёт в дóме №12. OR У меня́ есть тётя. Это её сын.

2. Say what his/her *name* is. (Егó/Её зовýт. . . . . .)

3. You might want to mention whether they are English or Russian or any other *nationality* (if you know it).

4. Speak about where he/she *lives*. Specify whether this is a village/a town/a big city.

5. Say whether he/she *works*. If they don't, see whether you can explain why not. If yes, try to say where.

6. Talk about his/her *family*. (У негó есть/У неё есть. . . . . .).

7. Think about their *hobbies and interests*: whether they play any games or musical instruments, whether they swim or know any other languages, have any pets etc.

Now you can try speaking about a different person without looking at the Step-by-step guide above. Make sure you use the same pattern for each person.

Try speaking about a different person every day. Speak about your neighbours, colleagues, celebrities, famous musicians, politicians etc. It does not matter who they are, as long as you have enough information about them to make 4–7 phrases in Russian. If you are working with someone else, you can play a "Guess who" game, speaking about somebody you both are likely to know without naming him/her. Make sure you take turns.

That is it for now, but I am not saying «До свидáния» – I am saying «До встречи», and I hope to meet you soon in my next book. Until then, THINK RUSSIAN - Дýмай пο-рýсски!

Russian alphabet

А а	like *a* in *father*	**К к**	like *k* in *kangaroo*	**Ф ф**	like *f* in *foot*
	(but not as back or as long)	**Л л**	like *l* in *fall,*	**Х х**	like *k* in *kangaroo*
Б б	like *b* in *bar*		*(sometimes like l in lit)*		*(but gentler and flowing)*
В в	like *v* in *van*	**М м**	like *m* in *empty*	**Ц ц**	like *ts* in *its*
Г г	like *g* in *golf*	**Н н**	like *n* in *nut*	**Ч ч**	like *ch* in *child*
Д д	like *d* in *dog*	**О о**	like *o* in *for*	**Ш ш**	like *sh* in *shop (but shorter*
Е е	like *ye* in *yes*		*(but not as back or as long)*		*and more to the back)*
Ё ё	like *your*	**П п**	like *p* in *pot*	**Щ щ**	like *shsh* in *Welsh sheep*
	(but not as back or as long)	**Р р**	like *r* in *error* but rolling		*(long and close to the palate)*
Ж ж	like *s* in *pleasure*	**С с**	like *c* in *cinema*	**Ъ ъ**	*The Hard Sign*
З з	like *z* in *zebra*	**Т т**	like *t* in *tent*	**Ы ы**	like *i at the back* of your mouth
И и	like *ee* in *see*	**У у**	like *oo* in *moon*		with teeth closed and a smile
	(the longer the better)			**Ь ь**	*The Soft Sign*
Й й	like *y* in *employ*			**Э э**	like *e* in *end*
	(but tense and rapid)			**Ю ю**	like *you*
				Я я	like *ya* in *yak*

Cultural and historical background

Terms and information

Dictionary

А

а	and (at the start of a sentence or a clause)
áдрес	address
Алло́.	Hello (on the phone)
Аме́рика	America
америка́нец	an American (male)
америка́нка	an American (female)
англи́йский	English (NOT about nationality)
англича́нин	an English man
англича́нка	an English woman
А́нглия	England

Б

ба́бушка	Grandmother, elderly lady
бе́лый	white
боле́л/а	(I/you/he/she) was ill/unwell
больни́ца	hospital
большо́й	big, large
брат/ья	brother/s
бу́дет	will (be)

В

в	in, to, at
ва́нна	bath, (often) bathroom
вас	you (formal, a form of «вы»)
ваш/а/е/и	your/s (formal)
Великобрита́ния	Great Britain
ве́чер	evening

ве́чером	in the evening
ви́за	visa
вино́	wine
вода́	water
вокза́л	big station (terminal, but not in the airport)
во́семь	eight
Вот.	Here you are./Here you go.(but NOT "here")
вре́мя	time
Всего́ хоро́шего.	All the best.
всё	everything
вход	entrance
вы	you (formal)
вы́ход	exit

Г

газе́та	newspaper
гара́ж	garage (personal)
где	where
го́род	city, town
гости́ница	hotel

Д

да	yes
два	two
де́вочка	girl (0–15 years old)
де́вушка	girl (15–30 years old), girlfriend

де́душка	Grandfather, elderly gentleman	жить	to live, (often) to stay
де́вять	nine	журна́л	magazine
день	day, afternoon	журнали́ст	journalist
де́ньги	money		
дере́вня	village, (often) countryside	**З**	
де́сять	ten	заво́д	factory
де́ти	children	за́втра	tomorrow
дива́н	sofa, settee	Здра́вствуй/те.	Hello. (formal)
До встре́чи.	= See you soon.	знать	to know
До за́втра.	= See you tomorrow.		
До свида́ния.	Good-bye.	**И**	
Добро́ пожа́ловать.	Welcome. (only when somebody arrives)	и	and (normally inside sentences)
до́брый	kind, good (in greetings)	игра́ть (в/на)	to play (games/instruments)
до́ктор	doctor	Извини́/те.	Excuse me. Sorry. (in/formal)
дом	house, block of flats, cottage, mansion, bungalow	и́ли	or
		инжене́р	engineer
до́ма	at home	иногда́	sometimes
дорого́й	dear, expensive	интере́сный	interesting
до́чка	daughter		
друг	friend (normally male)	**Й**	
друзья́	friends	-	No words start with «Й».
ду́мать	to think		
дя́дя	uncle	**К**	
		ка́сса	cash-desk, till, box-office, "Pay Here"
Е		как	how
его́	his, him	Как вас (тебя́) зову́т?	= What is your name? (How do they call you?)
её	her/s		
ем	(I) eat /am eating	Как дела́?	= How are you? (How are the doings?)
ест	(he/she) eats/is eating		
Есть . . .	There is/are . . .	каранда́ш	pencil
ешь	you (informal) eat /are eating	ка́рта	map
ещё	more, on top of, in addition to	карти́на	painting
		карти́нка	picture (not a photograph)
Ё		кафе́	café
ёлка	Christmas tree	кварти́ра	flat, apartment
		кино́	cinema (also film, colloquial)
Ж		класс	class (of children), classroom
жена́	wife	кни́га	book (to read)
же́нщина	woman	коро́бка	box (made of paper or cardboard)
живу́	(I) live, (often) stay (am staying)		

ко́мната	room	муж	husband
компью́тер	computer	мужчи́на *(m)*	man
коне́чно	of course, certainly	му́зыка	music
конфе́та	a sweet, a chocolate	мя́со	meat
кот	cat (male)		
ко́фе	coffee	**Н**	
ко́шка	cat (female)	на	on, on top of, at, to
краси́вый	beautiful (about how things/ people look)	не	not
		немно́го	a little, a bit, a drop, some
кра́сный	red	непра́вда	wrong (not true)
кто	who	нет	no
		ничего́	1) nothing; 2) It's OK./Fine
Л		но	but
ле́том	in summer	ноль	zero
люби́ть	to like (also stands for "love" if used with animates)	но́вый	new
		но́мер	hotel room, number
люблю́	(I) like (also stands for "I love" if used with animates)		(on something, e.g., a house)
лю́ди	people	Норма́льно.	Fine. (only as an answer to «Как дела́?»)
М		ночь *(f)*	night
ма́ленький	little, small		
ма́льчик	boy (0–15 years old)	**О**	
ма́ма	Mum	о́вощ	vegetable
магази́н	shop	оди́н	one
ма́рка	postage stamp	окно́	window
ма́сло	butter	он	he, it (for masculine nouns), him (only in «Э́то он»)
матрёшка	Russian doll, a set of Russian dolls	она́	she, it (for feminine nouns), her (only in «Э́то она́»)
маши́на	car, lorry, van		
медсестра́	nurse (female)	они́	they
меня́	me (a form of «я»)	оно́	it (only for neuter nouns)
метро́	underground	отли́чно	Excellent./ Great.
мно́го	many, much, a lot	о́фис	office
молодо́й	young (for over 15 years old)	о́чень	very, very much (with some verbs, e.g., «люби́ть»)
мо́жно	It is possible./It's OK./(You) may/ May I?	О́чень прия́тно.	Nice to meet you.
мой/моя́/моё/мой	my, mine		
молоко́	milk	**П**	
мо́ре	sea	паке́т	plastic bag
мост	bridge	па́па	Dad

па́рень	(colloquial) young man, boyfriend (15–30)
пенсионе́р/ка	retired
письмо́	letter (from somebody)
пла́вать	to swim
пло́хо	bad/ly
пло́щадь (f)	square (in a city/town)
подру́га	female friend (not a girlfriend)
пожа́луйста	1) please; 2) You are welcome (as a reply to Thank you); 3) Here you go.
Пока́.	Bye.
помога́ть	to help
понима́ть	to understand
пото́м	then, afterwards
потому́ что	because
по́чта	post-office, post, mail, (often) email
пра́вда	truth, true, (often) right, correct
прекра́сный	wonderful, beautiful (about how things feel and taste)
Приве́т.	Hello. (informal)
прия́тный	pleasant
проду́кты	food (food in a shop or a cupboard or a fridge, not prepared for eating yet, groceries; often the sign on food shop/kiosk)
пять	five

Р

рабо́та	work (a piece of work; a place of work); job
рабо́тать	to work (to do work)
рад/а	glad, happy (about something in particular)
ребёнок	child
река́	river
Росси́я	Russia
ру́сская	Russian (feminine), a Russian woman
ру́сский	Russian (masculine), a Russian man
ру́чка	pen

С

сад	garden
сала́т	salad
са́хар	sugar
сего́дня	today
сейча́с	now (at the moment)
семь	seven
семья́	family
сестра́	sister
Ско́лько?	How much? How many?
сло́во	word
соба́ка	dog
собо́р	cathedral
сок	juice
Сове́тский Сою́з	Soviet Union
сосе́д/ка	neighbour
Спаси́бо.	Thank you.
Споко́йной но́чи.	Good night.
стадио́н	stadium, sports ground, (often) sports centre
стака́н	glass, tumbler
ста́нция	station (where trains cannot terminate, e.g., ста́нция метро́)
ста́рый	old
стена́	wall
стол	table, desk
студе́нт/ка	student
стул	chair
су́мка	bag, handbag, travel bag (not a plastic bag or a suitcase)
сын	son
сыр	cheese

Т

такси́	taxi
там	there (not "There is")
таре́лка	plate, dish

тебя	you (informal, a form of «ты»)
телефóн	telephone, (often) mobile
тетрáдь (f)	book (to write in)
тётя	aunt
твой/я́/ё/й	your/s
тóже	also, too, as well, (often) either, neither
торт	gateau (the whole)
три	three
тут	here

У

Удáчи!	Good luck!
У вас есть	You have (formal)
У меня́ есть	I have
У тебя́ есть	You have (informal)
У негó есть	He has
У неё есть	She has
у́лица	street
у́тро	morning
устáл/а	tired
учи́тель/ница	teacher
учу́	(I) learn/am learning

Ф

фами́лия	surname, family name (not a family)
фéрма	farm
фи́рма	firm, (often) company
фотоаппарáт	camera (not a video camera)
фрукт(ы)	fruit

Х

Хвáтит.	(That would be) enough.
хлеб	bread
хорóший (adj.)	good, nice
хорошó (adv.)	well, good at something

Ц

цветы́	flowers
центр	centre

цéрковь (f)	church
цирк	circus

Ч

чай	tea
чáшка	teacup
человéк	person
четы́ре	four
Чёрное мóре	the Black Sea
читáть	to read
что	what, that (in clauses)

Ш

шáхматы	chess
шесть	six
шкóла	school
шоколáд	chocolate (an ingredient or a bar of)

Щ

щи	shchi (Russian soup)

Ъ

-

Ы

-

Ь

-

Э

э́то	this, that (on the phone)

Ю

Я

я	I ("me" in «Э́то я.»)
я́блоко	apple
язы́к	language

Grammar index

Grammatical term			Unit	Page
ADJECTIVE	dictionary form (masculine form)		Unit 9	220
	feminine form		Unit 9	221
	neuter form		Unit 9	226
CONJUNCTIONS	«И» *(as "and" inside the sentence)*		Unit 1	9
	«А» *(as "and" at the start of a sentence or a clause)*		Revision of Unit 2	17
	«НО» *(as "but")*		Unit 4	86
	«ЧТО» *(as "that")*		Unit 9	217
NOUN	Articles (a/the)		Unit 1	3
	Gender	masculine nouns	Unit 3	49
		feminine nouns	Unit 3, 6, 9	49, 135, 227
		neuter nouns	Unit 9	225
	Case (Prepositional)	«В»-locations	Unit 6	132, 134, 135, 136
		«НА»-locations	Unit 7	153–154
		«НА» + musical instruments	Unit 8	192
	Case (Accusative)	destinations	Unit 6	132
		«В» + games	Unit 7	167
	Plural	with «Ы»	Unit 6, 9	142, 210
		with «И» *(7-letter rule)*	Unit 7, 9	163, 210
		irregular	Unit 7, 8	163, 193

PERSONAL PRONOUNS	1st person Singular *(I/me)*	Я		Unit 1	13
		МЕН8	in «У мен* есть . . .»	Unit 4	84
			in «Мен* зов)т . . .»	Unit 10	245
	2nd person Singular *(you, informal)*	ТЫ		Unit 5	117
		ТЕБ8	in «У теб* есть . . .»	Unit 5	118
			in «Как теб* зов)т?»	Unit 10	245
	3rd person Singular *(he/him; she/her)*	ОН/ОН2		Unit 2	27
		ЕГ5 ЕЁ	in «У нег%/неё есть . . .»	Unit 10	247
			in «Ег%/её зов)т . . .»	Unit 10	246
	2nd person Plural *(you, formal)*	ВЫ		Unit 5	114
		ВАС	in «У вас есть . . .»	Unit 4	85
			in «Как вас зов)т?»	Unit 10	245
	3rd person Plural *(they)*	ОН4		Unit 8	193
POSSESSIVE PRONOUNS	1st person Singular *(my/mine)* МОЙ	Singular forms	masculine form	Unit 3	49
			feminine form	Unit 3	49
			neuter form	Unit 9	227
		Plural form		Unit 8	194
	2nd person Singular *(your/s, informal)* ТВОЙ	Singular forms	masculine form	Unit 3	49
			feminine form	Unit 3	49
			neuter form	Unit 9	227
		Plural form		Unit 8	194
	3rd person Singular *(his, her/s)* ЕГ5 / ЕЁ			Unit 10	242
	2nd person Plural *(your/s, formal)* ВАШ	Singular forms	masculine form	Unit 6	138
			feminine form	Unit 6	138
			neuter form	Unit 9	227
		Plural form		Unit 8	194
PREPOSITIONS	«В»			Unit 6, 7	132, 167
	«НА»			Unit 7, 8	153–154, 192
	«НА» and «В» as *at*			Unit 7	156

VERB	1st Conjugation		1st person Singular	Unit 3, 7, 8	56, 165, 187
			2nd person Singular	Unit 5, 8	117, 189, 191
			2nd person Plural	Unit 8	195
			3rd persons Singular	Unit 3, 9	56, 215, 216
	2nd Conjugation			Unit 10	249
	Infinitive (dictionary form)			Unit 7, 8, 10	165, 169, 187, 249
	Monosyllabic verbs			Unit 3, 8	56, 187
	Negative verb forms			Unit 3, 7	59, 165
	to be in Present			Unit 1	3
SYNTAX	Clauses			Revision of Unit 2, Unit 4, 9	17, 86, 217
	Fixed structures	"Having" construction		Unit 4, 5, 10	84–85, 115, 247
		"There is/are"		Unit 10	254
		"This is" (positive, interrogative, negative)		Unit 1, 2, 3	8, 26, 57
	Negative sentences			Unit 3, 5, 7	57, 59, 124, 131, 165
	Questions			Unit 2, 4, 8	26, 85–86, 90, 189
	Word order			Unit 2, 3, 4, 7, 10	24, 49, 86, 165, 254

Pronunciation index, including letter-sound correspondences

Pairs of Russian vowel letters

Normal vowels: (+ «Ы»)	А а	Э э	О о	У у	Ы ы
	(*a* in *father*)	(*e* in *end*)	(*o* in *for*)	(*oo* in *moon*)	(like *i* at the back)
Two-in-one vowels (+ «И») :	Я я	Е е	Ё ё	Ю ю	И и
	(*ya* in *yak*)	(*ye* in *yes*)	(like *your*)	(like *you*)	(like *ee* in *see*)

Pronunciation of sound/s
corresponding to each letter

А а	Unit 1	1	Р р	Unit 2, 3	32, 33, 58
Б б	Unit 3	51, 52, 58	С с	Unit 1, 3	4, 9–10, 58
В в	Unit 1, 3, 6	10, 12, 58, 131, 132	Т т	Unit 1, 3	1, 58
Г г	Unit 4, 6	87, 88, 90, 138	У у	Unit 4	81
Д д	Unit 2, 3	26, 28–29, 58	Ф ф	Unit 6	136, 141
Е е	Unit 3, 4, 5, 8, 9	55, 56–58, 68, 75, 192, 211	Х х	Unit 6	129–130
Ё ё	Unit 7, 8	158, 159, 161, 192	Ц ц	Unit 8	181, 183, 186
Ж ж	Unit 5, 7, 8	103, 107, 108, 161, 186	Ч ч	Unit 2, 3, 7	30, 75, 107, 161
З з	Unit 3, 5	53, 108	Ш ш	Unit 4, 5, 7, 8, 9	73, 103, 107, 161, 186, 209
И и	Unit 1, 2, 5, 8, 9	9, 36, 63, 112, 186, 209	Щ щ	Unit 9	208, 209, 211
Й й	Unit 2, 3,	36, 37, 48, 63	Ъ ъ	Unit 9	212–213

К к	Unit 1, 6	1, 129–130	**Ы ы**	Unit 5, 6	111, 112, 142
Л л	Unit 2, 4	21, 25, 80	**Ь ь**	Unit 4, 5, 8	78, 80, 117, 192
М м	Unit 1, 3	1, 58	**Э э**	Unit 1, 3	8, 55
Н н	Unit 1, 3	6, 9–10, 56–57	**Ю ю**	Unit 7, 8	161, 162, 192
О о	Unit 1	1, 7	**Я я**	Unit 1, 2, 3, 8	12, 18, 48, 55, 58, 192
П п	Unit 3	60, 62			

Pronunciation features index

Pronunciation term		*Unit*	*Page*
Assimilation		Unit 6, 7	131, 132, 160
Consonant clusters		Unit 1, 3, 6, 7, 9	XV, 70, 131, 160, 223
Devoicing of «Б»		Unit 3	52
Devoicing of «В»		Unit 1	12
Devoicing of «Г»		Unit 4	88
Devoicing of «Д»		Unit 2	29
Devoicing of «Ж»		Unit 5	108
Hushers		Unit 4, 5, 7, 8, 9	73, 103, 107, 117, 161, 208–211
Intonation in Questions		Unit 2	26
Long consonants (double consonants)		Unit 1	10
Palatalization	general	Unit 3, 4, 5,	56–58, 84, 107, 112, 117, 137
	indicated by «Е» and «Я»	Unit 3	56–57
	indicated by «Ё» and «Ю»	Unit 7	159, 162
	indicated by the Soft Sign «Ь»	Unit 4	78, 80
	of «Л»	Unit 2, 4	21, 25, 80
Reduction	general	Unit 1	7
	of «О»	Unit 1	7
	of «Е»	Unit 4	75
Soft vowels		Unit 2, 3, 7, 8	18, 55–56, 58, 158–159, 161, 192
Stress		Unit 1, 4, 6, 9	5, 7, 12, 83, 134, 220
Vowel length		Unit 1	2, 5, 7

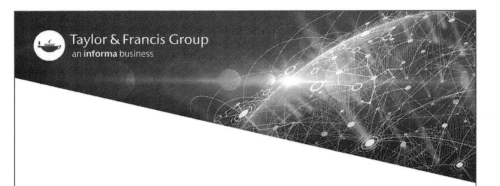

Made in United States
Orlando, FL
17 January 2022

13676584R00165